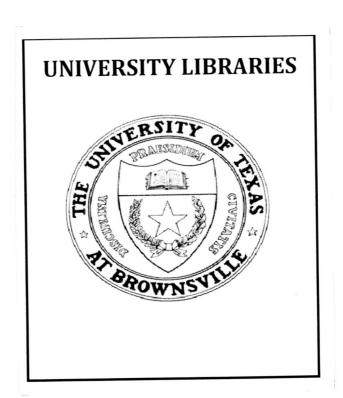

A Thousand Darknesses

Ruth Franklin

A Thousand Darknesses

Lies and Truth in Holocaust Fiction

OXFORD
UNIVERSITY PRESS

2011

OXFORD
UNIVERSITY PRESS

Oxford University Press, Inc., publishes works that further
Oxford University's objective of excellence
in research, scholarship, and education.

Oxford   New York
Auckland   Cape Town   Dar es Salaam   Hong Kong   Karachi
Kuala Lumpur   Madrid   Melbourne   Mexico City   Nairobi
New Delhi   Shanghai   Taipei   Toronto

With offices in
Argentina   Austria   Brazil   Chile   Czech Republic   France   Greece
Guatemala   Hungary   Italy   Japan   Poland   Portugal   Singapore
South Korea   Switzerland   Thailand   Turkey   Ukraine   Vietnam

Copyright © 2011 by Oxford University Press, Inc.

Published by Oxford University Press, Inc.
198 Madison Avenue, New York, New York 10016

www.oup.com

Library of Congress Cataloging-in-Publication Data
Franklin, Ruth.
A thousand darknesses : lies and truth in Holocaust fiction / Ruth Franklin.
    p.   cm.
Includes bibliographical references and index.
ISBN 978-0-19-531396-3 (cloth : alk. paper)   1. Holocaust, Jewish (1939–1945), in literature.
2. Jewish fiction—History and criticism.   3. Truth in literature.   4. Memory in literature.
I. Title.
PN56.3.J4F73 2010
809.33'9358405318—dc22   2010013590

1 3 5 7 9 8 6 4 2

Printed in the United States of America
on acid-free paper

To my grandmother, Esther Korzec
and in memory of my grandfather David Korzec

Acknowledgments

Some of the chapters in this book appeared in different form in *The New Republic*, the magazine I have been proud to call my home for the past decade. I thank my colleagues there for their support and intellectual stimulation over the years. Erin Leib, Chloë Schama, Francesca Mari, and Sophia Lear were meticulous and dependable assistants. Amanda Silverman was endlessly patient with my requests from the archives. Deborah Friedell went above and beyond in more ways than I can list here. James Wood was the first person to suggest that I might want to review books, and the first to encourage me to turn some of my pieces into a book of their own.

I conducted research mainly at the Library of Congress, the Brooklyn Public Library, and the New York Public Library. I give deepest thanks to the staff of those institutions for their help. I am very grateful to the Corporation of Yaddo and all the residents in June 2009 for two very happy and productive weeks there. Back home, Scott Adkins and Erin Courtney provided a stellar working environment at the Brooklyn Writers Space. At the New York Institute for the Humanities, I found camaraderie and inspiration.

I am lucky to have a group of friends and colleagues who are both brilliant and generous with their time. Jaroslaw Anders, Alessandra Bastagli, Blake Eskin, Arnon Grunberg, Katy Lederer, James Luria, Jenny McPhee, Zia Haider Rahman, and Catherine Toal all read and offered suggestions on individual chapters. I spent a lovely evening with Alicia Nitecki and Barbara Girs looking at original editions of Tadeusz Borowski's books. Adam Zagajewski's comments forced me to reconsider some of my initial assumptions about Borowski's self-representation. Atossa Abrahamian conducted covert operations at the Bibliothèque Nationale. Tatjana Suchy and Martin Zelewitz fielded queries about German. At the eleventh hour, Jerome Copulsky offered invaluable critiques of the entire manuscript.

Larissa MacFarquhar and Philip Gourevitch proved themselves the truest of friends in a time of need, as did Stephanie Steiker and Kate Galbraith. Stanley Kauffmann has been an inconceivably deep wellspring of expertise and encouragement. Ever since his first phone call about Wolfgang Koeppen, I have been grateful to Bob Weil for his loyal support. In graduate school, Miryam Sas first awakened me intellectually to "the literature of the disaster." In very different ways, Kenneth Greif, Wallace Gray, Edward Tayler, and Barbara Johnson taught me how to read.

This book could never have come into existence without the tireless labors of Sarah Burnes, the most devoted agent any writer could want. At Oxford University Press, Shannon McLachlan was a dedicated and perceptive editor. The copyeditor Ben Sadock astonished me with his linguistic expertise.

I also could not have written this book without the support of my family, particularly my parents and my in-laws. Danny Franklin bore with me valiantly through my obsession with this most difficult of subjects. Sam and Phoebe, the next one is for you.

Leon Wieseltier has been my inspiration as well as my editor, my mentor, and my friend. Only he knows how much I owe him.

Contents

A Thousand Darknesses

Introduction

The Anvil and the Crucible

"How can one write music after Auschwitz?" inquired Adorno....
"And how can you eat lunch?" the American poet Mark Strand once
retorted.
> —Joseph Brodsky, Nobel Lecture, 1987

I believe that we can promise to tell the truth; I believe in the transparency
of language, and in the existence of a complete subject who expresses himself
through it; I believe that my proper name guarantees my autonomy and my
singularity...I believe that when I say "I," it is I who am speaking: I believe
in the Holy Ghost of the first person. And who doesn't believe in it? But of
course it also happens that I believe the contrary, or at least claim to believe it.
> —Philippe Lejeune, "The Autobiographical Pact (bis)"

In the late 1990s, more than fifty years after the end of the war, Holocaust
memoirs were guaranteed an uncritical reception: responses to them tended
to range anywhere on the spectrum from respectful attention to outright
fawning. But one book was greeted with a level of excitement unusual even
for those enthusiastic times. Its author was compared to Jean Améry, Paul
Celan, and Primo Levi. The historian Daniel Jonah Goldhagen, who was
among the first to testify to its importance, wrote that "even those conversant
with the literature of the Holocaust will be educated by this arresting book."

In *The New York Times,* Julie Salamon described it as an "extraordinary memoir" that "recalls the Holocaust with the powerful immediacy of innocence, injecting well-documented events with fresh terror and poignancy." Writing in the *Nation,* Jonathan Kozol called it "so morally important, and so free from literary artifice of any kind at all, that I wonder if I even have the right to try to offer praise."

The book was *Fragments* by Binjamin Wilkomirski. Within just a few years, its author was determined to be a fraud: the gentile son of Swiss parents, he had been adopted as a young child by a prosperous Zurich family who raised him as their own son. He took on the identity of "Binjamin Wilkomirski," Jewish child Holocaust survivor, based on the most tenuous connections and suggestions by friends, including a psychologist who helped him with the "recovery" of some of his "memories." His unmasking—delivered in unsparing detail by exposés in both *Granta* and *The New Yorker*—hit students and scholars of the Holocaust, almost all of whom had embraced him, with the force of a tsunami. Wilkomirski's prizes were retracted, his speaking engagements canceled, his book withdrawn from bookstores and museum shops. Critics and academics alike wrung their hands. How, they wondered, could this have been allowed to happen?

But the real surprise is that it did not happen sooner. For the pathetic fraud perpetrated by Wilkomirski was the inevitable consequence of the way Holocaust literature has been read, discussed, and understood—in America especially, but also in Europe—over the last sixty years. Ever since Theodor Adorno's famous negation of poetry after Auschwitz, which dates from 1949, a fog of suspicion has clouded the very possibility of creating art in the wake of the Holocaust. We are all familiar with Adorno's dictum, warning, prohibition, whatever we want to call it; I'll quote it only because it has been so often misquoted, and because Adorno's exact phrasing matters. *Nach Auschwitz ein Gedicht zu schreiben, ist barbarisch:* "To write a poem after Auschwitz is barbaric." As critic after critic has interpreted and reinterpreted this statement, it has been stripped of its original context: a brand of highly ideological Marxist literary criticism in which the Holocaust serves as the ultimate paradigm of the intersection between culture and barbarism. The dictum is almost never understood in this context, which very few of those who approvingly cite it are aware of or would be likely to accept. Nor is it understood as it literally reads—as a comment, we should notice, on the act of writing a single poem. It is taken, rather, as a general prohibition against imaginative literature about the Holocaust, a condemnation of the moral callousness of aestheticizing horror.

There is something ethically dubious, so the usual argument goes, about using—literally or figuratively profiting from—atrocity as an inspiration for literature, or indeed any form of art. Aesthetically, the literary representation of horror has an inherent falsity, in that it requires the writer to impose a coherent pattern or form where in reality there was only chaos. And speaking practically, many have argued that as long as at least a few survivors are still alive, it's more important to focus on getting their stories down, to preserve their memories while that is still possible. And so the testimonial memoir, rather than the novel, has become the dominant form of Holocaust writing—resulting in a slew of unintended interpretive consequences.

It is unsurprising that the first generation of Holocaust scholars placed primary emphasis on establishing evidence—facts, proof—rather than on literary or aesthetic representation. This was, after all, the period of the Auschwitz trials. Swept in alongside the sea of documentation that the Nazis left behind, the voices of eyewitnesses emerged to tell their stories in every form imaginable, from the milk cans containing diaries of residents in the Warsaw Ghetto that were unearthed from the ashes of the city to the reams of testimonials that began to see publication immediately after the war and continue to appear at a steady clip. (The original Yiddish version of Elie Wiesel's *Night,* appearing in 1956, was the 117th volume in a series of personal testimonies.) All these sources were scoured for what they could tell us about life and death under the Nazis, and many continue to be of great importance and interest today. They are indispensible resources.

At the same time, imaginative literature about the Holocaust—fiction, poetry, literary memoir—was already starting to appear. Tadeusz Borowski published his first stories about Auschwitz in 1946, while working in Munich to help reunite refugee families. As if to emphasize how close the world of the camps still was, his publisher bound a few copies of the book, called *We Were in Auschwitz,* in the actual striped cloth of the uniforms worn by prisoners. *Sunrise Over Hell,* published in Israel in 1946 by the author who wrote under the name Ka-Tzetnik 135633 (literally "concentration camp inmate"), is generally considered to be the first Holocaust novel. Paul Celan's iconic poem "Todesfuge"—said to have provoked Adorno's outburst—appeared in a Romanian newspaper in 1947.

By the early 1980s, Yosef Hayim Yerushalmi would write that "the Holocaust has already engendered more historical research than any single event in Jewish history, but I have no doubt whatever that its image is being shaped, not at the historian's anvil, but in the novelist's crucible." While Yerushalmi worried about the ability of historiography to stir individuals and communities, and believed in the greater power of the artistic imagination, at the same time he lamented what he saw as an antihistorical trend among modern Jews. But one could just as easily argue, to the contrary, that the great surge of interest in literature and theater and film about the Holocaust that began in this country in the 1960s and continues still—despite periodically renewed complaints of "Holocaust fatigue"—seems to demonstrate our culture's almost too-intense fascination with its history, at least its immediate history in the form of the Holocaust. The critic Robert Alter worried presciently nearly thirty years ago that the Holocaust had come to play too great a role in contemporary Jewish life as a kind of touchstone of Jewish political and religious values. A controversial article published in the *New York Times Magazine* around the same time quoted scholar Jacob Neusner saying that "the Holocaust and the Redemption"—that is, the founding of the state of Israel—had come to "constitute the central myth by which American Jews seek to make sense of themselves."

This article noted the creation of a Holocaust studies department at Temple University, the first such program in America. Now degrees in the Holocaust are offered everywhere from Big Ten universities to regional state colleges; academic books on the subject appear by the dozen every year. What started out as a field distinguished by the production of enormous and definitive historical tomes such as Raul Hilberg's *Destruction of the European Jews* (1961) and popular histories such as Lucy Dawidowicz's *The War Against the Jews* (1975) has turned into a diverse discipline influenced heavily by trends in critical theory, philosophy, and historiography.

But while it hardly needs to be pointed out that interest in the Holocaust remains extremely strong in both the academy and in popular culture, the ways in which these two realms understand the Holocaust are so divergent as to be incompatible. The dominant academic approach, which has been called a "realist" approach, assumes that the Holocaust is basically knowable—that it can be understood through the usual means of scholarly investigation: reading, interviewing participants, looking at photographs. The leading philosophers and historians of the Holocaust are all realists. Yehuda Bauer, to give one example, has argued that emphasizing the mysteriousness of the Holocaust is an "elegant form of escapism" that results in obscuring its contemporary relevance.

The dominant popular approach, on the other hand, is more mystical. Understood thus, the Holocaust is not knowable; it is a unique event that cannot be meaningfully compared to any other historical phenomenon; it can be understood only by those who personally experienced it and is not transmissible to anyone else; and, most significantly for our concerns, it "could well be inaccessible to all attempts at a significant representation and interpretation," as Saul Friedlander has written. It is, quite literally, unspeakable. This approach fundamentally denies the possibility of creating a valid art and literature about the Holocaust. In contrast to Yerushalmi's fears, it smashes the novelist's crucible, emphasizing preservation rather than transformation.

Elie Wiesel, by any estimation the most influential Holocaust survivor in America if not the world, has been the leading proponent of this position, promoting it in countless essays, articles, and lectures. "Let us repeat it once again," he wrote in an article in the *Times* headlined "Art and the Holocaust: Trivializing Memory," which appeared in 1989 and offered a particularly blunt statement of his argument, but not an exceptional one. "Auschwitz is something else, always something else.... Then, it defeated culture; later, it defeated art, because just as no one could imagine Auschwitz before Auschwitz, no one can now retell Auschwitz after Auschwitz.... Only those who lived it in their flesh and in their minds can possibly transform their experience into knowledge." Wiesel exhorted his readers to shun imaginative representations of the Holocaust and instead read testimonies and watch documentaries. He concluded, bitterly, "Stop insulting the dead."

So, sixty years after Adorno, we are caught in a paradox. We have yet to sate our voracious cultural hunger for novels, films, plays that might somehow help us understand the Holocaust—which, whether one believes it was a unique event or not, is beyond question one of the most obscene catastrophes in history. If we look to literature, even in this age of lapsed humanism, to teach us about life, then it is no wonder that we desperately desire it to teach us also about the Holocaust. And yet we cannot quite get over our suspicion that there is something shameful in this desire. We worry that we are insulting the dead. A phenomenon such as the Holocaust evokes a kind of reticence of expression—a fear that to speak openly and bluntly about such matters is somehow improper or simply vulgar. And it evokes a more general anxiety about the ways in which we respond to and value art and the uses to which we are prepared to put it.

In *The Holocaust and Literary Imagination,* Lawrence Langer, one of the pioneers in this field, acknowledged that there seems to be "something disagreeable, almost dishonorable" about converting the suffering of the victims into art that is then offered for the delectation of the world that murdered them. In

addition to the ethical difficulty, Langer writes, there is also an aesthetic difficulty: the danger that art can impose a false meaning on events and thus imply
that "the inconceivable fate of the victims appears to have had some sense after
all." He continues: "The prospect of art denying what it seeks to affirm (the
hideous chaos of dehumanization during the Holocaust) raises a spectre of
paradox for the critic, the reader, and the artist himself." The philosopher and
theologian Michael Wyschogrod put it more succinctly: "Art takes the sting
out of suffering.... Any attempt to transform the holocaust into art demeans
the holocaust and must result in poor art."

Even if we welcome the idea of art on this subject (as Langer does), we
are confused about how we ought to treat it. In his introduction to *Probing
the Limits of Representation,* a touchstone collection of critical essays on the
subject of representing the Holocaust, Friedlander asks: "Is it not unacceptable to debate formal and abstract issues in relation to this catastrophe?" Note
the double negative—"is it not unacceptable"—which is symptomatic of the
extreme delicacy with which the question of representing the Holocaust is
always approached. This phrasing manages to imply that even as we debate
such issues, it is in fact not quite legitimate to do so. The possibility that there
might *not* be limits on representation is not considered.

If it is barbaric to write a poem about the Holocaust, is it not also barbaric to
read one—or at least to read one critically? This is a fundamental insecurity of
many of the critics who address themselves to this body of literature—a canon
that is vast, diffuse, and growing steadily, not to mention extremely demand-
ing on the reader. Critics and scholars tend to proceed hesitantly, offering
caveats, prefacing and concluding their arguments by emphasizing their own
inadequacy to the subject. The fallback position is to embrace the paradox:
confronting the Holocaust is impossible, yet the Holocaust requires us to confront it. "The Holocaust demands speech even as it threatens speech," Alvin
Rosenfeld writes in *The Double Dying,* his landmark 1980 study of Holocaust
literature. "The speech may be flawed, stuttering, and inadequate...but it is
still speech.... If it is a blasphemy, then, to attempt to write about the Holocaust, and an injustice against the victims, how much greater the injustice and
more terrible the blasphemy to remain silent." Rosenfeld's reference to the
"injustice" of silence inevitably recalls the terrible silence of the general European and American population in the face of the Holocaust; since the failure
of onlookers to speak out at the time helped to permit the Holocaust to occur,
to speak about it now becomes a moral imperative of the highest order. (The
original title of Wiesel's *Night* was *And the World Was Silent.*)

Rosenfeld emphasizes his deferential position with regard to his subject through his use of this religious terminology. (Here he follows Wiesel, who has famously and shockingly said that "Auschwitz is as important as Sinai"—the ultimate confirmation of Alter's worry that the Holocaust was taking on too dominant a role in Jewish culture.) But the problem with a criticism based in religion is that it is forced to take a tone that is more ecstatic than rational. And so Rosenfeld winds up claiming—passionately, but ultimately absurdly—that books about the Holocaust are almost magical objects. "The object in our hands looks like a book but seems to have turned into something else," he writes. "Its birth, a testament to more than silence, more than madness, more even than language itself, must be seen as a miracle of some sort, not only an overcoming of mute despair but an assertion and affirmation of faith." Such generalities about faith and affirmation are inadequate to the vast thematic variety of Holocaust literature, which runs from Tadeusz Borowski's rage to Primo Levi's rationality to Imre Kertész's irony and beyond.

Rosenfeld is right to be astonished that certain books have managed to reach us at all. But does this mean that "we can never distance ourselves from an accompanying and transfiguring sense of awe as we encounter them"? It is telling that the example he gives is not a novel or another work of imaginative literature—the ostensible subject of his discussion—but "a manuscript written secretly and at the daily risk of life in the Warsaw ghetto, buried in milk tins or transmitted through the ghetto walls at the last moment.... Such a manuscript begins to carry with it the aura of a holy text. Surely we do not take it in our hands and read it as we do those books that reach us through the normal channels of composition and publication." Here is the holy grail of Holocaust literature: that forever desired and never-to-be-attained text that will provide us with a direct channel to the Holocaust. If we believe, with Wiesel, that only those who experienced the Holocaust can understand it, then anyone who did not experience the Holocaust but still wishes to understand it must find his or her own way to experience it. And since to do this is clearly impossible, we are left desiring the next best thing—an authentic document, straight from the concentration camp or ghetto, that will offer us unmediated access to the experience; that will tell us, in Wiesel's words, "how it really was." But to say, as Rosenfeld does, that "we can never distance ourselves" from such texts is to prohibit literary criticism. In an age when false memoirs proliferate, this is simply irresponsible.

Yet this is precisely where we find ourselves. When faced with an ostensibly nonfiction book having to do with the Holocaust, the default response of scholars and critics, as well as the general reading public, has been to extinguish the critical faculty and retreat to a position of all-accepting deference. We saw this in the reviews of *Fragments*—how those critics must now regret their naive statements of credulity!—but this tendency has been common for decades. In a review originally published in 1968, of a documentary novel about Treblinka and a diary from the Warsaw Ghetto, even George Steiner— whose family background, linguistic facility, and depth of literary knowledge ought to have qualified him, as much as anyone, to intelligently assess Holocaust literature—explicitly abdicated the critical role:

> These books and the documents that have survived are not for "review." Not unless "review" signifies, as perhaps it should in these instances, a "seeing-again," over and over. As in some Borges fable, the only completely decent 'review' of the *Warsaw Diary* or Elie Wiesel's *Night* would be to re-copy the book, line by line, pausing at the names of the dead and the names of the children as the orthodox scribe pauses, when re-copying the Bible, at the hallowed name of God. Until we know many of the words by *heart* (knowledge deeper than mind) and can repeat a few at the break of morning to remind ourselves that we live *after*, that the end of the day may bring inhuman trial or a remembrance stranger than death.
>
> In the Warsaw Ghetto a child wrote in its diary: "I am hungry, I am cold; when I grow up I want to be a German, and then I shall no longer be hungry, and no longer cold." And now I want to write that sentence again: "I am hungry, I am cold; when I grow up I want to be a German, and then I shall no longer be hungry, and no longer cold." And say it many times over, in prayer for the child, in prayer for myself. Because when that sentence was written I was fed, beyond my need, and slept warm, and was silent.

The emotional pull of Steiner's desire here is strong; and over the years it has often been echoed. How can we who "live *after*"—who experienced no persecution or privation—judge the actions of those who lived *during*? (Or, as Steiner asks of himself, how can a person who lived during the Holocaust but separate from it, safely removed to the United States as a child before the occupation of his native France, judge those who were not as lucky?) This has become an ethical cliché, but it is not without validity. What does surprise, however, is how quickly it is translated into the literary realm. Perhaps we may not judge the deeds of someone who came through the Holocaust, but are we truly not to judge his or her words?

It might be argued that different standards of criticism should apply to works of nonfiction about the Holocaust and to works of fiction. By this logic, it is acceptable to coolly dissect the metaphors in a work such as Piotr Rawicz's *Blood from the Sky,* a deliberately surreal novel, whereas it is morally dubious, or at least beside the point, to do so for Elie Wiesel's *Night,* which continues to be accepted as the ultimately canonical Holocaust memoir. The problem is that these categories are perpetually fluid. *Night*—like the stories of Tadeusz Borowski, the autobiographical works of Primo Levi, and *virtually every other important work of literature about the Holocaust*—has been understood, at different times, as *both* a novel and a memoir. In his perceptive book *Writing and Rewriting the Holocaust,* James E. Young analyzes in detail the essential narrative component of diaries and testimonies, and concludes: "If there is a line between fact and fiction, it may by necessity be a winding border that tends to bind these two categories as much as it separates them, allowing each side to dissolve occasionally into the other."

Textual evidence alone is insufficient to help us distinguish between the two forms. In his seminal work *On Autobiography,* the French literary theorist Philip Lejeune despaired at the "seemingly insoluble problem of establishing a distinction between autobiography and fiction." He argued that it is the reader's response that makes the difference: autobiography, he wrote, is "a mode of reading as much as it is a type of writing." But it is up to the author to guide the reader in his or her definition of the category. Lejeune posited the existence of what he called "the autobiographical pact": "an implicit or explicit contract" between author and reader in which the autobiographer commits him- or herself not to some impossible historical exactitude but rather to the sincere effort to come to terms with and to represent his or her own life. The autobiographical pact, he wrote, "determines the mode of reading of the text and engenders the effects which...seem to define it as autobiography."

Such an autobiographical pact is a familiar feature of the Holocaust memoir, which is often prefaced by an assertion of the truth-value of its own content, ranging from the handwritten oath that appeared on the frontispiece to what is, as far as I know, the very first published testimony about the concentration camps—German political prisoner Gerhart Seger's memoir of his time at Oranienburg, which appeared in 1934 ("I swear that to the best of my knowledge I have pursued pure truth, concealing nothing and adding nothing")—to

Primo Levi's understated declaration at the start of *Survival in Auschwitz* that "it seems to me unnecessary to add that none of the facts are invented." An implicit form is to be found in *We Were in Auschwitz,* the three authors of which were listed on the title page by their concentration camp numbers. The narrators of the stories share the authors' first names (another feature of the autobiographical pact), and the publisher explicitly declares in the preface that the book constitutes "the history of a certain concentration camp.... Obviously, it does not subsume all of the circumstances of this camp, but very cautiously and, one is tempted to say, intimately, it gives a few fragments of what the authors themselves experienced and saw with their own eyes." Even the book's extraordinary physical appearance—the binding incorporating the fabric of the camp uniform—amounts to a unique assertion of reliability.

Unfortunately, the situation is not always so clear cut. Even Lejeune, who emphasizes the significance of the editorial apparatus as an integral part of any text, recognizes that the autobiographical pact is ridiculously easy to fake. In his recent history of the memoir as a literary form, Ben Yagoda notes that the novel itself began as a form of fake memoir, pioneered by Daniel Defoe: the title page of *Robinson Crusoe* (1719) asserted the book's identity as an authentic account. In *Moll Flanders* (1722), Defoe went further, claiming (as the book's "editor") that "the world is so taken up nowadays with novels and romances, that it will be hard for a private history to be taken as genuine." Though some readers were stymied by the question of how to read these books, Yagoda argues that attitudes toward literary truth up to that point were exceedingly flexible, with the majority of narratives occupying "an indeterminate middle ground" between fact and fiction. "The truth was of a general quality," he writes. "It wouldn't have occurred to anyone that every detail happened precisely as described." Regardless, the authentification trope took off, and has found expression in hundreds of novels over the form's nearly three-hundred-year history.

At the beginning of the modern "memoir boom"—Yagoda credits Tobias Wolff with inaugurating its current form with his book *This Boy's Life,* in 1989—readers were similarly inclined to be forgiving: what mattered was the author's good faith, not whether he or she could accurately reproduce every word of dialogue from conversations that had taken place thirty years earlier. But in the wake of a series of fraudulent memoirs—in addition to Wilkomirski, there was James Frey, discovered to have exaggerated many of the events in his addiction memoir *A Million Little Pieces,* and J. T. Leroy, the supposedly teenaged male author of an autobiographical novel about a childhood spent among truck-stop prostitutes, who turned out to be a middle-aged Brooklyn woman—the pendulum has swung entirely to the other side. Suddenly, the slightest hint that even a single passage in a memoir might not be literally true is enough to cast doubt on the entire enterprise.

Such insistence on literal truth is particularly absurd in the light of all that scientists have learned about memory in the past few decades, confirming what poets and novelists have been telling us for centuries. The fundamental unreliability of the human mind has been established over and over again; it has become a truism that our memories are not the tape recorders they were once thought to be, playing back duplicate copies of original experiences on demand, but are rather more like mosaics: pieced-together scraps of experience from various sources that generate the appearance of coherence. "Every person carries within himself a rough draft, perpetually reshaped, of the story of his life," Lejeune wrote. In one of the most famous studies, psychologist Ulric Neisser, on the day after the explosion of the *Challenger* space shuttle in 1986, asked around a hundred students to write down exactly where they were and what they were doing when they heard the news. When he interviewed them two and a half years later, the students had great confidence in the accuracy of their own memories, but they answered his questions correctly less than half the time. Many of them asserted the truth of their memory narratives—the form of the story they had established for themselves in the intervening time—even over the evidence of their own reports.

By emphasizing the fallibility of memory, I do not mean in any way to impugn the truth-value of survivors' testimonies, as some revisionists have done by seizing on certain discrepancies (such as a survivor's mistaken memory of the number of crematoria at Auschwitz) to question the facticity of the Holocaust in general. But I do want to question fundamentally the idea that testimonials about the Holocaust—the "holy writ," in Rosenfeld's words—are pure, authentic documents that exempt themselves from criticism and interpretation. If we start examining these manuscripts closely, we discover that there can be no such authentic document, because all written texts are in some way mediated. To consider any text "pure testimony," completely free from aestheticizing influences and narrative conventions, is naïve.

Every canonical work of Holocaust literature involves some graying of the line between fiction and reality. We now know that Anne Frank's diary was edited not only by her father, who deleted her musings on her awakening sexuality and on her complex relationship with her mother, but also by Anne herself, who (as Francine Prose has written) rewrote her diary during the last few weeks before her arrest with an eye toward its publication. *Night,* far from being scribbled in a fever of divine inspiration, did indeed reach us through something like "the normal channels of composition and publication": it was heavily edited, both by Wiesel himself and by an editor at his publishing house, and the French version ultimately took quite a different shape from the original Yiddish, as Naomi Seidman and others have shown. Even the testimonials that seem the most ragged, and thus the most pure—the interviews with survivors collected at Yale's Holocaust Video Archive, for instance—still reveal the pressure of external influence. ("Someone comes with a story to tell—how, alone of all his family, friends, and townspeople, he survived the Nazi Holocaust," David Roskies once wrote in an article criticizing the artifice of video testimony. "So you put him in a bare room and sit him down in front of a video camera, and a stranger asks him questions in English to which he replies with a heavy accent.")

Every act of memory is also an act of narrative. Total recall is beyond human capabilities, and so our minds distill and pound the chaos of life into something resembling a coherent shape. From the very moment we begin the activity of remembering, we place some kind of editorial framework, some principle of selection—no matter how simple, how neutral, or how unconscious—around the events of the past. Of course there is an important difference between the "editing" that our minds do instinctively (it could also be called "forgetting") and the deliberate, goal-driven work that an editor performs on a text. But the end result is very similar: a narrative, whether written or contained within the mind, that is a faithful and yet inevitably incomplete representation of actual events. In the context of today's belief in the infallibility of the survivor, it is ironic to read the words of a scholar who wrote in 1950 that "most of the [Holocaust] memoirs and reports are full of preposterous verbosity, graphomaniac exaggerations, dramatic effects, overestimated self-inflation, dilettante philosophizing, would-be lyricism, unchecked rumors, bias, partisan attacks, and apologies." This is harshly put, but we have all read testimonies that fit this description.

"We do not simplify the challenge of interpretation, which is difficult enough, by seeing around the books we read the aura of a holy text," Langer has written. "The literature of the Holocaust is neither awesome nor holy, only painful, and if a distance remains between us and this literature, the fault is ours."

Up to this point I have tried to make the case for why we shouldn't *not* write literature about the Holocaust. But there is an additional case to be made for

why we *should* write literature about the Holocaust, though it is an argument
not about the Holocaust, but about literature. We need literature about the
Holocaust not only because testimony is inevitably incomplete, but because of
what literature uniquely offers: an imaginative access to past events, together
with new and different ways of understanding them that are unavailable to
strictly factual forms of writing.

Literature's aesthetic pleasures have often been seen as evidence that it is
inappropriate to an event such as the Holocaust. As George Steiner has written, "the aesthetic makes endurable" even that which ought not to be. But
there is a practical argument to counterbalance this fear: the fact that literature, by virtue of its ability to make difficult ideas easier to contemplate, also
increases the possibility of the listener's or reader's empathetic response. This
seemed self-evident to Jorge Semprun—the author of *The Long Goodbye,* a
highly regarded Holocaust novel—whose memoir *Literature or Life* defends
the value of literature in the camps themselves. Semprun, who was a student
and a member of the French Resistance at the time of his deportation, writes of
exchanging poems with other inmates in the latrines at Buchenwald and quot-
ing Baudelaire to comfort a professor dying in the camp. In contrast to writers
such as Wiesel, who emphasize the inadequacy of language, Semprun believes
deeply in its ability to communicate the experience to others. "Only the artifice of a masterly narrative will prove capable of conveying some of the truth of
such testimony," he writes. "But there's nothing exceptional about this: it's the
same with all great historical experiences." Instead, he worries about the ability
of the listeners of the future: "Will they have the necessary patience, passion,
compassion, and fortitude?"

Semprun does not believe naively in the power of literature as a humanizing impulse: his memoir contains an extraordinary scene in which one of the
American lieutenants present at the liberation of Buchenwald confronts the
citizens of the nearby town of Weimar, home of Goethe and Schiller. "Your
pretty town, so clean, so neat, brimming with cultural memories, the heart of
classical and enlightened Germany, seems not to have had the slightest qualm
about living in the smoke of Nazi crematoria!" the soldier exclaims. But Semprun also recognizes that literature, while not perfect, is the best chance the
survivors have.

A few days after liberation, Semprun comes upon a group of inmates discussing how to tell the story of the camps. "We were trying to figure out how
we should talk about all this, so that people would understand us," says a man
named Yves, who is about to be repatriated.

"That's not the problem," someone else exclaims immediately. "The real problem isn't talking about it, whatever the difficulties might be. It's hearing about it.... Will people want to hear our stories, even if they're well told?"...

"What does that mean, 'well-told'?" asks someone indignantly. "You have to tell things the way they are, with no fancy stuff!"

This blunt affirmation seems to have the support of most of the future repatriates present. Most of the potential future narrators. Then I stick my nose in, pointing out something that seems obvious to me.

"Telling a story well, that means: so as to be understood. You can't manage it without a bit of artifice. Enough artifice to make it art!"

To some of the other men, though, this isn't obvious at all. Their argument exactly prefigures the debate that would play out over the coming decades between the opposing camps of testimony and literature, between telling things "the way they are, with no fancy stuff" and putting in "enough artifice to make it art." Semprun argues that it is precisely because the stories are not "easily believable"—even, he says, "unimaginable"—that artifice is all the more necessary to render them convincing. ("That's right!" says another of the men. "It's so unbelievable that I myself plan to stop believing it, as soon as possible!") How do you "foster the imagination of the unimaginable, if not by elaborating, by reworking reality, by putting it in perspective?" Semprun asks. Finally he receives some backup from an inmate who was once a professor.

"I imagine there'll be a flood of accounts," [the professor says.] "Their value will depend on the worth of the witness, his insight, his judgment.... And then there will be documents.... Later, historians will collect, classify, analyze this material, drawing on it for scholarly works.... Everything will be said, put on record.... Everything in these books will be true...except that they won't contain the essential truth, which no historical reconstruction will ever be able to grasp, no matter how thorough and all-inclusive it may be.... The other kind of understanding, the essential truth of the experience, cannot be imparted.... Or should I say, it can be imparted only through literary writing."...

"If I understand you correctly," says Yves, "they'll never know, those who haven't been there!"

"They'll never really know.... That leaves books. Novels, preferably. Literary narratives, at least, that will go beyond simple eyewitness accounts, that will let you imagine, even if they can't let you see.... Perhaps there will be a literature of the camps.... And I do mean literature, not just reportage."

That will let you imagine, even if they can't let you see. This is the true value of literature and of humanism more generally—a value, it should be pointed out, that stands in direct contrast to the Nazis' program of dehumanization. Observing Eichmann's tendency to speak almost entirely in meaningless formulas, Hannah Arendt wrote that "the longer one listened to him, the more obvious it became that his inability to speak [without using clichés] was closely connected with an inability to *think*, namely, to think from the standpoint of somebody else." The act of imagination, on the other hand, is an act of empathy.

In her uncommonly sensible and perceptive work *Reading the Holocaust*, the Australian scholar Inga Clendinnen both questions and acknowledges the value of such empathy. As a historian, Clendinnen has a tendency to privilege the historical account; but she is also a reader, and she recognizes what fiction has to offer:

This is a difficult issue, especially in these post-postmodernist days, but it is central, and worth taking time over. In my view the largest single difference between History and Fiction (at moments like these they require capitalization) is that each establishes quite different relationships between writer and subject, and writer and reader. Had I discovered the nature of Humbert Humbert's secret joys in real life, I would have had him locked up.... Snug between the covers of the fiction called *Lolita* I can revel in his eely escapades, his delirious descriptions; weep with him when his child slave escapes; yearn with him for her recapture. Through giving me access to the inner thoughts and secret actions of closed others, fiction has taught me most of what I know, or think I know, about life.

But does it matter, she wonders, that such identification is itself a fiction?

This fictional world, however, contains a curious absence. The reason for its exhilarating freedom is that it is a kind of game, a circumscribed place of play. Once inside I have no responsibility beyond my responsibility to respond to the text. I may tremble for its people, I may weep for them—but I want to relish their anguish, not heal it. I do not want

Anna reconciled with Karenin and living to plump and comfortable grandmotherhood....Although they may be more intimately known than my most intimate actual others, although they may often seem very much more 'real,' in the end my compassion is a fiction too, because I know they are fictions.

Yes, Humbert Humbert and Anna Karenina are fictions. But in a way they are *not* fictions, because to be plausible they must to some degree come from life. In a sense, all great fictional characters are composites, because the novelist's imagination is necessarily inspired by people whom he or she has known or encountered, whether in life or in fiction. Remember the childhood exercises: it's impossible to dream up an animal totally unrelated to any other, just as it's impossible to imagine a color one has never seen. Even the most far-fetched imaginary creatures will have heads, or wings, or scales; they will be composed out of familiar parts. In the same way, fictional characters too are never "either wholly true or wholly invented," as Primo Levi once told an interviewer. "However much a writer struggles to be objective—even a writer of history or historical novels—he always leaves his own mark and every character is distorted in some way as a result," Levi continued. "Conversely, if you set out to invent a character from scratch, to make a montage, you cannot help but draw on your own experiences, your own previous human contacts, and so in both cases the character is a hybrid." If fiction could ever be a complete invention, then it wouldn't be able to teach us what we know, or think we know, about life—as Clendinnen so aptly puts it. The historian's anvil and the novelist's crucible perform different functions, but they are made out of the same material.

And it is for this reason that we do no favors to writers such as Borowski, Levi, or Wiesel when we continue to insist that their books are strictly, purely, factual. For to do so is to underrate the extraordinary level of literary sophistication displayed in their work. The critic A. Alvarez was guilty of this in his famous assessment of *Night*. Everybody cites the first part of his statement: "*Night* is almost unbearably painful, and certainly beyond criticism." Yet in the next breath he went on: "But it is a failure as a work of art." His argument, as I understand it, is based on style: Wiesel's language has the effect of seeming "excessive, even a bit journalistic," Alvarez writes, because "the feelings are so fiercely present in the barest recital of the facts that any attempt to elaborate, underline, or explain them seems like wild overstatement." At times this might be true, but I argue that it is less true of Wiesel than of many less skilled writer-survivors. Alvarez also fails to consider the extraordinarily effective way in which Wiesel's narrative unfolds simultaneously on two levels, at once a testimonial to the evils of the camps and a chronicle of the loss of faith. He favors Borowski's "curt, icy, and brutally direct" style, arguing that "around [his] stories there is a kind of moral silence, like the pause which follows a scream." Yet this reading of Borowski's works, which has become standard, fails to recognize the undercurrent of moral condemnation that beats at the heart of his Auschwitz stories and poems.

Levi's memoir *Survival in Auschwitz,* normally considered one of the most straightforward works of Holocaust literature, also deserves reconsideration from a literary perspective. This book is often described as being written in the style of a laboratory report, but to dispute that, we need only compare another text by Levi that has only recently become available in English. In the spring of 1945, the Soviet authorities in Poland asked Levi, together with his friend and fellow survivor Leonardo de Benedetti, to write an essay documenting the conditions in the camp. It was published in November 1946 in an Italian medical journal; its title in English is *Auschwitz Report.* Much of the material from this essay would find its way into *Survival in Auschwitz,* in greatly revised form. Levi's biographers have observed that despite the "legend" that Levi would come to construct around his memoir, the book was not written "in furious haste immediately on his return from exile," but rather was "the product of a gradual maturation [that] involved many different phases of drafting." As Wiesel did when revising *Night* for French publication, Levi removed several Jewish allusions to give the text a more universal appeal. He also added more of his own personal experiences and impressions, as well as some of the book's more colorful characters, including Steinlauf, the memorable compulsive washer. Though Paul Steinberg, the man known as "Henri," would acknowledge the truth of Levi's ugly portrait of him, others would gently dispute Levi's portrayals, especially the family of Alberto Dalla Volta, another Italian who was Levi's close companion in Auschwitz. But if we take Levi seriously as a writer, why should we not grant him the creative freedom to do with his characters what he will, to alter them in ways that will make his narrative more effective?

"One of the main problems for the Holocaust writer," Langer has written, "is to find a secure place, somewhere between memory and imagination, for all those corpses who, like the ghost of Hamlet's father, cry out against the injustice of their end, but for whom no act of vengeance or ritual of remembrance exists sufficient to bring them to a peaceful place of rest." The best literature about the

Holocaust manages to accomplish exactly this. I am thinking not only of writers from the "first category" of witnesses, such as Wiesel, Borowski, and Levi, but also of a host of later writers who more explicitly characterized their works as fiction—and who took radically different approaches. In *Blood from the Sky* (1961), a classic in France that is mysteriously almost unknown in English, Piotr Rawicz writes of his own experiences in an intricately layered narrative whose disjointed form discourages any effort to understand the book as a chronicle or testimony. The postscript on the book's last page, in contrast to the avowals of truth found in many Holocaust texts, explicitly disavows its authority: "*This book is not a historical record.* If the notion of chance (like most other notions) did not strike the author as absurd, he would gladly say that any reference to a particular period, territory, or race is purely coincidental." Similarly, *Fatelessness* (1975) is a factually based account of Imre Kertész's experience in Buchenwald, but the book's ironic, disaffected tone is light years removed from the fervor of Wiesel, imprisoned in the same camp at around the same age. Jerzy Kosinski, on the other hand, used variations on the theme of his own autobiography to authenticate *The Painted Bird,* his novel about the experiences of a boy savagely persecuted by Poles during the war. When the truth about his history came out, his book also was discredited—despite the fact that he had always insisted it was fiction.

The 1980s and 1990s saw an increasing reliance on documentation, even among fiction writers. Thomas Keneally called *Schindler's Ark* a "non-fiction novel," arguing that he had used novelistic means to tell a story based entirely on fact because "fiction would debase the record." When Spielberg adapted Keneally's book into a fiction film, however, he had very different goals in mind. And when the German novelist Wolfgang Koeppen republished a memoir he had ghostwritten for a survivor shortly after the war—this time calling it a novel and attaching his own name—he ignited an enormous controversy over the questions of appropriation and authorship.

Meanwhile, among the generation of writers Brecht called "*die Nachgeborenen*"—those born after the war, whose lives were shaped by it even though they were not directly affected—W. G. Sebald stands out for his profound understanding of the ethical conflicts inherent in representing another person's life story. In works such as *The Emigrants* and *Austerlitz,* he employed a unique method of documentary fiction, incorporating interviews, letters, diaries, and photographs, which tease and unbalance the reader by simultaneously asserting and undermining the authority of the texts. Bernhard Schlink's novels, by contrast, have obsessively investigated the concept of collective guilt and responsibility, but stagnate in moral confusion. And the fiction by the self-identified members of the "second generation" in America—the sons and daughters of survivors—has often committed the unexpected crime of substituting the children for the parents as primary victims of the Holocaust.

If we have learned anything in the last sixty-five years, it is that—as even this brief and incomplete list of works demonstrates—there is an infinite number of stories to be told about the Holocaust. Recall Adorno's overused dictum once more: *Nach Auschwitz ein Gedicht zu schreiben, ist barbarisch.* Notice that he wrote *"ein Gedicht"*—not "poems" or "poetry" but "a poem." Sometimes I imagine that he might, perhaps even subconsciously, have meant the statement literally. It would be horrific to write only *one* poem after Auschwitz. But to write a hundred poems, a thousand poems, a million—that might be better, because it would take an infinite number of works of literature to represent the vast multiplicity of voices and experiences that constitute the Holocaust. In his Bremen Prize speech, Paul Celan said that "it, the language, remained, not lost, yes in spite of everything. But it had to pass through its own answerlessness, pass through frightful muting, pass through the thousand darknesses of deathbringing speech." The thousand darknesses are the stories of the Holocaust: endlessly echoing, ever terrifying, infinitely variable.

Part One

The Witnesses

1

Angry Young Man: Tadeusz Borowski

It is impossible to write about Auschwitz impersonally. The first duty
of Auschwitzers is to make clear just what a camp is.... But let them
not forget that the reader will unfailingly ask: how did it happen that
you survived?... Explain, then, how you bought places in the hospital,
easy posts; how you shoved the *"Muselmänner"* into the oven; how
you bought women, men; what you did in the barracks, unloading the
transports, at the gypsy camp; tell about the daily life of the camp, about
the hierarchy of fear, about the loneliness of every man. But write that
you, you were the ones who did this. That a portion of the sad fame of
Auschwitz belongs to you as well.

           —from Borowski's review of a Holocaust testimony

The book is small, about the size of an ordinary paperback, and heavier than it
looks. Its cover bears neither a title nor the name of an author, just an upside-
down red triangle with the letter "P" inside and the number 6643. Its cardboard binding is covered in fabric: a soft, flannel-like material, warm and fuzzy
to the touch, striped blue-gray.

This book is one of the most remarkable documents to emerge from World
War II. It is called *Byliśmy w Oświęcimiu,* or *We Were in Auschwitz,* and it was
published in Munich in 1946. The three authors, all non-Jewish Polish survivors of the death camp, were listed on the title page by their camp numbers.

Number 6643, the engineer Janusz Nel Siedlecki, was an "old-timer," as his low number demonstrates: he came to the camp in 1940, at its very beginnings, as a political prisoner. Number 75817, Krystyn Olszewski, was an architect who would go on to become one of the chief city planners for Warsaw, Baghdad, and Singapore. Number 119198 was Tadeusz Borowski.

Borowski published his first book of poetry in 1942, at the age of twenty, while he was a student at the underground Warsaw University. His fiancée, Maria Rundo (known by her nickname, Tuśka), was carrying what might have become his second book, a cycle of love poems, when she was arrested by the Gestapo the following year. Searching for her, Borowski too was arrested. He was sent first to Warsaw's Pawiak Prison and then to Auschwitz, where he remained for a year and a half before being transferred to various camps in Germany. He, Siedlecki, and Olszewski, along with Anatol Girs, the man who would become their publisher, were liberated from Dachau in May 1945 by the U.S. Army, to which they dedicated *We Were in Auschwitz*.

In Poland before the war, Girs had been a successful graphic artist and book designer. Now, in Munich, he established the Family Tracing Service—an offshoot of the Polish Red Cross devoted to reuniting the mass of refugees separated by the war—and brought the three survivors into his employ. It was he who originally conceived *We Were in Auschwitz,* intending the book to offer, as he wrote in the preface, "the history of a certain concentration camp...." Obviously, it does not subsume all of the circumstances of this camp, but very cautiously and, one is tempted to say, intimately, it gives a few fragments of what the authors themselves experienced and saw with their own eyes." Siedlecki, Olszewski, and Borowski each contributed chapters, ranging in length from a few pages to more than forty, told by narrators who share the authors' first names.

As if to put the book's authenticity beyond dispute, its cardboard covers imitated the blue and gray stripes of the clothing worn by Auschwitz inmates, along with Siedlecki's number. A few copies—only a handful are known to exist—were bound in the actual fabric used for the camp uniforms; Barbara Girs, Anatol Girs's daughter, showed one of them to me. (Several years ago Welcome Rain Publishers released an English translation of the book, by Alicia Nitecki, that reproduces this macabre binding.) The book's title was *We Were in Auschwitz,* but by binding it with clothing worn in the concentration camp—clothing they might have worn themselves—the authors make an even stronger declaration. "We *were* Auschwitz," they seem to say.

And the book's contents, which were even more shocking than its "fantastical binding" (as Borowski described it), reinforce this impression. The stories bear coldly ironic titles such as "I Don't Recommend Getting Sick" and "This Way for the Gas, Ladies and Gentlemen." (The latter, one of Borowski's contributions, would eventually be anthologized as a classic of Holocaust literature.) They established the harshest perspective yet seen on the universe of the concentration camp, regarding not just its perpetrators but also its victims. The writers did not shrink from offering details of torture discreetly omitted by other memoirists: prisoners in the arduous penal company lining up for voluntary hangings, an escapee forced to march around the camp in a clown costume before his execution. But the most horrific aspect of the stories—which ignited a controversy over the purposes of literature that would have drastic consequences for Borowski's future as a writer—is the utterly unforgiving way in which they portray the behavior of the prisoners toward each other.

This Auschwitz, in contrast to the myths that sprang up immediately in the war's aftermath, is not a place of martyrdom or heroism. It is a place where inmates higher up in the camp hierarchy, the Polish political prisoners and others with special privileges, jeer at the Jews and Gypsies lower on the totem pole; where even a minor offense will be brutally avenged; where a prisoner, wondering if his girlfriend might have been sent to the gas chamber, muses, "What's gone is gone." All this is recounted in a chillingly unsentimental and brazenly nihilistic voice that emphasizes its own detachment from the horrors that it records. Yet this detachment, it soon becomes clear, is a literary device for containing the speaker's fury, which bubbles up between the lines of each story even as he tries to choke it back.

Though the three former prisoners claimed joint authorship to the stories, this unforgettable voice has come to be associated with Borowski, and it is most pronounced in the four stories that he personally wrote for the volume, which he later reprinted under his own name in his first collection of fiction. When the stories first appeared in English translation—one in an anthology of Polish writing published in 1962, another in *Commentary* the same year—they were immediately recognized as singular in the burgeoning genre of Holocaust literature. But in the politically sensitive literary climate of Poland in the late 1940s, Borowski was more repudiated than celebrated. The editors of a prominent literary journal reprinted two of the *We Were in Auschwitz* stories, but accompanied them with a note in which the editors distanced themselves from Borowski's work. Critics in both the Catholic and the Communist press disparaged his writing as distasteful and even immoral. By the final years of the decade, Borowski had renounced his own fiction and launched himself into a new career as a journalist, writing propagandistic columns that promoted socialist realism and the dream of the Communist society.

In July 1951, shortly before his thirtieth birthday, Borowski committed suicide. It was an act that many critics, most prominently Czesław Miłosz, have understood as the unavoidable consequence of his political compromises. As Miłosz mercilessly portrayed him (under the pseudonym "Beta") in *The Captive Mind,* Borowski, who as a youth had been "a real poet," succumbed after Auschwitz to hatred and bitterness: "Pitiless and intolerant, he was one open wound." In propaganda, according to Miłosz, he found the ideal vehicle for his fury, and he grew addicted to the esteem that his "malignant articles" brought him. "His mind, like that of so many Eastern [European] intellectuals, was impelled toward self-annihilation," Miłosz concluded. Miłosz also repeated the rumor that Borowski, after surviving Auschwitz with Tuśka and later settling in Poland with her, had been unfaithful and found the guilt too much to bear.

But Borowski's suicide can also be read as a final act of rage against a world that turned out, in his estimation, to be more or less identical to Auschwitz itself, a world filled with robbers, swindlers, and murderers, and governed by similarly corrupt codes of conduct. A. Alvarez has famously written that "around Borowski's stories there is a kind of moral silence, like the pause which follows a scream." But the scream, for Borowski, was the essence of his work. If Elie Wiesel was the great mystic of the Holocaust and Primo Levi was its great analyst, Borowski was its angry young man, a pent-up vessel of pressurized fury that finally could do nothing but explode.

The story of Borowski's life has all the makings of a myth: a meteoric rise followed just as quickly by a meteoric fall, not to mention the horrific irony of his death (he gassed himself at home in his kitchen). And like all myths, the myth of Tadeusz Borowski has come to overshadow his work. To make matters worse, for years his poetry and his fiction have been relatively inaccessible, existing in incomplete and scattered versions. An authoritative edition of his complete work has appeared in Polish only in the last few years. In English, a collection of short stories under the title *This Way for the Gas, Ladies and Gentlemen* was one of the volumes published in the 1970s by Philip Roth in his seminal series "Writers from the Other Europe," devoted to promoting the work of Eastern European authors, and is still available in a Penguin Classics edition, but it includes only the best-known of his stories. A bilingual volume of his poetry, translated by Tadeusz Pióro, is out of print. The Polish literary critic Tadeusz Drewnowski published a biography of Borowski in 1972, but it has not been translated. The agonizing questions raised by Borowski's life and work have by and large gone unanswered. Why did he switch abruptly from poetry to prose after the war, only to renounce literature altogether a few years later? What led him to embrace the Communist Party, and what eventually disillusioned him? And why did he commit suicide?

The appearance of Borowski's correspondence, selected and edited by Tadeusz Drewnowski and published in Poland in 2001 and in America in 2007 as *Postal Indiscretions: The Correspondence of Tadeusz Borowski,* seemed to offer the possibility of some answers. But even these letters—which include postcards that Borowski sent to his parents from Auschwitz, love letters to his fiancée from the period when they were separated after the war, and editorial correspondence from Borowski's career as a literary critic and journalist—tend to be revealing primarily for what they do not reveal. The title of the volume is misleading: very few "postal indiscretions" are committed here. Borowski's letters can be candid and affecting, but they are more often very guarded. And yet, while it leaves more than a few mysteries maddeningly unsolved, the book offers a view of a Borowski far different from the furious narrator of his stories: a gentle, joking man who encouraged and supported his literary friends even as he struggled with the morality of creating literature after the horror of the concentration camps, a man who pined for his great love even as he despaired of ever again feeling like a whole human being.

And so the letters force a reconsideration of how exactly to understand Borowski's work. Virtually unanimously, critics have read the stories as testimonial. The "autobiographical pact" (to use Philippe Lejeune's phrase) at the start of *We Were in Auschwitz*—the concentration camp numbers as bylines, the "fantastical binding," the insistence in the preface on the stories' authenticity—could hardly be more explicit. Barbara Vedder, in her translator's preface to the first American edition of the stories, refers to Borowski's "documentary technique." More than a matter of style, the question of whether Borowski speaks in his own voice is crucial to his vision of Auschwitz. "The identification of the author with the narrator was the moral decision of a prisoner who had lived through Auschwitz—an acceptance of mutual responsibility, mutual participation, and mutual guilt for the concentration camp," wrote the Polish literary critic Jan Kott in his introduction to the Penguin volume.

But despite the apparently confessional tone of these stories, despite the apparent identity of author and narrator, a haze persists regarding the matter of their genre. How can we account for their double publication: first as "fragments of what the authors themselves experienced and saw with their own eyes" (as Anatol Girs wrote), then in the Polish press as short stories?

It is up to the reader to decide in which category they belong: nonfiction or fiction, neither or both. And this decision has important implications for the way we understand Borowski's "moral decision" in his portrayal of the camp. Is the "Tadek" who narrates the stories—pitiless, privileged, opportunistic—an accurate representation of Borowski himself? ("Tadek" is a common nickname for Tadeusz.) Since little is known about Borowski's actual behavior in the camp, this cannot be assumed. Miłosz, in the single sympathetic sentence of his otherwise unsparing depiction of Borowski in *The Captive Mind,* notes that "the truth about [Borowski's] behavior in Auschwitz, according to his fellow-prisoners, is utterly different from what his stories would lead one to suppose; he acted heroically, and was a model of comradeship." And so perhaps the narrator is best understood more generally, as a stand-in for the camp mentality as a whole…but then what of the authors' insistence on their book's authenticity? Where are their personal stories?

The writer of the letters is a gentler, more optimistic, less cynical man than the narrator of the stories. But when it comes to describing the conditions in the camps, the fiction is more accurate. Borowski's initial letters, sent to his mother first from Pawiak prison and soon from Auschwitz, reveal the impress of the censor metaphorically if not literally: their contents are restricted to the careful explanation of what sorts of food items he was permitted to receive. "Send me whatever, and as much as, you are able, and preferably as often as you wrote in the letter. Don't worry about me, I am completely healthy and feel fine," he writes on May 30, 1943, in his first letter from the camp. "If you can, send more, and more often," the second letter pleads. A few weeks later, the businesslike language does not conceal his desperation: "Send bigger packages and as often as possible.…More dried bread, also loaves of bread, as much fat as you can…whole packages of onion, garlic, and other vegetables." It was, of course, a sign of Borowski's relatively privileged position as a Polish political prisoner that he was permitted to receive such packages; the Jews were not even allowed to write letters.

And the stories demonstrate that Borowski was intensely aware of the injustice of privileged status. In "A Day at Harmenz," a Jew who has been selected for the gas chamber begs Tadek to share his food. "Okay, Jew, come on up and eat," Tadek replies. "And when you've had enough, take the rest with you to the cremo." (According to Drewnowski's notes on the letters, at the same time as Borowski's mother was sending her son the packages that cushioned for him the brutality of Auschwitz, she managed to shelter a Jewish child at the family's home in Warsaw.) Christopher Bigsby, whose excellent book *Remember-*

ing and Imagining the Holocaust offers one of the only sustained studies of Borowski's work in English, draws attention to the almost edenic vision of life among the functionaries: "Perversely, this appears to be a place of plenty." It can be no accident that the high-level prisoners occupy the top bunks; their exalted position contrasts sharply with that of the Jews lying in excrement in the hell down below.

Borowski was lucky in another way as well: he was able to pass letters to his fiancée in the women's camp, and even occasionally to see her. The first time, Kott writes, was when Borowski was sent to the women's camp to pick up the corpses of infants. Tuśka's head was shaved, and her body was covered with scabies. "Don't worry; our children won't be bald," Borowski is reported to have said to her. Later, assigned to a roofing commando working in the women's camp, he was able at least to catch sight of her every day. Of course, there is no mention of any of this in the letters home, composed with the knowledge that the authorities were reading every word. A single cryptic comment—"I'm happy that Tuśka often sees her husband"—is all that he will dare.

But the story "Auschwitz, Our Home" reconstructs the letters that Borowski sent to his beloved, which describe a particularly tranquil period when he was training to become an orderly at the Auschwitz hospital—a position highly preferable to hard labor. The inmates who have experienced Birkenau depict Auschwitz as a place not far from paradise: the distinction here is between "Auschwitz I," the camp's administrative headquarters, and "Auschwitz II/ Birkenau," the much larger and better-known extermination camp. (There was also Auschwitz III/Monowitz, site of the Buna chemical factory, where Primo Levi worked for a time.) "These people over here are crazy about Auschwitz," Borowski writes. " 'Auschwitz, our home,' they say with pride." The story's narrator, too, speaks of the camp with something like affection: he describes "the Puff," the camp bordello, which functions in the usual way, except that its users must undergo disinfection before and after their visits; and a wedding that takes place to the accompaniment of the prison orchestra. "Now everyone at the camp walks proudly, head high. 'We even have weddings in Auschwitz!' "

But life at Auschwitz I was hardly all sex and romance. In this story, Borowski offers his bluntest assessment of the evil of the Nazi system, which he describes with a chilling simplicity:

> If I had said to you as we danced together in my room in the light of the paraffin lamp: listen, take a million people, or two million, or three, kill them in such a way that no one knows about it, not even they themselves,

enslave several hundred thousand more, destroy their mutual loyalty, pit man against man...surely you would have thought me mad....But this is how it is done: first just one ordinary barn, brightly whitewashed— and here they proceed to asphyxiate people. Later, four large buildings, accommodating twenty thousand at a time without any trouble. No hocus-pocus, no poison, no hypnosis. Only several men directing traffic to keep operations running smoothly, and the thousands flow along like water from an open tap.

"One ordinary barn"; "only several men directing traffic"—what disturbs Borowski particularly is the apparent normalcy with which business at Auschwitz is conducted. The recent conventional wisdom, supported by scholars of Auschwitz such as Raul Hilberg and Hannah Arendt, has presented the Final Solution as a giant bureaucracy that required the participation of millions, from janitors to high-level strategists, to keep the machine running. But Borowski saw it differently, emphasizing the relatively small amount of infrastructure and labor required for Auschwitz to function. What was most necessary, he believed, was the cooperation of the prisoners themselves. As Bigsby succinctly puts it, "Because he was fed and clothed as a result of those brought to this place to die, when the transports ceased to arrive with regularity he found himself lamenting their non-appearance....His survival depended upon the death of others." In order to survive, the inmates had to assume this double role of victim and executioner, and they did so automatically, as a matter of course. Even those responsible for the cruelest tasks—unloading the transports of prisoners arriving at the camp, despoiling them of their valuables, and leading them to the gas chamber—were not "bad people," Borowski wrote in "This Way for the Gas, Ladies and Gentlemen," his most famous story. "They were simply accustomed."

A reader who did not know the context of Borowski's Auschwitz letters might think their writer was taking the cure at some particularly unluxurious spa. "All's well with me, I'm just a bit tired," he wrote to his mother in January 1944. "I myself am, of course, well and cheerful, a normal person who accepts the present as though it were already the past, who is full of hope and not without a future," he reported the following summer. Again, a truer picture can be found in Borowski's fiction. "This Way for the Gas" is based on a harrowing day spent working on the platform where the transports arrived. A friend invites the story's narrator, again called Tadek, to serve as a substitute worker on the "Canada" commando, which is in charge of unloading the train cars. It is a relatively cushy post: the workers get to keep some of the food and clothing they find, and the labor is not physically challenging. The catch, Tadek quickly discovers, is that he is forced to confront the Jews headed to their deaths. Here he is no longer an onlooker to the thousands who "flow along like water from an open tap," and accordingly, his formerly disingenuous tone is now cynical and knowing. But still he is not beyond all possibility of shock—and it is at these moments that the story's moral voice, often over-looked amid the onslaught of cynicism, can be made out.

The language of the story, relentlessly impersonal, works against any recog-nition of the Jews' humanity: "heads" and "mouths" appear at the train win-dows instead of people; the Jews are a "crowd," a "wave," or a "river," rather than individuals. (The critics Sidra Ezrahi and James E. Young have noted that Borowski allows himself to use only comparisons that reflect the world of the camp: the pavement glistens "like a black leather strap." This works, in Young's words, to "keep both the writer's and the reader's minds fenced into the camp.... Through this kind of figuring, Borowski also reflects a consciousness that in itself has become subject to the norms of the camp.") Tadek describes his own actions with a distinctly impersonal Polish verb form: rather than say-ing "I jumped into the car," he uses a construction that would translate literally as something like "The car was jumped into." In contrast, vehicles start up on their own, as if they were living beings. "Trucks are given more agency than those they carry," writes Christopher Bigsby.

But human contact cannot be avoided for long. Several times Tadek must acknowledge his victims, and each encounter is profoundly distressing. Clean-ing out one of the cattle cars, he finds a pile of dead babies. An SS officer tells him to make the Jewish women carry them onto trucks destined for the gas chambers. Most of the women run in horror, but an older woman, taking the babies from his arms, looks into his eyes. " 'Child, child,' she whispered and smiled at me." Another woman refuses to acknowledge her own child, who runs after her, screaming; she is beaten by an outraged member of the com-mando. Finally Tadek encounters a blond girl who reminds him of Tuśka. She faces him with unusual poise:

"Listen, listen, tell me, where are they taking us?"
    I looked at her. Here standing before me is a girl with marvelous blond hair, with lovely breasts, in an embroidered summer blouse, with a wise, mature gaze. She stands, looks me straight in the eye, and waits. Over there is the gas chamber: communal death, hideous and disgusting. On

the other side, the camp: the shaved head, the padded Soviet trousers in the heat, the repulsive, sickening stench of dirty, overheated women's bodies, the animalistic hunger, the inhuman labor, and then that same chimney, but a death still more hideous, still more disgusting, still more terrifying. No one who comes here—even if his ashes do not rise into the air above the chain of guards—will ever return to his former life....

"Answer."

I was silent. Her mouth tightened.

"I already know," she said with a shade of haughty disdain in her voice, tossing her head. She walked boldly toward the trucks. Someone tried to hold her back, but resolutely she pushed him away and ran to the steps of the truck, which was already almost full. I could see from afar only her flowing blond hair, blowing in the wind.[1]

The girl's question, of course, cannot be answered. "It is the law of the camp that people going to their deaths are deceived until the very last moment," Tadek says earlier in the story. "This is the only permissible form of mercy." The story's title, then, is the height of irony; it represents precisely what cannot be said. Tadek has no choice but to be silent, but he recognizes his silence, too, as a form of complicity. In the last scene, the commando, returning to the camp, passes a division of SS officers marching and singing the Nazi anthem *Und morgen die ganze Welt* ("And tomorrow the world"). "'*Rechts ran!* To the right!' someone calls from the front of the command. We get out of their way."

We get out of their way. The camp permits no resistance. This is the crux of the moral problem in Borowski's stories: there can be no heroism in surviving, because the camp is a zero-sum game. Those who live do so at the expense of others. "In the framework of a 'criminal system' the very idea of a criminal and his victim becomes relative, because the system turns victims into criminals," the Polish critic Andrzej Wirth has written. Wirth gives as an example the dilemma faced by a prisoner in the story "Death of a Freedom Fighter," in which a man dying of hunger begs another prisoner for a beet. He will die of starvation without it, but he will also die if he eats it, because the beet is poisonous if consumed raw. The solution Borowski's story offers, Wirth writes, is "even more criminal than these two": the second prisoner sells the beet to the first man in return for his last ration of bread. Likewise, the narrator of "This

1. The translations from this story, as well as the translations of Borowski's poetry, are my own. Translations from the other stories are adapted from the versions by Alicia Nitecki and Barbara Vedder.

Way for the Gas" finds himself worrying about what will happen if the transports stop, since he and his fellow functionaries depend upon the steady influx
of food and clothing.

Through the depiction of "almost unimaginable crimes as if they were something quite natural," Wirth argues, Borowski achieves an "alienation effect, in
the flash of which [he] portrays the truth about the camps." This "natural,"
straightforward voice had already been seen in Erich Maria Remarque's anti-
war novel *All Quiet on the Western Front,* which uses a casual, unsanitized tone
to depict horrors of the greatest magnitude and the matter-of-fact behavior
of the German soldiers. Borowski, who is likely to have read Remarque—
the novel appeared in Polish translation in 1930—brings this style of cynical
realism to the camps. One of the most notorious examples is an exchange in
"Auschwitz, Our Home" in which another prisoner proudly describes to the
narrator "a new way to burn people":—the heads of four children are placed
together and their hair is set on fire, so that their bodies become a kind of
torch. Lawrence Langer writes that "the casual exchange…leaps with chilling
effect from the pages in a kind of verbal counterpoint, as the harmony of con-
versational tone is constantly disrupted by the dissonance of its theme."

In the story's last line, which follows directly upon the passage about the
burning children, this tone falters. Here the "fourth wall" breaks down; the
author appears to address the reader in his own voice. "But this is a monstrous
lie, a grotesque lie, like the whole camp, like the whole world." Wirth objects
to this, arguing that the weakest moments in Borowski are the ones in which
"the author identifies himself with the narrator and offers *direct* comments."
Langer, too, finds it jarring:

> Borowski is outraged by man's acquiescence to forces that dehumanize,
> humiliate, and ultimately destroy him; but in this passage he appears
> even more apprehensive over the possibility of the reader's failing to
> recognize the implications of such acquiescence—hence his angry out-
> burst. It is almost as if he feared too great a success for his literary art:
> the ostensible indifference in the tone of the speakers inculcates a com-
> parable detachment in the reader, and creates the danger of his "passing
> by" without acknowledging the insidious change that has been wrought
> in the characters."

But it is important to recognize that the "ostensible indifference" is itself an
illusion, beneath which beats the moral heart of these stories. If there were

nothing exceptional about the world of Auschwitz, if it were truly an extension of the daily life of humanity, there would be no reason to write about it at all. Borowski's outburst underlines his own dilemma as a prisoner turned writer.

After Dachau was liberated, at the end of April 1945, Borowski was transported to Munich, only about ten miles from the camp. For some time, as he reports in his letters, he could find no civilian clothes, and had to go around in his "prison stripes." When he was finally able to exchange them, the only available replacement was an SS uniform, which he was still wearing the following fall. The war had ended, but its traces were not so easily shaken off.

In his letters from Munich, in which he debated whether to return to Poland, Borowski was generally laconic about his experience in the camp. "You probably haven't got the slightest idea how long a person can live without food," he wrote to a former schoolmate, describing the journey from Auschwitz to Dachau. In another letter ten days later, he was even more succinct: "I survived, it was awful, but no matter." Of course, it did matter, more than anything. As he would write in "This Way for the Gas," "No one who comes here...will ever return to his former life."

For one thing, there was very little left of Borowski's former life to return to. He was thrilled to discover that a few of his friends from university were still alive, but they brought the terrible news that many others had not survived the war. Much of his poetry had also been lost. "If you remember anything, write it down and send it to me," he begged. It took him months to trace Tuśka, whom he had not seen since August 1944, when she had been transferred to Ravensbrück. "Tell her, if she's alive, that I exist," he wrote to his friend Stanisław Kazimierz Marczak, in words that appear nearly verbatim in one of his poems. "That I will return at her slightest summons leaving everything behind: writing, stories, promises." In late 1945 he finally learned that she was living in Sweden, but it was another year before they would reunite and marry in Poland.

Separated from his love, Borowski was uncannily nostalgic for the time they had spent together at Auschwitz, a nostalgia that appears in both his letters and his poetry. "*Światło i cień*" ("Light and Shadow"), a cycle of love poems that he began in Warsaw before they were both arrested, includes what might be the only published love poem set in the death camp, a pastoral reverie that begins "You remember the sun of Auschwitz" and goes on to imagine the countryside around the camp, the "far-off green meadow and white-celadon clouds," as if the landscape itself were the poet's lover. Another poem written at Dachau finds evidence for the beloved's survival in the natural world:

I know you are alive. Otherwise
what sense would there be in the shadow and light
of faraway cold stars, reflections
of a crystal world? The black earth
seems to blaze with dew, the woods
rise up darkly above the horizon
as if it were the sea's blue depths,
and my blood pulses as if its beat answered
the beat of the waves of all the seas in the universe,
so close to me and yet so far,
pulsing with your blood.
I feel you are here, I know you are.

These dense, allusive lyrics, deeply romantic and infused with a shimmering, corporeal vision of nature, would be remarkable regardless of the circumstances of their creation. That they were written in the camps makes them nearly miraculous.

But as he waited in "faraway, hateful Munich" for word from Tuśka on whether she would return to Poland with him, Borowski began to grow skeptical about the value of his poetry—of any poetry at all. "Our era hurts too much to write poems about the setting of the moon," he wrote in early 1946. In another letter around the same time, he expressed a withering condemnation of some earlier Polish poets and their preference for florid description and "Byronic grief" over reality: "Please believe me when I say that some parts of Germany (Dresden, Württemberg, the Alps, for example) are as beautiful as the landscapes in the novels of bygone centuries. But when we walked across them in prison stripes, we did not extol the beauty of this country.... The most beautiful city? Frankfurt reduced to rubble.... What I'm writing is, of course, only effective barbarism."

In his Munich poems, Borowski cultivated a voice even more powerful in its constrained ferocity than the voice of his stories. The poems' tight, almost singsong rhythm and ingenious multilingual rhymes serve as an ironic contrast to the subject matter: the wreckage of Europe in the wake of the camps. (What other poet has devised so many rhymes for "crematorium"?) In "Résumé of a Good German," he traces the career path of an SS soldier—the Hitler Youth, battles in Africa and Russia, finally Auschwitz—along with his reading material along the way: Goethe, Hegel, Hitler. (Borowski rhymes "Hitler *Jugend*" with "*Tugend*"—German for virtue—and "*Mein Kampf*" with "ramp," the platform where the transports were unloaded.) "Friends" affects an ironic sneer at his fellow students who died in the war:

> All of my friends
> SOBs
> knew life in the damp
> of KZs.

(KZ is the abbreviation for *Konzentrationslager für Zivilpersonen,* the German term for concentration camp.)

These flashes of angry humor cannot entirely lighten the immeasurable sadness at the core of Borowski's poetry. Grounding his pyrotechnics is a mournful vision of a world unable to leave Auschwitz behind. In a heartbreaking inversion of his love lyrics, "Farewell to Maria" warns his beloved not to return to Poland with him: "My love / was devoured by the crematorium fire." In "Fairy Tale for Children," he imagines legends of the camps passed down through generations, with no redemption: "Our children will build gas chambers, / they will murder people inside." A poem dedicated to Stanisław Wygodzki, a Jewish poet who had also survived Auschwitz, predicts the circumstances under which each of them would return to Poland. Wygodzki, Borowski wrote, would be "alone, unneeded / like a shred of stripped-off bark," his wife and daughter both having perished. In contrast, Borowski imagines himself sharing a meal with his family, but fundamentally no less alone.

> "That was interesting," someone will say.
> "My poor boy," someone will sigh.
> And I will feel myself far away
> with a world beyond waking in my sight.

"I saw the death of a million people—literally, not metaphorically," Borowski wrote in one of his letters. The burden of bearing witness to this enormity was overpowering. As early as summer 1946, he declared in a letter to Tuśka that he had given up poetry, though he continued writing poems for at least another year. But prose was not the answer, either. Borowski was ambivalent about *We Were in Auschwitz* even before the book appeared, describing it as "an unfortunate mix of encyclopedia, symphony, proclamation, and anecdote....I wrote two stories for it to which I will admit, and a few other things that I'd willingly foist off on my friends." (In fact, Borowski not only wrote four stories for the book, but he edited those written by Siedlecki and Olszewski, and reportedly also wrote the book's extensive editorial remarks as well as its indispensible "glossary" of Auschwitz terms.) "There is nothing artistic about it, since it was written in haste and to order," he wrote to Tuśka's uncle, the editor of a literary journal, about the book. "I am sending you one of the stories as a sample of no worth."

After his return to Poland in June 1946, Borowski continued to publish stories on what he called "camp themes," many just a few pages long, which were collected in 1948 as *Kamienny świat* (*Stony World*). Some of these were based on his experiences in the German camps; others were intended to demonstrate how "concentration camp reality" persisted into the postwar period. He also threw himself into writing literary journalism, producing numerous reviews and essays for the journals and magazines that had sprung up or resurrected themselves after the war, and even starting one of his own, though it folded after a few issues. The letters from this period, largely business correspondence concerning deadlines and manuscripts, give almost no hint of the commotion that Borowski's work was causing. His most notorious piece was a devastating review of *Z otchłani* (*Out of the Abyss*), a highly regarded memoir by the Catholic Auschwitz survivor Zofia Kossak-Szczucka. Borowski alleged that she had doctored facts in order to conceal her privileged status at the camp and accused her of promulgating the Polish "martyrological myth" by suggesting, for example, that Polish women could tolerate hunger for longer than others because they were accustomed to observing the Catholic fast days. (As if there were no fast days in Judaism!)

The review provoked a concerted attack on Borowski in both the Catholic and the Communist press. "The public was expecting martyrologies; the Communist Party called for works that were ideological, that divided the world into the righteous and the unrighteous, heroes and traitors," Kott writes. Of course, this was the exact antithesis of Borowski's view of the camps. Borowski was accused of immorality for his stories' portrayal of the savagery of Auschwitz— for daring to suggest that anyone might have been more focused on survival than on good deeds—and was told that he lacked the ethical right to judge the writing of others. Several editors demanded that he be brought before the court of the Polish Writers' Union.

If these attacks disturbed Borowski, he did not acknowledge it in his letters. But he did hint at the government's growing interest in literary activities. In a letter to a friend on January 10, 1948, Borowski refers jokingly to "the Ministry of…and…(of Art and Culture, but since there is neither art nor culture there, I maintain that only 'and' remains)." He joined the Communist Party later that year, but his membership did not alter the official position on his fiction. At a meeting of the Polish Writers' Union in January 1949, Władysław Sikorski, the minister of culture, referred to Borowski as "a dangerous phenomenon, sometimes even positively harmful," and the editor of one of Poland's most prominent literary journals, formerly a supporter of Borowski's, joined in the chorus of condemnation. "He declared my creative work youthful, pointed out and condemned its immorality, left the door open for the future with the words that 'it is hard to assess him as yet,'" Borowski reported. "It'll be easier if they just hit me on the head."

It goes without saying that these attacks were unfair. Borowski's critics were judging him on religious and ideological grounds, not on his literary merits; and they had their own obvious political motives. Yet his friends, too, were growing concerned about his unbearably pessimistic worldview, his conviction that the brutality of Auschwitz continued unabated in the "stony world" of the postwar years. A colleague wrote that Borowski's skewed perspective reminded him of "the Malayan girl in Conrad's story: a girl who, reading only the local paper consisting of reprints from European papers of news about accidents, comes to the conclusion that Europe is one great slaughterhouse." Anatol Girs, who by now had emigrated to America, repeatedly urged Borowski to abandon the camp theme: "One cannot always live in camp memories. It was written about and one needs to let it go.… There are, after all, enough subjects, as you well know."

But Borowski had no other subject. Auschwitz was an essential element of his conception of himself. "We're a pair of sick people, you and I," he had written to Tuśka a year after liberation." We suffer from some indefinable nostalgia and are weary of the world. But evil doesn't lie in the world, it lies in us. I think it is going to be hard for me to live like this."

On a trip to Belgrade in 1947, Borowski had found himself impressed by his Yugoslav colleagues' pragmatic approach to their careers. "Literature isn't the chief occupation of young and old writers, and there are three, maybe four, professional writers—making a living only off writing," he reported to Tuśka. "The rest concern themselves with matters that are often far from literary, and that are primarily useful, and only after that beautiful. Perhaps this is better."

As socialist realism was promoted more and more stringently in Poland—it was officially espoused for the first time at that 1949 writers' conference—Borowski struggled to find a way to function within the system. In June 1949, he accepted a job in East Berlin as a cultural attaché at the Polish Press Office. He seems to have thought that the post would provide him with a salary while still allowing him time for his own work. In fact, the job may have been intentionally designed to frustrate him; forced to do administrative work all day, he was unable to write.

But the German Democratic State was established in October, not long after Borowski's arrival, and he seems to have found in it his inspiration. "Infant cries in Berlin: a new people's democracy is being born," he wrote to Aleksander Wat a few weeks after the state was established. "May we have ever more of such infants!" Returning to Warsaw the following March, he devoted himself entirely to journalism, producing a weekly column in which he promoted socialist realism and denounced the decadence of the West. "I don't care if they lament my wasting myself on journalism," he wrote. "I don't consider myself a vestal virgin consecrated to prose." Miłosz, in *The Captive Mind,* describes this final stage of his career:

> For all their violence and precision of language, his articles were so dull and one-dimensional that this debasement of a gifted prose writer stirred my curiosity. He was certainly intelligent enough to understand that he was wasting his talent. In conversation with several literary authorities whose word determines a writer's place in the official hierarchy, I asked why such measures were being applied to him...." No one makes him write articles," came the reply, "that's the whole misfortune. The editor of the weekly can't drive him away. He himself insists on writing them. He thinks there is no time, today, for art, that you have to act on the masses more directly and elementally. He wants to be as useful as possible."

How did Borowski so quickly jump from party scourge to Communist darling—from joking about "the Ministry of...and..." to serving as its official mouthpiece? His letters offer no explanation. In Berlin, we see him for the first time writing in Communist boilerplate, admiring the maturity of the city's young workers and observing "the class struggle in the area of culture." In a letter dated around the same time, Tuśka coolly assesses West Berlin: "Luxury behind window displays, prostitution on the streets, and despair in the heart." But only a single letter written during the last year of Borowski's life seems to have survived, a superficial note to his brother that offers a report of a factory visited on a recent trip to Berlin and the news that Tuśka was expecting a baby. (Their daughter was born on June 27, 1951, less than a week before Borowski's suicide.) There are, however, some excoriating letters from friends and colleagues who were amazed at Borowski's transformation. "Do you think, Sir, that a great literature can arise without being based on the literary output of older generations, even though…[they] concerned themselves with 'bourgeois' problems?" the journalist and theater critic Jan Paweł Gawlik inquired sharply. The editor Stefan Kisielewski, who had supported Borowski during the initial attack on him, now turned unsparing: "I consider you a journalist of great talent and equally great ignorance.…I doubt that I can stop you on the intellectual slope down which you are heading. But I want my conscience to be clear: that I warned you."

The circumstances of Borowski's suicide left the doors wide open for speculation about his motives. Drewnowski notes that he tried to kill himself several times during the last year of his life, citing a letter from 1946 as explanation: "Sometimes it seems it would be good to leave the field of battle before one commits some kind of compromise." But this does not really explain anything, since by the year before his death it was already far too late for Borowski to avoid compromise. Two weeks before Borowski's suicide, according to Kott, Czesław Mankiewicz, an old friend of his who had previously been tortured by the Gestapo, was arrested by the Polish Security Service. Borowski tried to intercede on his behalf, but was told that "the people's justice was never mistaken."

Kott writes also that Borowski confided to his closest friends that, "like Mayakovsky, he had 'stepped on the throat of his own song.'" In a poem written on the occasion of Borowski's death, Miłosz too compares Borowski to Mayakovsky: "*Noc, do siebie strzela / I nie masz, nie masz wtedy przyjaciela*": "At night, he shoots himself / And then you have no, you have no friends." In *The Captive Mind*, Miłosz commented that "those who observed him in the last months of his feverish activity were of the opinion that the discrepancy between what he said in his public statements and what his quick mind could perceive was increasing daily. He behaved too nervously for them not to suspect that he was acutely aware of this contrast."

In England and America, by contrast, readers have followed the usual tendency to assume that the suicide of a Holocaust survivor is a direct consequence of his or her experience during the war. "Having escaped the Zyklon B of Auschwitz, he gassed himself at home," A. Alvarez concluded. Yet this assumption seems in many cases facile, an oversimplification. To say of the suicide of Primo Levi (which has in the twenty years since his death become the prime example of this tendency) that "Auschwitz killed him forty years later" is to overlook the severity of Levi's depression, which plagued him throughout his life, as all his biographers attest. (Borowski, too, may have suffered from manic depression.) The temperaments, the inclinations, the psychologies of the survivors are surely as relevant as the historical factors, if not more so: as Lionel Trilling once observed, it is in our particularity that we suffer. Anyway, speculations about the motivations for suicide always have an air of ghoulish futility. Who can ever understand why another person, especially a stranger known only through his writing, commits this most hopeless of acts?

In the case of Borowski, however, the Auschwitz interpretation does seem to have a certain plausibility, although in a way quite different from the easy correlation that is normally suggested. This requires some explaining. Unusually for a non-Jewish writer, Borowski's stories about the camp have been unquestioningly accepted into what has become established, for better or for worse, as the canon of Holocaust literature. His work is taught in college courses alongside the memoirs of Wiesel and Levi, and he is assumed, like them, to have been among the victims of the Holocaust, not among the perpetrators. Yet it is important to remember that Borowski—at least for the purposes of his fiction—viewed himself as a kind of perpetrator.

There can be no doubt that Borowski suffered terribly at Auschwitz; but he experienced the camp at a certain remove. As a Polish political prisoner, he was exempt from the very worst threat: three weeks before his arrival at Auschwitz, the Nazis had stopped gassing Aryan prisoners. And thanks to the food that he received from home, he did not have to subsist on the Auschwitz starvation diet, which Levi painstakingly documented as consisting of about eight hundred calories per day. Levi, too, as he readily admitted, for a time occupied a relatively privileged position as a laboratory worker, but as a Jew he lived in a state of constant threat from which Borowski was—at least in certain ways— exempt. Since "his survival depended upon the death of others," Chrisopher Bigsby writes, it was "morally tainted."

The gulf between Borowski's experience of Auschwitz and Levi's experience of it can be seen in two particularly telling passages. In a story called "The People Who Walked On," included in *We Were in Auschwitz,* Borowski describes playing soccer on a field at the camp directly adjacent to the ramp where the transports were unloaded. One day Borowski was tending goal, and as he went to retrieve the ball, he noticed that the people from a newly arrived transport had just assembled on the platform. He returned to the game and continued playing, then looked back a few minutes later. The platform was now empty. "Between two throw-ins in a soccer game," he writes, "right behind my back, three thousand people had been put to death." This line has become notorious as an example of the indifference affected by Borowski's narrator—a transport is being unloaded, and he plays soccer! It can also be read as a judgment less on the narrator than on the entire apparatus that disposed of human beings in such a preternaturally efficient manner. What can it be like to realize that the population of a small town was sent to the gas chamber while one's back was turned? But no matter how one reads the line, there can be no doubt that the Borowski figure in the story is on the soccer field, not on the ramp.

Compare this description, in Levi's book *The Drowned and the Saved,* of what might have been the same soccer game. It occurs in a chapter titled "The Gray Zone," in which Levi analyzes the cases of certain groups of privileged prisoners at Auschwitz, and the varying levels of collaboration with the system required of virtually everyone who survived the camp. (Levi mordantly notes that "privileged prisoners were a minority within the *Lager* population; nevertheless they represent a potent majority among survivors.") He devotes particular attention to the prisoners who served on the *Sonderkommandos,* the work forces who escorted the prisoners to the gas chambers and disposed of their bodies afterward. These prisoners were kept segregated from the general population of the camp, and thus they attained a certain legendary status as the personification of collaboration and degradation. "It has been testified that a large amount of alcohol was put at the disposal of those wretches," Levi writes, "and that they were in a permanent state of complete debasement and prostration." To emphasize their utterly depraved condition, he tells of a soccer game played between a team representing the SS crematorium guards and a team representing the *Sonderkommando.* "Nothing of this kind ever took place, nor would it have been conceivable, with other categories of prisoners," Levi writes. "But with them, with the 'crematorium ravens,' the SS could enter the field on an equal footing, or almost. Behind this armistice one hears satanic laughter.... We have embraced you, corrupted you, dragged you to the bottom with us.... You too, like us and like Cain, have killed the brother. Come, we can play together."

Borowski was no "crematorium raven." According to his biographer Drewnowski, he worked on the *Sonderkommando* for only one day—the day that he depicts in "This Way for the Gas." But many of the details that he provides in that story—the commandos' use of alcohol on the ramp, for instance, or the psychological makeup of the squad members—corroborate Levi's analysis. He was not one of the brutes Levi imagines, men psychologically destroyed by the inhumanities they were forced to perpetrate. And who is to say that any prisoner, faced with the offer of delicacies from all over Europe, new clothes, maybe even a watch, could have turned that down? Yet the fact remains that it was Levi who starved with the hordes of miserable Jews, and Borowski who mocked them when they begged him for food: "Okay, Jew, come on up and eat. And when you've had enough, take the rest with you to the cremo." It was Levi who incredulously heard the report of a soccer game in Auschwitz, and Borowski, with his back to the ramp, who tended the goal.

Or was it? Is "The People Who Walked On," together with Borowski's other stories, the equivalent of an eyewitness report—a "fiction virtually indistinguishable from fact," in Bigsby's phrase—or an imagined episode? The stories and letters are the only documentation that exists on Borowski's actual conduct in Auschwitz, and the eyewitness reports differ. Remember Miłosz's assertion that he "acted heroically, and was a model of comradeship." Andrzej Wirth writes that Borowski voluntarily gave up his post as a hospital orderly "to share the common lot of the other prisoners." But Wirth published his essay in 1967; at that point, just a year before a renewed wave of anti-Semitism would drive out many of the country's remaining Jews, Polish critics may not have completely understood what the "common lot" of Auschwitz prisoners was. Another Polish critic, writing in 1960, described the narrator of the stories as a "typical inmate," a mistake that could perhaps only have been made in postwar Poland, where there persisted for decades a highly distorted view of the Holocaust that downplayed the experience of the Jews and focused on the Polish "martyrs."

"The worst—that is, the fittest—survived," Levi wrote also in *The Drowned and the Saved*. "The best all died." What he meant, as he had already written repeatedly, is that it was impossible to survive in Auschwitz without resorting to theft, to trickery, even to collaboration—at the very least, to selfishness and deception. Those who did not—who shared their food rations, who picked up the slack for those unable to perform heavy labor, who extended a hand to help a prisoner who had fallen—were guaranteed to perish. This is hardly a moral judgment; no one can fault survivors for the ferocity of their will to survive. And it is also not universally true: Levi's writings are full of evidence of the help he received from others, from the non-Jew Lorenzo who brought him extra portions of soup to his partnership with his friend Alberto Dalla Volta, with whom he shared "everything."

No one who has read Levi's scrupulous and intelligent writings can believe that their author could have been among "the worst." The same goes for Borowski: a writer of extraordinary talent and perception, whose moral rage at an incomprehensibly vast injustice was so all-consuming that in the end it overpowered his political judgment. But this is the way he saw himself. In the end, we cannot know how he behaved at Auschwitz. All we know is how he presented his own behavior—or, if not exactly his own, then the behavior of a narrator who must be understood as a representation of himself. Borowski concurred fully with Levi's philosophy of the camp. And the psychological wound suffered by a person who believes that about himself is unimaginable. In a terrible way, in a pitiful way, Borowski was not only *in* Auschwitz; he *was* Auschwitz. His privileges came at an annihilating cost. The Nazis spared his body, but they exterminated his soul.

2

The Alchemist: Primo Levi

A batch that spoils is one that solidifies halfway through the preparation: the liquid becomes gelatinous, or even hard, like horn. It's a phenomenon that is called by fancy names like gelatinization or premature polymerization, but it's a traumatic event, an ugly sight, not to mention the money that's lost. It shouldn't happen, but sometimes it does happen, even if you're paying attention, and when it happens it leaves its mark.... Among all my experiences of work, none is so alien and inimical as that of a batch that spoils, whatever the cause, whether the damage is serious or slight, if you're guilty or not. A fire or an explosion can be a much more destructive accident, even tragic, but it's not disgraceful, like a gelatinization. The spoiled batch contains a mocking quality: a gesture of scorn, the derisiveness of soulless things that ought to obey you and instead rise up, defying your prudence and foresight. The unique "molecule," deformed but gigantic, that is born and dies in your hands is an obscene message and symbol: a symbol of other ugly things without reversal or remedy that obscure our future, of the prevalence of confusion over order, and of unseemly death over life.

—from "The Molecule's Defiance"

Primo Levi, the most clear-eyed chronicler of the twentieth century's darkest inferno, has often been compared to Dante. Like Dante, Levi maps out the full panorama of his hell, carefully detailing its geography and its regulations, and paying special attention to its human inhabitants. Often in *If This Is a Man* (*Se questo è un uomo*), his memoir of his time in Auschwitz,[1] Levi pauses to introduce characters as pathetic and as terrifying as the *Inferno*'s Francesca or Ugolino—each marked, like Dante's lost souls, by a story or a behavior that cauterizes their essence. We meet the compulsive Steinlauf, who insists that washing his face is a meaningful way of defying the Nazis. We meet Elias the dwarf, who has superhuman strength and a variety of skills—tailoring, wood-working, and the ability to "ingest ten, fifteen, twenty pints of soup without vomiting and without having diarrhea." And we meet Henri, the supreme organizer, "once seen in the act of eating a real hard-boiled egg," whose special talent is for human exploitation, and who is the only one of his fellow prison-ers whom Levi says that he does not want ever to see again.

Still more haunting than any of these characters is one who appears after libera-tion, as Levi is recovering from scarlet fever. In a nearby bed lies a three-year-old boy, "a child of death, a child of Auschwitz," who may have been born in the camp, and who never learned to speak. Another boy discovers that the child, whom a nurse has named "Hurbinek," can say one word, but it is a word that nobody rec-ognizes. "In the following days everybody listened to him in silence, anxious to understand, and among us there were speakers of all the languages of Europe; but Hurbinek's word remained secret." No one ever learns the meaning of Hurbinek's word. He dies in March 1945, "free but not redeemed."

Hurbinek embodies a classic survivor's nightmare: to speak and not to be heard. While at Auschwitz, Levi dreamed about speaking of the hunger, the lice, the cruelty of the Kapos, to people who ignore him; in the dream his sister "looks at me, gets up, and goes away without a word." After his return from the camp, Levi would spend the rest of his life testifying as compulsively as the Ancient Mariner: a citation from Coleridge's poem serves as the epigraph to *The Drowned and the Saved,* his final book. Ian Thomson, the author of an excel-lent biography of Levi, reports that soon after Levi returned home, he began to feel a need "as strong as hunger" to tell his story, buttonholing his fellow passengers on trains and trams. His audiences were receptive: on one occasion

1. This book was published in America under the title *Survival in Auschwitz,* but I have chosen to use its British title, which is much closer to the original Italian. Sam Magavern, in his perceptive study *Primo Levi's Universe,* points out that the tension between the two titles "signals a confu-sion that exists in Levi's reputation and that perhaps existed even within him: the urge to poeti-cize and philosophize competing at times with the need to bear witness, to record in as literal and straightforward a manner as possible the Nazi war against Western civilization in general and Jews in particular."

a passenger told Levi he was hard of hearing and asked him to speak up, and another asked permission to eavesdrop. "Only once did a commuter, a priest, ask Levi why he had to address strangers with such a malignant-sounding story," Thomson writes. "Levi replied that he could not help himself."

But if Levi's storytelling drive was very nearly beyond his control, the way in which he told his story was as important to him as the act of telling it. At Auschwitz, as his memoirs make clear, the wrong word could literally mean the difference between life and death. In his writings—which would eventually span the genres from laboratory report to novel, newspaper column to play script—the stakes, obviously, were not quite the same. But for Levi the importance of finding the right word never diminished. In his late short story "A Tranquil Star," the narrator, seeking to describe an ordinary star, writes that it was "very big and very hot, and its weight was enormous," but at once he is brought up short by the poverty of his language: "We have written 'very far,' 'big,' 'hot,' 'enormous.' Australia is very far, an elephant is big and a house is bigger.... It's clear that something in our lexicon isn't working." Even superlatives are useless: "For a discussion of stars our language is inadequate and seems laughable, as if someone were trying to plow with a feather."

If our language is inadequate to the task of describing a common natural object, how can it cope with what Levi would refer to as "the greatest of the structural defects" in the "moral universe"? This is one of the primary dilemmas of Holocaust writing, the question to which everyone who writes—or reads—about the Holocaust must find his or her own answer. Levi's answer, which he credited to his training as a scientist (he had recently finished his degree in chemistry and started his professional work as a chemist when he was deported to Auschwitz), was to seek the supreme clarity of language that would ultimately be the hallmark of all his writing, fiction and nonfiction. (It is charmingly evident in the elegant simile in his statement of skepticism about language above: "as if someone were trying to plow with a feather.") "It is not true that disorder is necessary to depict disorder; it is not true that the chaos of the written page is the best symbol of the ultimate chaos to which we are fated," he wrote in an essay titled "On Obscure Writing," in which he took the poet Paul Celan, also a Holocaust survivor, harshly to task for his "indecipherable" work. "To believe this is a typical vice of our uncertain century."

Levi struggled with the dual responsibilities of writing his books while working full time as an industrial chemist: he often complained of not having enough time to do both, and the tension between his two careers was the source of great stress. "Being a chemist in the eyes of the world, yet feeling the blood of a writer in my veins, I felt as if I had two souls in my body, which is one too many," he once wrote. Yet he was always conscious of how crucial to his writing—more, to his identity—the chemist's trade was. On the most literal level, it saved his life in Auschwitz: after passing a chemistry exam, he was plucked off an outdoor forced-labor detail and sent to work in the more hospitable environs of the Buna factory. But it also prepared him for his work as a writer in other, less obvious ways.

He detailed some of these in an essay called "Ex-Chemist," one of the many newspaper columns that he published at the height of his writing career, when, in addition to his books, he turned out regular articles for Italian newspapers and magazines. Chemistry, Levi wrote, breathes life into dead metaphors: "The layman too knows what to filter, crystallize, and distill means, but he knows it only at second hand…he does not know the emotions that are tied to these gestures, has not perceived the symbolic shadow they cast." The writer who has incorporated the chemist's "habit of penetrating matter, of wanting to know its composition and structure," will be inclined "not to stop at the surface of things." It teaches precision: "Chemistry is the art of separating, weighing, and distinguishing…three useful exercises also for the person who sets out to describe events or give body to his own imagination." And finally Levi argued that, like chemistry,

> writing is a way of "producing," indeed a process of transformation: the writer transforms his experiences into a form that is accessible and attractive to the "customer" who will be the reader.…Now, the things I have seen, experienced, and done during my preceding [professional] incarnation are today for me as writer a precious source of raw materials, of events to narrate, and not only events: also of those fundamental emotions which are one's way of measuring oneself against matter (an impartial, imperturbable, but extremely harsh judge).

So Levi was not only a chemist, both at work in the laboratory and at home in his study; he was also a kind of alchemist. In the story "Nitrogen," one of the early chapters in *The Periodic Table,* he humorously described a youthful endeavor to extract nitrogen from chicken excrement—"gold from dung." As his biographer Carole Angier points out, this is exactly what he was doing with his first book, "extracting the gold of *If This Is a Man* from the dung of Auschwitz." (Anyone who has read that book's detailed descriptions of dysentery knows that this statement is not entirely metaphorical.)

And Levi's "process of transformation" was not simply the narration of "his experiences," no matter how "accessible and attractive" the form. The transformation, as it must be, is also a process of fictionalization. In addition to his two Holocaust memoirs, *If This Is a Man* and *The Truce* (published in America as *The Reawakening*), Levi wrote dozens of short stories and essays, two novels, and his uncategorizable masterwork, *The Periodic Table*. (Astonishingly, his short stories were out of print in the English-speaking world until 2007, when a small selection of previously untranslated pieces was published as *A Tranquil Star*. A new translation of Levi's complete works into English is planned for publication by W.W. Norton in 2012.) By no means did he begrudge the attention that his memoirs justly attracted, nor did he slight the importance of his role as an eyewitness to, and later reporter on, the Holocaust. But—especially later in his life—he thought of himself as a writer first and a witness second. "This Italian word, *testimone*, would settle on Levi like an albatross, and he came to resent it thoroughly," Thomson writes. "It seemed to him the most backhanded praise."

Like the vast majority of firsthand chroniclers of the Holocaust, Levi made it clear that his first loyalty was to the truth. He ended his preface to *If This Is a Man* with the somber statement, "It seems to me unnecessary to add that none of the facts are invented." But none of his other books bears such a disclaimer. And all of his works, without exception, are in their own ways works of imagination, whether they be sober memoirs or futuristic fantasies. Even *If This Is a Man,* as Levi's biographers have discovered, does not always maintain absolute fidelity to the facts. As Levi would later demonstrate in his story "Order on the Cheap," a satire about a kind of "copying machine" that can duplicate anything—a diamond, a spider, finally a human being—an exact copy is a freak of nature.

Levi presented *The Periodic Table,* the book with which he would finally achieve an international audience late in his career, as his autobiography through chemistry. But from the first chapter, in which he uses the element argon to represent his ancestors ("noble, inert, and rare"), it is clear that there is much we are not meant to take literally. To begin with, Angier—whose method in her biography is to attempt, as much as possible, to verify Levi's stories—discovered that the stories Levi tells in this chapter were not always about his own family members. "After *The Periodic Table* was published, he said, friends frequently remarked to him: 'It's odd, but my grandfather said exactly the same thing as yours,'" she reports. "The reason, of course, was that it was their grandfather." When the stories do concern Levi's relatives, they are carefully edited. He alludes to the suicide of his grandfather, but disguises the circumstances of his grandmother's remarriage; and he does not mention at all the suicide of his great-uncle. Their method of suicide, uncanny in retrospect, would be the means of his own death: *precipitazione dall'alto,* or "a fall from a high place," in the official terminology.

Levi was unhappy at school, despite his academic excellence: "Primo Levi *primo,*" a friend would say, reporting that he was first in the class. He was close to his sister, Anna Maria, and apparently also to his mother, with whom he would live, in the same Turin apartment, for his entire life, excepting only a brief period in Milan and the year he spent at Auschwitz. The marriage of Levi's parents is said to have been unhappy. Cesare Levi, Primo Levi's father, was a playboy who carried on a long affair with his secretary. Levi never spoke or wrote about his mother, giving as his reason that she was still alive. (She outlived him by four years.) Their relationship seems to have been both preternaturally close and stiflingly restrictive. Late in life, Levi would tell an interviewer that he could not remember a single time that his mother had kissed him. Nevertheless, he would care for her in her old age with striking devotion.

Levi entered Turin's Chemical Institute in 1937, just before racial laws were first established in Italy. He started learning German in order to read his inorganic chemistry textbook in the original—a whim seemingly insignificant at the time, but which would make all the difference in his survival. Zinc becomes the metaphor in *The Periodic Table* for this point in his life, in a chapter that focuses on questions of purity and impurity, in both metals and romance. Zinc, Levi learns, resists interaction when it is in a very pure state; he finds this imperturbability "disgustingly moralistic," and prefers the zinc impure, "which gives rise to changes, in other words, to life." When he discovers that Rita, a fellow student to whom he is attracted, is working on the same experiment, he uses it to bridge the racial barrier that separates them: "I...am Jewish and she is not: I am the impurity that makes the zinc react." He endeavors to walk her home, and in the last image of the chapter he triumphantly takes her arm. But when Angier tracks "Rita" down—her real name is Clara Moschino—she does not remember the walk home, nor Levi's gesture of affection. "Perhaps [Angier interjects] he did do it, on another occasion.... She can see that I would like at least this to be true. So she says firmly but gently that she does not think so. He may have wanted to do it, or dreamed of doing it, but he did not." His frustrations in love may have contributed to his first bouts of depression, which would recur with increasing frequency throughout his life; as early as 1938, according to one of his oldest friends, Levi had already contemplated suicide.

Levi graduated in 1941 with high honors, but because of the racial laws, he had difficulty finding a job. Eventually he was offered employment in a mine, where he had to work under a false name so as to hide his "abominable origin." Two percent of what the mine produced was asbestos; the rest was detritus, from which Levi was supposed to extract nickel. This alchemical dream of procuring "gold from dung" would become a central metaphor of *The Periodic Table;* Levi would later say that he wrote the "Lead" and "Mercury" chapters while working at the mine. But he quickly grew tired of this futile task and moved to a factory outside Milan for another nonsensical job: he was to extract pigments or phosphorous from certain plants and then inject them into rabbits as a possible cure for diabetes. Here he again fell in love, this time with Gabriella Garda, a former classmate from Turin. In the climax of the "Phosphorous" chapter of *The Periodic Table,* he chauffeurs her on the handlebars of his bicycle to her fiancé's house, where she hopes to convince his parents to allow her to marry him. Levi waits outside, hoping against hope that she will not succeed. This chapter, according to Angier, is almost entirely true. Yet a crucial detail is invented: that Garda threatened to embarrass Levi by screaming, "Get your hands off me, you pig!" on an evening when he refused to accompany her home from the cinema. When Levi showed her the manuscript, Angier reports, Garda asked him to remove this anecdote, but he refused, telling her that it revealed her nature better than anything that actually took place. Again, when the materials with which life provided him ran short, Levi improvised. His stories were autobiographical, but they were not autobiography.

On September 8, 1943, the Nazis occupied Italy, and Levi returned home to Turin. He joined a band of partisans fighting in the mountains, but the group lasted only a month and a half before they were betrayed. He was arrested by the Fascist police and held briefly in prison at Aosta, then sent with three friends to Fossoli, a holding camp. *If This Is a Man* begins on their last night in Fossoli, before deportation to Auschwitz.

Primo Levi's life as a writer began in earnest at almost the moment he arrived at Auschwitz. "I was conscious of living the fundamental experience of my life," he wrote later. "The idea of *having* to survive in order to tell what I had seen obsessed me night and day." He would say that he was "saved by [his] trade": his background in chemistry won him a job indoors in a laboratory, with an extra ration of soup. But it was also his vocation as a writer that saved him. He may have survived in order to become a writer, but he also became a writer in order to survive.

Levi "distilled" (as he put it) his eleven months at Auschwitz into the slim volume *If This Is a Man.* He wrote that he considered the camp "pre-eminently a gigantic biological and social experiment," and the book is in some ways similar to a laboratory report: it includes detailed analyses of the soup and the bread served at Auschwitz, and the "selections" in which the SS weeded out prisoners not of obvious utility, and the literally back-breaking labor required of even the weakest of those chosen for work rather than for death. In fact, in its original version it *was* a kind of laboratory report: in the spring of 1945, the Soviet authorities in Poland asked Levi, together with his friend and fellow survivor Leonardo de Benedetti, who was a medical doctor, to write an essay documenting the conditions in the camp. It was published in November 1946 in the Italian medical journal *Minerva Medica,* and appeared in book form in English several years ago under the title *Auschwitz Report.* Much of the material from this essay, albeit greatly revised, would find its way into *If This Is a Man.*

But *If This Is a Man* is also an experiment in itself, and what it distills is the essence of Auschwitz—the attempted "demolition," in Levi's term, of the prisoners' humanity. "It is not possible to sink lower than this; no human condition is more miserable than this, nor could it conceivably be so," he writes early on, as his transport of prisoners arrives at Auschwitz and they are stripped of their possessions, shaved, and tattooed. "Nothing belongs to us any more; they have taken away our clothes, our shoes, even our hair; if we speak, they will not listen to us, and if they listen, they will not understand. They will even take away our name: and if we want to keep it, we will have to find ourselves the strength to do so, to manage somehow so that behind the name something of us, of us as we were, still remains."

Yet Levi will soon discover that newly arrived prisoners cannot be the most wretched of all humanity: they are freezing and terrified, but they are still in reasonably good health. The most miserable, Levi will say later, are the ones who have been broken down by life in the camp: the *"Muselmänner,"* literally "Muslims,"[2] who are the thinnest, the weakest, the sickest. He describes them as "an anonymous mass, continually renewed and always identical.... If I could enclose all the evil of our time in one image, I would choose this image which is familiar to me: an emaciated man, with head dropped and shoulders curved, on whose face and in whose eyes not a trace of a thought is to be seen."

---

2. This name for the most wretched prisoners appears in numerous texts about the Holocaust. Kertész, in *Fatelessness,* calls them "mobile question marks" and writes that "you lost any will to live just looking at them." There are two common theories about the meaning behind the name: first, because the prisoners were often prostrate, they resembled Muslims at prayer; second, their lack of resistance to their imminent fate was apparently associated with Islam's fatalistic attitude toward death. In his memoir *The Tale of the Ring,* Frank Stiffel offers an alternative explanation that I have not seen anywhere else and which I find most convincing. He writes that prisoners who worked outside the camp would go after the evening roll call to the clinic to have their wounds dressed. They would leave with a white paper bandage around their heads, "which, in combination with their skinny bodies and starved faces, gave them the appearance of desert nomads."

Their image is familiar not only to Levi, but to all of us now: the *Muselmänner* are the bones piled up like sticks in mass graves, the empty faces peering out from the bunks after liberation—in short, the ultimate symbol of the Nazis' depravity.

When all the trappings of humanity are taken away, what remains? This question is at the heart of *If This Is a Man,* starting with the title, which comes from a poem by Levi called "Shema" (the book's epigraph). Here are the relevant lines:

> You who live safe
> In your warm houses,
> You who find, returning in the evening,
> Hot food and friendly faces:
> Consider if this is a man
> Who works in the mud
> Who does not know peace
> Who fights for a scrap of bread
> Who dies because of a yes or a no

"Consider if this is a man": if Auschwitz was a laboratory, then this was Primo Levi's hypothesis, and *If This Is a Man* is the record of its testing, which he approached as a chemist investigating the building blocks of nature, the materials of which man is made. He examines the workings of the camp and their effects on his own behavior and that of his fellow prisoners, who can be thought of as case studies of a sort. But unlike Levi's youthful experiments with nitrogen and phosphorous, this hypothesis could not be proved through scientific methods alone: a human being is not simply the sum total of all the molecules that make up our physical structure. Later Levi would humorously explore the same question in his short story "Our Fine Specifications," which appeared in his collection *Vizio di forma,* or *Structural Defect.* As in many of Levi's science-fiction stories, this one takes place in a future or perhaps parallel universe, in an office where workers are engaged in determining "specifications" defining the attributes for various items: castor oil, brooms, cardboard boxes. The placid atmosphere is disrupted one day when an employee comes upon "Specification No. 366478: Man," which stipulates certain "dimensional tolerances" and delineates methods of testing flexibility, sensitivity to heat and cold, memory, leadership skills, and so on. It seems no accident that the "specification number," like the typical Auschwitz tattoo, has six digits. For the project of the Nazis was precisely to push the boundaries of what human beings could endure, physically and emotionally. When the boundaries are breached, death results.

If the Nazis believed that men could be dehumanized—and Levi shows that this intent was evident in every detail of their plan, from the lack of latrines on the transports bringing prisoners to the camps (which forced the deportees to crouch shamelessly in plain view whenever the train made its infrequent stops) to the practice of addressing prisoners by number rather than by name—then Levi's question must be answered in the affirmative: yes, this *is* a man, even if he is battered and starved and wretched. To answer no is to think like a Nazi. Even among the "anonymous mass" of the *Muselmänner,* one character stands out: young "Null Achtzehn" (Zero Eighteen), addressed by everyone by these last three digits of his tattoo, "as if everyone was aware that only a man is worthy of a name, and that Null Achtzehn is no longer a man." As the Italian critic Risa Sodi has brilliantly pointed out, the number eighteen has a numerological significance in Judaism, meaning "life," and thus Null Achtzehn's name is code for "no life"—"a perfect designation for a *Muselman.*" But it can also be understood somewhat differently. By bringing zero and eighteen together in a single name, Levi emphasizes the dual condition of the *Muselmänner*—not quite dead yet, but also not alive in any meaningful way; not truly men, but not exactly inhuman, either.

In the end Levi will affirm his hypothesis. In the book's climax, Levi and a young man he calls Pikolo, the Kapo's assistant, have gone to collect the day's kettle of soup. (Pikolo has been identified as a Frenchman named Jean Samuel, who eventually would publish his own memoir about Auschwitz and Levi titled *Il m'appelait Pikolo,* or *He Called Me Pikolo.*) Pikolo mentions that he'd like to learn Italian, and Levi seizes the opportunity to recite the story of Ulysses from Dante's *Inferno:*

Here, listen Pikolo, open your ears and your mind, you have to understand, for my sake:

"Think of your breed; for brutish ignorance
Your mettle was not made; you were made men,
To follow after knowledge and excellence."

As if I also was hearing it for the first time: like the blast of a trumpet, like the voice of God. For a moment I forget who I am and where I am.

Jean Améry, in his essay on the fate of the intellectual in Auschwitz, lamented that poetry had no meaning for him in the camp; it was "an intellectual word game that here no longer had any social relevance." But for Levi, these lines from Dante served precisely the purpose that Améry sought: they "transcended reality," jolting him out of his miserable circumstances and back to a world in which the life of the mind does have meaning. Pikolo begs him to continue, and he recites a few more lines, explicating as he goes along, but then comes a gap: there are a few triplets he cannot recall, and he "would give today's soup" in order to remember them. (Here is the proof that the intellectual in Levi has won out, even for a moment: the idea that soup would be sacrificed for poetry.) By the time they reach the kitchen, he has nearly finished. "I keep Pikolo back, it is vitally necessary and urgent that he listen…tomorrow he or I might be dead, or we might never see each other again, I must tell him, I must explain to him about the Middle Ages…but still more, something gigantic that I myself have only just seen, in a flash of intuition, perhaps the reason for our fate, for our being here today." Levi will not stop with reciting Dante; he has had a glimpse of the possibilities for his own future. As he would tell Pikolo often during their time in the camp, his ambition was to record and report Auschwitz to the world.

This was particularly crucial, Levi felt, because of the special perversity of the Nazis' tactics: they tried to destroy men by beating them, by working them to death, by starving them, but also by taking away the essential tool of humanity, their language. By now the linguistic deformations of the Nazis are well known—most notoriously, the code words they used to disguise the truth about their tactics, such as "special treatment" (*Sonderbehandlung*) to signify extermination by gas. But Levi was among the first to document the extent to which the Nazis used language, or rather the deprivation and the distortion of language, as a tool of dehumanization.

From the start, all information is disseminated in German, and those who cannot understand it are more likely to be sent to the wrong side. People died "at first sight of hunger, cold, fatigue, disease; on closer examination, of insufficient information." Early on in the book, an inmate is forced to translate an officer's nasty remark: "One sees the words which are not his, the bad words, twist his mouth as they come out, as if he were spitting out a foul taste." Levi learns two German words right away: *Lager* (camp) and *Häftling* (prisoner). He uses them rather than their Italian equivalents throughout the book, to emphasize the distinctness of their meaning. "The *Lager's* language was a

German apart," Levi explained later. For the Nazis, linguistic confusion was also a means of sowing moral confusion. As Levi would later write, the concentration camp was "a world turned upside down, where *fair is foul and foul is fair,* where professors have to use shovels, murderers are supervisors, and hospitals are places where people are killed." In this world, as reversed as a photographic negative, the most basic concepts could lose their meaning, as Levi demonstrates in the following passage. "Theft in Buna [the chemical factory in Auschwitz III, where Levi worked], punished by the civil direction, is authorized and encouraged by the SS; theft in camp, severely repressed by the SS, is considered by the civilians as a normal exchange operation; theft among *Häftlinge* is generally punished, but the punishment strikes the thief and the victim with equal gravity," Levi wrote. "We now invite the reader to contemplate the possible meaning in the *Lager* of the words 'good' and 'evil', 'just' and 'unjust'; let everybody judge, on the basis of the picture we have outlined and of the examples given above, how much of our ordinary moral world could survive on this side of the barbed wire."

The camp, Levi finds, is a "perpetual Babel, in which everyone shouts orders and threats in languages never heard before, and woe betide whoever fails to grasp the meaning." Polish will always remain more or less incomprehensible to him: in an interview upon a return visit to Auschwitz in 1982, he described it as "spitting...a stream of consonants, a genuinely infernal language," epitomized by the Auschwitz "dawn command"—the single word *wstawać,* "get up." (Levi would write of the deep-seated dread this word evoked, the dread of waking to face another day in Auschwitz.) His first efforts at communicating with fellow prisoners are frustrated by his lack of linguistic skills: a Polish boy is incredulous that he is really Jewish, since he does not speak Yiddish, a *lingua franca* of the camp. Language will work its perversity until the end. During his last days at Auschwitz, spent in the infirmary, Levi hears dying men around him succumb to delirium: one mutters "*Jawohl*" for two days straight.

But amid the Babel Levi was formulating exact, potent phrases. He began making notes while working in the Buna laboratory, though for safety's sake he would soon commit them to memory and destroy them. Despite its adherence—mostly—to fact, *If This Is a Man* is a fundamentally literary book, with a highly stylized use of language. The prisoners, stripped and shaved, are "a hundred miserable and sordid puppets." The book is so detailed that one wishes prisoners entering the camp could have used it as a manual. All the camp's perverse rules and systems are elucidated: how many buttons one must have on one's shirt, how to exchange ill-fitting shoes, where to stand in line to receive the heartiest portion of soup. Levi does not shrink from the disgusting: there is an extended passage on the importance of properly timing one's night-time visits to the latrine bucket so as to avoid being the one who must empty it, since the contents will inevitably overflow onto one's feet. The Germans run the camp with "absurd precision," but Levi's own precision is eminently rational.

To say that the book is literary does not imply that its content is fictional. Many years later, Levi would remember his time at Auschwitz as "a period of exalted receptivity, during which not a detail was lost." Levi said numerous times that not one word or episode of *If This Is a Man* was invented. He wrote the first draft in the first year after the war, and the only changes that he made later, he said, were to add characters or his own commentary. No one has ever disputed the substance of his account.

And yet, as Ian Thomson notes, despite the "legend" that Levi would come to construct around *If This Is a Man,* the book—like Elie Wiesel's *Night*— was not written "in furious haste immediately on his return from exile," but rather was "the produce of a gradual maturation [that] involved many differ-ent phases of drafting."[3] Most of the changes were added when he revised *If This Is a Man* after its initial rejection (the book was turned down by Natalia Ginzburg at Einaudi, as well as by five other publishers). As Wiesel did when revising *Night* for French publication, Levi removed several Jewish allusions to give the text a more universal appeal. ("I know suffering and suffering is the same for us all," he said.) He also added more of his own personal experiences and impressions, as well as some of the book's more colorful characters, such as Steinlauf, the compulsive washer.

Though Paul Steinberg, the man known as "Henri," would acknowledge the truth of Levi's ugly portrait of him, others disputed Levi's portrayals. The fam-ily of Alberto Dalla Volta, another Italian who was Levi's close companion in Auschwitz, took issue with Levi's inaccurate depiction of Alberto as unable to speak German, and generally as more intuitive and less intellectual than Levi. (Alberto's linguistic skills were actually better than Levi's.) Thomson and Angier, both of whom assume that *If This Is a Man* is close a work of pure

---

3. Levi reflected on this in an interview with Germaine Greer in 1985. "The other people I've talked to about it accepted the legend," he said. "In fact, writing is never spontaneous. Now that I think about it, I can see that this book is full of literature, literature absorbed through the skin, even while I was rejecting it (because I was a bad student of Italian literature)."

testimony as is possible, are stymied by Levi's liberties with Alberto's character. Thomson speculates that Levi might have felt guilty for surviving when
Alberto had not and thus was reluctant to acknowledge Alberto's role in helping him: "Many survivors find some aspect of their survival intolerable and
prefer to bury whatever had been necessary for them to survive." Angier writes
that "the transformation of Alberto Dalla Volta into one of Primo's opposites
was not a literary device...but natural and unconscious." (Could it be insignificant that, according to one source, Alberto was in fact responsible for sav-
ing Levi's life by telling the Germans, upon their arrival at Auschwitz, that he
was a chemist and Levi his assistant?)

If we take Levi seriously as a writer, both these explanations give him too
little credit. Why should he not exploit his creative freedom to do with his
characters what he will, to alter them intentionally—not unconsciously—in
ways that will make his narrative more effective? But they also let him off the
hook too easily. Every writer who uses material from his life in his work—and
what writer does not fall into this category?—must acknowledge his or her
responsibility for the fact that not all of the subjects will be pleased to be used
in this way. Levi said often in interviews that he did not write about his family
because "one does not write about the living," yet he did not adhere consistently to this rule. Magavern notes that it is crucial to *If This Is a Man* that Levi
retains control over the narrative, that he remains its sole storyteller, since to
tell one's own story is to control one's own destiny—another element of the
tension within the book between those who are men and those who might
not be anymore. "Perhaps this is a small part of the reason that Lorenzo is the
great hero of the book: because he, a morose man who does his good deeds in
silence, does not threaten Levi's role as storyteller," Magavern writes. "Perhaps
this is why Levi never mentions that Alberto helped save him at the first selection with his better command of German. Perhaps it accounts for the fact that
Pikolo is portrayed as the ideal listener, the student of Italian, and never as
Levi's German teacher." (Levi bought German lessons from Jean Samuel, paying him in bread rations. The two men remained close friends throughout their
lives, but in Samuel's own memoir he gives a different version of the "Canto of
Ulysses" episode and of his relationship with Levi. "Today I still wonder about
this mystery of memory: both of us had the sensation of a crucial meeting,
unforgettable, and yet that memory was not based on the same gestures, on the
same words, on the same emotions," Samuel writes.)

Some critics have insisted that Levi erected a barrier between *If This Is a
Man,* with its essentially testimonial character, and the rest of his writing;

while he was willing to fictionalize about other subjects, they argue, he could not do so about the Holocaust. But this argument overlooks the many stories and essays—Magavern puts them all under the blanket heading "memoir-stories"—in which Levi openly did write more freely about Auschwitz. Many of these are collected in English in the volume *Moments of Reprieve,* a selection of short pieces in which Levi took the opportunity, years later, to describe certain "human figures" who "stood out against that tragic background…begging me one after another to help them survive and enjoy the ambiguous perennial existence of literary characters." Mainly short character sketches, they are all based, Levi says, on true stories. But while Levi insists that his memory of his "two years of life outside the law" is still intact, he nonetheless admits that "it is possible that the distance in time has accentuated the tendency to round out the facts or heighten the colors: this tendency, or temptation, is an integral part of writing, without it one does not write stories but rather accounts."

Like all great writers, Levi cannot be firmly placed in a single category. The tendency to do so seems particularly American. Magavern notes that in Italy *If This Is a Man* is read as an autobiographical novel, which seems absurd to American readers accustomed to our culture's stringent attempts to separate fact and fiction. But if to call the book a novel seems to go too far, it is likewise a category mistake to understand it as a chronicle or laboratory report. Magavern calls it "a literary work of uncertain genre, using the tools of a memoirist, novelist, short story writer, poet, essayist, historian, and scientist." He might also have added philosopher: as he explains, a single form would be inadequate to Levi's task, which was nothing less than "to explore the existential parameters of life."

Language is again the fundamental subject of *The Truce,* which begins with the arrival of the Russians liberating Auschwitz. As soon as Levi is well enough, he is sent to a transit camp in Kraków. Here he meets "the Greek," one of the remarkable mercantilists of Auschwitz, and the first of the fantastic characters to accompany him on his journey. He leads Levi to the market and tells him to find out the going rate for shirts. Whereas in the *Lager* language barriers meant death, in the post-Auschwitz world they are the stuff of comedy. And so Levi makes his way around the market, learning the Polish for "how much" and "what time" and "gentlemen," and even manages to sell a shirt. He stops a priest to find out where food might be available, and, with no other languages in common, they converse in Latin: "*Pater optime,*" Levi asks, "*ubi est mensa pauperorum?*"

These humorous episodes recur as Levi winds his circuitous way from Poland to the Soviet Union and finally down through Romania, Hungary, and Austria to Italy. After the Babel of Auschwitz, he cannot repress his glee at being able to make himself understood in language after language. When the war ends, he is in a transit camp in the Polish town of Katowice, and manages to follow the news even without understanding the language. "We read 'Vienna,' 'Koblenz,' 'Rhine'; then 'Bologna'; then, with emotion and joy, 'Turin' and 'Milan.' Finally, 'Mussolini,' in enormous letters, followed by an awesome and indecipherable past participle; and at last, in red ink, covering half a page, the final, cryptic, and exhilarating announcement: 'BERLIN UPADL!'" Even miscommunication, when it occurs, is largely for comic effect. The huckster Cesare wants Levi to teach him German so that he can woo a Polish girl, but "the things he wanted to learn from me are not taught in any German language course, nor had I had the slightest occasion to learn them in Auschwitz; moreover, they were such subtle and idiomatic questions that I suspect that they do not exist in any language other than Italian and French." Much of this comedy is almost certainly exaggerated for effect, and interviews with the man whom "Cesare" was based upon have turned up a number of discrepancies. Levi was playing with a much looser hand than in *If This Is a Man*.

Levi's newfound language skills are providential, because he is seized with the desire to speak about his experiences to anyone he sees. He tells his tale for the first time on a train platform in rural Poland. Getting off the train to stretch his legs, he immediately finds himself at the center of a group of curious people, all speaking excitedly in Polish, which he did not understand. "Perhaps I was among the first dressed in 'zebra' clothes"—the striped uniform of the camp—"to appear in that place," he speculated. Fortunately for Levi, "in the middle of the group of workers and peasants a bourgeois appeared, with a felt hat, glasses and a leather briefcase in his hand—a lawyer. He was Polish, he spoke French and German well, he was an extremely courteous and benevolent person; in short, he possessed all the requisites enabling me finally, after the long year of slavery and silence, to recognize in him the messenger, the spokesman of the civilized world, the first that I had met." The man questioned Levi, and he spoke "at dizzy speed of those so recent experiences of mine, of Auschwitz nearby, yet, it seemed, unknown to all, of the hecatomb from which I alone had escaped, of everything," and the lawyer translated for the crowd. But it did not take Levi long to figure out that something was amiss. "I do not know Polish, but I know how one says 'Jew' and how one says 'political'; and I soon realized that the translation of my account, although sympathetic, was not faithful to it. The lawyer described me to the public not as an Italian Jew, but as an Italian political prisoner. I asked him why, amazed and almost offended. He replied, embarrassed: '*C'est mieux pour vous. La guerre n'est pas finie.*'" It's better for you. The war isn't over. As if on cue, Levi's listeners begin to disperse; his nightmare has come true.

The ending of *The Truce* quietly annihilates the comedy that has preceded it. "A dream full of horror has still not ceased to visit me, at sometimes frequent, sometimes longer, intervals," Levi writes.

> I am sitting at a table with my family, or with friends, or at work, or in the green countryside; in short, in a peaceful relaxed environment, apparently without tension or affliction; yet I feel a deep and subtle anguish, the definite sensation of an impending threat. And in fact, as the dream proceeds, slowly or brutally, each time in a different way, everything collapses and disintegrates around me, the scenery, the walls, the people, while the anguish becomes more intense and more precise. Now everything has changed to chaos; I am alone in the center of a gray and turbid nothing, and now, I *know* what this thing means, and I also know that I have always known it. I am in the *Lager* once more, and nothing is true outside the *Lager*. All the rest was a brief pause, a deception of the senses, a dream; my family, nature in flower, my home. Now this inner dream, this dream of peace, is over, and in the outer dream, which continues, gelid, a well-known voice resounds: a single word, not imperious, but brief and subdued. It is the dawn command of Auschwitz, a foreign word, feared and expected: get up, "*wstawać.*"

"Nothing is true outside the *Lager*." This, perhaps even more than the fear of not being understood, is the survivor's nightmare. In the camp, the prisoners saw Auschwitz as a microcosm of the world; outside, they began to wonder if the world was actually a macrocosm of Auschwitz. ("Even Levi's most explicit messages depend on our realizing that, despite its uniqueness, Auschwitz is always a possibility slumbering in our current reality," Magavern writes.) Tadeusz Borowski wrote of this fear in poetry he published soon after the war; he killed himself in 1951. Sarah Kofman wrote of it in her remarkable memoir *Rue Ordener, Rue Labat,* published in 1994; she killed herself the same year. It seems self-evident: how could anyone living under the weight of so great a fear not commit suicide? Primo Levi's son was quoted after his father's death as saying, "Read the ending of *The Truce* and you'll understand."

But his remark was probably flippant. It is too easy to say, as so many people did at the time, that Auschwitz killed Levi forty years later. (Turin's rabbi called his death a case of "delayed murder.") To begin with, it can never be definitively established that Levi's death was in fact a suicide; some of those who knew him have speculated that he might have suffered a dizzy spell as a side effect of the medications he was taking, leading him to fall accidentally over the precipitously low railing of his apartment building's third-floor landing. Magavern sensibly suggests that Levi's death "occurred in a zone between accident and intention that defies clear explanation." More to the point, the fact that both Kofman and Levi killed themselves (or, in Levi's case, may have done so) shortly after writing these particular books—Kofman was writing about her experiences during the Holocaust for the first time, Levi, with *The Drowned and the Saved,* was returning to the topic after a long break—certainly does not mean that it was writing these books that killed them. It could just as easily be the other way around: that Auschwitz kept Levi alive for forty years as a writer, and that, after feeling he had had his final say on the matter, he was unable to recapture a sense of purpose in life.

Yet this interpretation, too, is inadequate, because it insists that we continue to regard Levi as a writer defined by the Holocaust. This mistaken conception predominates in America, where Levi is known almost exclusively as the writer of *Survival in Auschwitz* (even its title drowns out the greater philosophical thrust of the work) and *The Periodic Table.* But the Italian edition of Levi's collected works comprises 1,600 pages of dense type, of which the memoirs constitute a fraction. In Italy Levi was known during his later life as a popular newspaper columnist and a prolific (and prize-winning) writer of fiction. While much of his fiction can be read as commentary on the Holocaust (and many critics have insisted on reading it that way), such an interpretation is reductionist, even insulting, as Levi himself found it. "I refuse to be classified as a concentration camp writer," he once said in an interview. "I came out of the camps, I wrote about them, and possibly, in fact certainly, I have not finished writing about them, but I think I can say something worthwhile about other topics as well."

Starting already in 1946, as he was writing and revising *If This Is a Man,* Levi began publishing short stories about science, some based on his experiences in the laboratory at the paint factory where he spent nearly his entire career. They were collected in two volumes: *Storie naturali* (Natural stories), which appeared in 1966, and *Vizio di forma* (Structural defect), in 1971; selections of these stories appear in English in the collections *The Sixth Day* and *A Tranquil*

Star. While some of the stories have much in common with classic science fiction, they are better seen as quasi-Borgesian metaphysical fables, by turns haunting and humorous, written in Levi's signature dry, plainspoken tone. Speaking at a conference on Jewish literature in 1982, Levi linked his stories to the parables of the midrashic tradition; in an earlier interview, he called them "moral tales dressed up, in disguise." Often they are tales of technology gone too far: a glorified photocopier that is put to use cloning people, or a telephone network that tries to initiate its own connections between human beings. Levi wrote in a mission statement printed on the cover of *Storie naturali* that he had tried to explore "the perception that in the world we live in there is a discrepancy, a small or large gap, a structural defect which cancels out one aspect or another of our civilization." Indeed, the stories give a sense of how finely tuned our world truly is, in that a minor alteration can throw everything off kilter. Like certain Greek myths, they reveal the danger in wishing for something without thinking through its possible consequences.

Of course, the Holocaust was the twentieth century's prime instance of technology gone wrong, and Levi did not wish to ignore the obvious thematic connections that often exist between the camps and his fiction: the link, he said, was "mankind violated." Indeed, the first two stories he wrote were set in postwar Germany, and another later story also takes place there. The first, "The Sleeping Beauty in the Fridge: A Winter's Tale," written in the form of a short play, is set in Berlin in 2115. The title character is a woman who has undergone a cryogenics experiment; frozen in 1975, she is woken for only a few hours every year, so that, despite being 163 years old, she has hardly aged. Levi portrays her experience as dual-edged: roused for important family occasions and historical events, she gets to experience only the high points of life, without all the dull parts in between; but she is also a prisoner of her circumstances and of her guardians, one of whom, in a sinister twist, regularly defrosts her enough to rape her but not enough for her to resist. In the second, "Angelic Butterfly," a group of Allied soldiers patrolling postwar Berlin come upon the remnants of the laboratory in which a "Dr. Leeb," inspired by the axolotl (a type of salamander that can reproduce while still in the larval stage), has been experimenting with methods of organic transformation in humans. A girl living across the street reports that one day the professor brought four subjects into the lab, civilians who were "very thin and did not lift their heads"; they transformed into vulture-like beasts, but could not fly. Eventually, in the desperation of the last days of the war, they were slaughtered for food, the mob who killed them perhaps led by the nurse who was their guardian. The connections here with

Nazi eugenics experiments are obvious: the guano found in Dr. Leeb's lab contains "blood, cement, cat piss and mouse piss, sauerkraut, beer—in short, the quintessence of Germany." But it is also interesting that Dr. Leeb's crimes are reported on by a German civilian who observed them, in contrast to the many who claimed to have no idea about the camps.

Yet the most provocative and unsettling—and also the most successful—of Levi's stories are not directly connected with the Holocaust, and these go far toward vindicating his refusal to classify himself as a "concentration camp writer." Particularly effective are a series of six satires revolving around an American company called NATCA, which produces technological innovations, and its representative Mr. Simpson, who tries to sell them to the unnamed chemist who serves as the narrator. In "Order on the Cheap," the chemist tests out a device called the Mimer, a "three-dimensional duplicator" that is advertised for use with paper: unlike a photocopier, however, it produces exact copies. At first the chemist objects to the idea of creating something from nothing, but Simpson hastily corrects him: "Not just from nothing, obviously. I meant to say from chaos. . . . That's what the Mimer does: it creates order from disorder." Intrigued, the narrator spends a week testing it out. On the first three days he creates inanimate objects; on the fourth day, plants and food; on the fifth day, a spider; on the sixth day, a lizard; "on the seventh day [he] rested." (Levi's scientific background is evident in his attention to physical detail: the matches look perfect but will not light, and the lizard has a weak skeleton and soon dies.) Mr. Simpson is horrified by the narrator's reports on his experiments, and will not listen to his exhortations that the device could be commercially successful. Eventually the narrator receives a warning from NATCA forbidding the use of the Mimer for reproducing anything other than documents. "It is my opinion that these limitations will not contribute to the Mimer's commercial success. . . . It is incredible how reputably reasonable people will do things that are in such obvious conflict with their interests," he laments. Of course, there is nothing to stop customers from using the Mimer for whatever they wish; and in another story we learn that one of the narrator's friends has used it to clone his wife.

In subsequent NATCA fables, we find Simpson using a device called the Kalometer to measure male and female beauty, or putting the animal kingdom to work for his own purposes: he trains the dragonflies in his garden to pick blueberries and strikes a treaty with the mosquitoes that they will not bite if he provides them regularly with a quantity of cows' blood every day. What starts as a mutual agreement quickly transforms into a kind of slavery; and at the story's end Simpson's partner is arrested for training eels to smuggle heroin on their annual migration. Again, the slightest alteration in the natural world leads to everything being thrown askew.

It would be disingenuous to argue that there is no connection between the world of the camps and the world of these stories. The critic Lucie Benchouiha has pointed out that the crimes against human or animal life committed in the stories are identical to those committed in the concentration camps: exploitation of labor, violation of privacy, treatment of humans as objects, death through scientific experimentation, loss of creativity and reason—in sum, the violent transformation of men into beasts. "Levi's subject matter has not altered significantly," she writes, "it has merely changed form, from autobiographical to fictional, from the issues of the concentration camp world to similar issues arising in a highly credible, fictitious world." Mirna Cicioni, in *Primo Levi: Bridges of Knowledge,* also sees a "clear continuity" between the themes addressed in *If This Is a Man* and some of the stories, particularly "those which emphasize people's loss of human identity, and which define what is 'human' cumulatively and negatively." Remember also "Our Fine Specifications," in which the office employees are anxious about the implications of judging human beings according to technical specifications but in the end consent to doing so.

Though Levi complained about such interpretations, even he admitted that they had a certain amount of validity. In an interview in 1979, asked if he was ever surprised by what critics saw in his work, Levi took the opportunity to revisit this question:

> A typical case is the polemic that has pursued me for my whole career, the relationship between my first two books and my two books of stories, *Storie naturali* and *Vizio di forma.* The issue is clearer to my readers than to myself. I see relatively little in the latter of the *Lager* revisited, of an attempt to reproduce or to review the world of the *Lager* in the world of today. I don't wholly agree with those who make these links, that alienation in today's world is no different from the alienation of the camps. Try spending some time in a concentration camp....On the other hand, readers can probably find in my stories contours of the figure of the camp-prisoner that I did not know I had put there. It's probable and in some cases, quite apparent. In "Versamina" [another story set in Germany] and "Angelic Butterfly," for instance, I deliberately set up links with my earlier experiences. In other stories, there may well be such links but that does not mean I intended them.

Levi resisted this idea because he knew that the Holocaust, like the black holes to which he often compared it, has the effect of sucking the life out of everything around it. If a story is judged to be about the Holocaust, that interpretation cannot help but dominate; everything else loses significance beside it. But if there exists a world outside Auschwitz, there must also exist a world of fiction outside and greater than Auschwitz. Magavern writes that "Levi believed in stories as a path to truth, and, in particular, to truths about human nature." Must the road to truths about human nature always lead back to Auschwitz?

Despite Levi's professional success, the frequency of his bouts of depression increased toward the end of his life. They often came at times when Levi was aware of his own fragility; he suffered from debilitating attacks of shingles, and had "a terror of physical ailment" of any kind. A diary kept by a woman with whom (according to Angier) Levi had a long romantic relationship, from 1974 until his death, makes for heartbreaking reading. "I have nothing more to say," he reportedly told her during a deep depression in 1982. "I don't know what to do with myself.... My novel has won three prizes, but the very thought of it makes me sick.... I want to end it. But the third floor is not high enough."

I have nothing more to say. This quintessential writer's anxiety surfaces with particular poignancy in a few of Levi's stories. "The Fugitive" describes a poet whose muse visits him only occasionally. One day, while at work, he writes a poem that he finds particularly beautiful, but when he returns to the office the next day, the sheet of paper on which he has written it is no longer where he left it. He puts it back in his drawer, but the next day the same thing happens. "He realized that for some reason, perhaps precisely because of its uniqueness, because of the life that openly animated it, the poem was trying to escape, to get away from him," Levi explains. In a final fruitless effort to pin it down, he glues it to a piece of wood, but it disintegrates in its effort to escape. And rewriting it is impossible: "He tried many times, during the rest of his life, to call to memory the lost text; in fact, at increasingly rare intervals, he wrote other versions of it, but they were increasingly thin, bloodless, and weak," the story concludes. More humorously, in "Man's Friend" a professor discovers that the cells of certain tapeworms reveal patterns that correspond to *terza rima*. The tapeworms, he realizes, encode within their bodies passionate love poems addressed to their hosts: "Your strength penetrates me, your joy descends into me.... I love you, oh sacred man." Alas, they go unread, since the hosts are largely uninterested in missives from their intestines.

Both of these stories can be interpreted, if one is so inclined, from the perspective of the Holocaust. Seen thus, "The Fugitive" expresses the survivor's lack of control over his testimony once it is committed to paper and released into the world, while the tapeworm is a personification of the survivor in Levi's nightmare, speaking his words into a void. But such interpretations illustrate the inadequacy of reading a writer's biography in all his works. Are the stories not more powerful if they are understood as being about any writer, not only the survivor? Must the world be a macrocosm of Auschwitz? "Whoever writes... writes in his own code, which others do not know; and whoever speaks as well," Levi once wrote.

This is not relativizing, but universalizing. On the subject of human disaster, Levi was no exceptionalist. His story "The Hard-Sellers" describes a group of people who recruit supernatural beings—perhaps angels or aliens—to experience life on earth. The subject who is being recruited discerns that life is not always as positive as the salesmen portray it. In addition to ordinary human tragedies, such as a man who works in the post office for the rest of his life after receiving his doctorate, there is the possibility of great calamity:

> One could see a multiple cannon shoot into darkness, lighting up with its glare collapsed houses and factories in ruins; then mounds of skeletal corpses at the foot of a bonfire, within a gloomy frame of smoke and barbed wire; then a hut made of cane beneath a tropical rain and inside on the bare earthen floor a child dying; then a squalid expanse of uncultivated fields reduced to swamp, and of forests without leaves; then a village, and an entire valley, invaded and buried by a gigantic tide of mud. There were many others.

These "mounds of skeletal corpses" framed by smoke and barbed wire—the only direct reference to the Holocaust in Levi's stories—are just one of a list of human disasters. *There were many others.* To say that Levi came to understand Auschwitz itself as just one possibility for human catastrophe is not to diminish it through comparison, just as it does not diminish Levi's suicide (as some have claimed) to attribute its cause not to the Holocaust but to depression. His depression, after all, seems to have stemmed from despair not only about what had happened in Auschwitz, but about the human condition in general. And the fiction demonstrates that evil, even Auschwitz-level evil, was hardly unique to the camps; it exists in all aspects of human life. The horrors of human slavery and genetic experimentation are not restricted to SS officers; they can be perpetrated, or at least facilitated, by the cheerful, hardworking Mr. Simpson.

Levi will always be known as the author of one of the defining texts of Auschwitz. But in addition to being a witness and a chronicler, he was also a scientist who was unafraid to let his profound physical understanding of the universe and all its components shade into the metaphysical. And he was a writer who took seriously the discrepancies between the way the world appears on paper and the way people actually experience it, a writer who tried to alchemize each of his stories—no matter what their form—into "a fable that awakens echoes," as he wrote in "A Tranquil Star," "and in which each of us can perceive distant reflections of himself and the human race."

3

The Kabbalist in the Death Camps: Elie Wiesel

"What are you writing?" the Rebbe asked. "Stories," I said. He wanted
to know what kind of stories: true stories. "About people you knew?"
Yes, about people I might have known. "About things that happened?"
Yes, about things that happened or could have happened. "But they did
not?" No, not all of them did. In fact, some were invented from almost
the beginning to almost the end. The Rebbe leaned forward as if to
measure me up and said with more sorrow than anger: "That means you
are writing lies!" I did not answer immediately. The scolded child within
me had nothing to say in his defense. Yet, I had to justify myself: "Things
are not that simple, Rebbe. Some events do take place but are not true;
others are—although they never occurred."

—from *Legends of Our Time*

Elie Wiesel's *Night*, together with *Anne Frank's* Diary of a Young Girl, told the story
of the Holocaust to the world. In the fifty-plus years since its original publication, it
has been translated into thirty languages and has sold more than six million copies in
the United States alone. This book has a special status as a touchstone for countless
readers, for whom it was likely their first encounter with Holocaust literature. I still
have the copy I was given as a child, with its dramatic blue and black lettering and
the graphic of an indistinct figure behind curls of barbed wire. The book carried a
blurb from A. Alvarez, who had famously written in *Commentary* that it was "almost

unbearably painful, and certainly beyond criticism." And for me, *Night* remains as devastating to read now as it did when I first encountered it.

Night is devastating first because of its simplicity. The basic outline is this: After the Germans invade Hungary in March 1944, the teenaged Eliezer and his family, religious Jews who live comfortably in their community, are deported to Auschwitz. Eliezer and his father, separated from the rest of their family, are assigned to hard labor. As the last days of the war tick on endlessly, they survive transfers, work assignments, selections, illnesses, and all the other daily threats of life in the camp, as their friends and neighbors fall dead around them. In January 1945, the SS evacuate Auschwitz before the imminent arrival of the Soviet army. The prisoners march through the snow for days before being transferred to Buchenwald. There Eliezer watches his father slowly die.

In *Night* there are no epiphanies like Primo Levi's epiphany in *Survival in Auschwitz,* when he recalls the story of Ulysses from Dante's *Inferno* and remembers that he, too, is a thinking, feeling human being. And there is no irony like Imre Kertész's irony in *Fatelessness,* when the narrator, mistaken for a corpse and carted away, protests that he would "like to live a bit longer in this beautiful concentration camp." There is no extraneous detail, no analysis, no speculation. There is only a story: Eliezer's account of what happened, delivered in his plainspoken voice.

The story itself is by now familiar. We know, or we think we know, all about Dr. Mengele and people being sent to the left and to the right, about the Zyklon B and the crematoria, about the bizarre systems and hierarchies that allowed some prisoners to discover mechanisms for survival and condemned others to a quick death. And the story's familiarity etherizes our minds into complacency: it becomes possible for us to think that because we know *about* all these things, we actually *know* them. Auschwitz is no longer just a place but a shorthand for the Holocaust, a common metaphor for uncommon evil, the almost platitudinous reference for the very embodiment of hell on earth. Amazingly, such complacency had already set in just a decade after the war, when François Mauriac wrote in his foreword to the French edition of *Night* that "this personal record, coming as it does after so many others and describing an abomination such as we might have thought no longer had any secrets for us, is different, distinct, and unique nevertheless." He suggested that *Night*'s uniqueness resides in the circumstances of its coming to exist—that is, its author's experiences during the war years—which "would surely have sufficed to inspire a book to which, I believe, no other can be compared."

By that standard, however, every Holocaust memoir is "unique," since each survivor tells his or her own terrible story. The reason that *Night* is particularly devastating has less to do with the facts of Wiesel's story than with the book's exquisite construction. I do not mean that it is beautifully written: its language and style are plain. But every sentence feels weighted and deliberate, every episode carefully chosen and delineated. It is also disarmingly brief; it can be carried in a pocket and read in an hour. One has the sense of merciless experience mercilessly distilled to its essence, because to take a story as fundamentally brutal as this one and clutter it with embellishments would be grotesque. By refusing to add the rationality of explanation or the cynicism of hindsight, *Night* takes us back to its terrible story with something resembling innocence, the innocence of a young boy who, like most of the rest of the Jews of Europe, had no idea what was coming. To read it is to lose one's own innocence about the Holocaust all over again.

Night's potency has been somewhat diluted by its canonicity. Relegated to high school reading lists, the small book was overshadowed by the subsequent fame of its Nobel Peace Prize–winning author, who during the 1970s and 1980s became known, for better or for worse, as a—or perhaps *the*—representative of the Holocaust. But in 2007, another chapter opened in *Night's* strange career. A lucid new translation of the book by Marion Wiesel, the author's wife, was selected by Oprah Winfrey for her book club. A few weeks later, fully half a century after its publication, *Night* made its first appearance at the top of the *New York Times* best-seller list, where it remained for a year and a half, until the newspaper decided to remove it owing to its status as an "evergreen."

Night's resuscitation came when the genre of memoir was in the midst of a crisis. James Frey had just been flagellated by none other than Winfrey for fabricating large parts of *A Million Little Pieces,* his supposed addiction memoir, which had been a previous Oprah selection. Less than a month later, the writer Laura Albert was unmasked as the mastermind behind "JT Leroy," the persona under which she had published allegedly autobiographical works of fiction describing the life of an HIV-positive teenage male prostitute and former drug addict. Considering the circumstances, Winfrey's endorsement of *Night* seemed typically canny: what could better restore credibility to her book club—and to the genre of memoir itself—than a book that, as Alvarez had written, was "beyond criticism"? And in fact *Night* was immediately seized as a lodestar of authenticity by the many commentators who had lambasted Winfrey's judgment in the Frey affair.

Unfortunately, *Night* is an imperfect ambassador for the infallibility of the memoir, owing to the fact that it has been treated very often as a novel—by journalists, by scholars, and even by its publishers. Lawrence Langer, in his landmark study *The Holocaust and the Literary Imagination,* notes that *Night* "continues to be classified and critically acclaimed as a novel, and not without reason." The book "yields the effect of an authentic *Bildungsroman,*" though it reverses the formula: Wiesel's "youthful protagonist becomes an initiate into death rather than in life," Langer writes. He finds literary antecedents for *Night* in *King Lear, The Brothers Karamazov,* and even *A Portrait of the Artist as a Young Man.* "Wiesel's account is ballasted with the freight of fiction: scenic organization, characterization through dialogue, periodic climaxes, elimination of superfluous or repetitive episodes, and especially an ability to arouse the empathy of his readers, which is an elusive ideal of the writer bound by fidelity to fact," Langer concludes.

Nonetheless, in 1997 *Publishers Weekly* columnist Paul Nathan had to issue a correction apologizing for referring to the book as an "autobiographical novel"; he had been misled, he said, by the entry on Wiesel in *The International Dictionary of Twentieth-Century Biography.* In response, the correction itself was challenged by the director of Penguin Reference Books, publishers of the biography dictionary, who cited half a dozen sources to the effect that *Night* was in fact a novel. Together with most critics, Gary Weissman, who recounted the above history in his book *Fantasies of Witnessing: Postwar Efforts to Experience the Holocaust,* seems to concur with Ernst Pawel's remark in an early magazine survey of Holocaust fiction that "the line between fact and fiction, tenuous at best, tends to vanish altogether in autobiographical novels" such as *Night.* The hybrid terms used to describe it include "novel/autobiography," "non-fictional novel," "semi-fictional memoir," "fictional-autobiographical memoir," "fictionalized autobiographical memoir," and "memoir-novel."

Matters are further confused by Wiesel's comment in the preface to the new edition that his wife's editing had helped him "to correct and revise a number of important details." He did not elaborate on what these were, but the statement was quickly seized and investigated by the news media. ("Old Questions Are Raised" was the ominous headline of a *New York Times* article about the issue.) The discrepancies, it turned out, amounted to errors such as the narrator's age upon his arrival at Auschwitz: in the first English translation he is said to be "almost fifteen," while in the new edition he is fifteen. Understandably angered by any suggestion of similarity between his book and Frey's, Wiesel asserted to a reporter that since *Night* is a memoir, his "experiences in the book—A to Z—must be true.... I object angrily if someone mentions it as a novel."

But if *Night* may not be a novel, even an autobiographical novel, it is not exactly a memoir, either—assuming memoir can be defined, following *Times* book critic Michiko Kakutani (one of the many to join the crusade against

Frey), as a form that prizes "authenticity above all else." The story of how *Night* came into existence reveals just how many factors come into play in the creation of a memoir: the obligation to remember and to testify, certainly, but also the artistic and even moral obligation to construct a true persona and to craft a beautiful work. Fact, we know, can be stranger than fiction; but truth in prose, it turns out, is not always the same thing as truth in life.

Night was first published in Buenos Aires in 1956, as the 117th volume in a series of Yiddish memoirs of prewar and wartime Europe. Its original title was *Un di velt hot geshvign* (And the world was silent). In *The Modern Jewish Canon,* Ruth R. Wisse notes that, in contrast to the other works in the series, which were traditional testimonials that aimed to memorialize as many of the murdered as possible, Wiesel's book was a "highly selective and isolating literary narrative" clearly influenced by its young author's reading of the French existentialists. When the book was translated—or, as Wisse puts it, "transposed"—into French, this distinction sharpened, beginning with the title, which shifts the book's emphasis from the world's indifference in the face of the fate of the Jews to the abstract "night": at once the darkness of the camps and the moral and spiritual darkness of the world during and after World War II. Wiesel—or his publisher—was reimagining his book not for his shrinking Yiddish readership, but for the global audience it would eventually attain.

In the first volume of the memoirs he wrote later in life, *All Rivers Run to the Sea,* Wiesel claims that his Yiddish manuscript was more than eight hundred pages long. *La Nuit,* published in 1958 in France (where Wiesel had temporarily settled), amounted to 178 pages. Wiesel writes that he made a number of cuts on his own, with further editing from his French publisher, which he then approved. All material not directly related to the story was pruned away. "Substance alone mattered," Wiesel writes in the preface to the new American edition (which, like all translations of *Night,* is based on the French version, not the Yiddish original). "I was more afraid of having said too much than too little." But his revisions had other implications as well. As Naomi Seidman writes in her well-known essay "Elie Wiesel and the Scandal of Jewish Rage," which examines Wiesel's revisions to *Un di velt,* "There are two survivors...a Yiddish and a French." The first wrote a testimonial intended largely for the historical record; the second had grander ambitions.

The book originally began with a passage in which the author, in lines that reflect his deep religious education, lamented the Jews' self-deception during the war years:

In the beginning there was faith—which is childish; trust—which is vain; and illusion—which is dangerous.

We believed in God, trusted in man, and lived with the illusion that every one of us has been entrusted with a sacred spark from the Shekhinah's flame; that every one of us carries in his eyes and in his soul a reflection of God's image.

That was the source if not the cause of all our ordeals.

And it ended with what Wiesel, in his new preface, calls a "gloomy meditation" on the global response to the Holocaust:

Now, scarcely ten years after Buchenwald, I realize that the world forgets quickly. Today, Germany is a sovereign state. The German army has been resuscitated. Ilse Koch, the notorious sadistic monster of Buchenwald, was allowed to have children and live happily ever after. War criminals stroll through the streets of Hamburg and Munich. The past seems to have been erased, relegated to oblivion.

Today, there are anti-Semites in Germany, France, and even the United States who tell the world that the "story" of six million assassinated Jews is nothing but a hoax, and many people, not knowing any better, may well believe them, if not today then tomorrow or the day after...

I am not so naïve as to believe that this slim volume will change the course of history or shake the conscience of the world.

Books no longer have the power they once did.

Those who kept silent yesterday will remain silent tomorrow.

As Wisse points out, there may well have been a political motivation behind the disappearance of these lines from the text: Wiesel could have been reluctant to expose the "collective self-blame" of the Jews or his own fury at Gentiles before a primarily Gentile audience. But, more importantly, there is an aesthetic imperative at work as well. These passages have their own didactic force: Wiesel's bitterness as he speaks of the Jews' belief as an "illusion," his expression of his own impotence in the face of Holocaust denial. But their moralizing tone is at odds with the simplicity of the main narrative, and it detracts from the power of the story. There is a terrifying finality to the last scene of the edited version, in which the narrator, after his liberation from Buchenwald and a brief stay in the hospital, looks at himself in the mirror for the first time since his imprisonment: "From the depths of the mirror, a corpse was contemplating me. The look in his eyes as he gazed at me has never left me."

Like every memoir, *Night* balances unsteadily between fidelity to the events it portrays and the making of literature. The book's poetic austerity comes at a cost to the literal truth. This cost, it must be said, does not detract in the least from *Night*'s validity as a Holocaust testimonial. (To Seidman's horror, her essay has been outrageously appropriated by Holocaust deniers who exploit her analysis of the differences between Wiesel's Yiddish and French texts to question his standing as a witness.) But it is worth recognizing that such a cost exists, if only to remind ourselves that no memoir can be at once an unerring representation of reality and a genuine artistic achievement. We do writers such as Wiesel (and Borowski and Levi) no credit by continuing to insist that their work is strictly, purely factual. For to insist this is to underrate their extraordinary level of literary sophistication.

To understand the problem, we need to return to A. Alvarez's famous quote from *Commentary*. Here it is in its entirety: "As a human document, *Night* is almost unbearably painful, and certainly beyond criticism." But Alvarez draws a distinction between the "human document" of a testimony and a literary text; and in this latter category the book does not measure up. He continues: "Like *The Terezín Requiem* [a novel published around the same time] and dozens of other equally sincere, equally distressing books, it is a failure as a work of art." He is right, of course, that sincerity is not enough to make a work of art successful. His complaint against Wiesel is primarily stylistic: the language in *Night* can sound "excessive, even journalistic," because "the feelings are so fiercely present in the barest recital of the facts that any attempt to elaborate, underline, or explain them seems like wild overstatement.... When what Wiesel has to say becomes intolerable for him, he falls back on rhetoric." Alvarez prefers the tone of Borowski, "curt, icy, and brutally direct."

But to dismiss the literary achievement of *Night* (which Alvarez, adding to the cacophony of categories, identifies as "a scantily fictionalized autobiography") in the same breath as *The Terezín Requiem*—a sentimental and almost entirely fictional account of the efforts to produce a performance of Verdi's Requiem in the concentration camp—is to undermine the extraordinary effectiveness of Wiesel's narrative, which unfolds simultaneously on two levels. It is at once a testimonial to the evils of the camps and a chronicle of its protagonist's loss of faith—a spiritual journey that, evidence from Wiesel's other books shows, may well be fictional. For it is by no means clear that Wiesel himself underwent the rebellion against God that unfolds in his text. "In one of its aspects, Wiesel's text is a study of fathers and sons in Auschwitz, with all inmates being the children of God the Father," Langer has written. "This lifts the narrative, to its credit, to be sure, beyond the constraints of autobiography into the realm of imagined fiction; nothing is more 'literary' or stylized in the story than the young boy's denunciation of God's world and implied renunciation of its Creator, the seeds of both of which are nurtured by passages in Dostoevsky and Camus, in addition to the conditions of Auschwitz itself."

The book begins in 1942, when Eliezer (as Wiesel calls himself here) is twelve years old. He describes himself as "deeply observant" and immersed in religious study, and laments having been unable to find anyone willing to tutor him in kabbalah, an esoteric field generally restricted to older men. One day at the synagogue he falls into conversation with Moishe the Beadle, a poor man who reveals a surprising depth of knowledge and who becomes his teacher. Eliezer recounts one of their talks:

> Man comes closer to God through the questions he asks Him, [Moishe] liked to say. Therein lies true dialogue. Man asks and God replies. But we don't understand His replies. We cannot understand them. Because they dwell in the depths of our souls and remain there until we die. The real answers, Eliezer, you will find only within yourself.
>
> "And why do you pray, Moishe?" I asked him.
>
> "I pray to the God within me for the strength to ask him the real questions."
>
> ...And in the course of those evenings I became convinced that Moishe the Beadle would help me enter eternity, into that time when question and answer would become ONE.

These talks end when Moishe, along with the rest of the town's foreign Jews, is deported. He returns with a horrifying tale. The Jews, he said, traveled first by train and then by truck to a forest in Galicia, where they were forced to dig trenches. After they finished, they were shot, one by one. Moishe escaped, miraculously, after being wounded in the leg and left for dead. But no matter how many times he repeats his story, no one believes him; even as late as the spring of 1944, as German troops are invading Budapest, the Jews of Sighet (now in Romania, the town was under Hungarian administration during the war) do not think the army will reach their town. They do not even really believe that Hitler intends to exterminate the Jews. The narrator does not try to explain their naïveté, just as later he does not try to explain the Nazis' brutality. He relies on factual statements: "In less than three days, German army vehicles made their appearance on our streets."

"Night fell....Night had fallen....Night." This is the book's only stylistic flourish: an almost incantatory repetition, in steady beats at the beginning of a sentence or passage bearing some new agony. The Jews of Sighet are first restricted to two small ghettoes; soon they learn they are all to be deported. Eliezer's family is in the last group to go, packed eighty to a train car. In the car with them is a woman named Mrs. Schächter, who has lost her mind and cries out continually: "Fire!...I see a fire! I see flames, huge flames!" The other passengers tie her down and gag her. Finally they arrive at a train station bearing the sign "Auschwitz." Here Mrs. Schächter screams of fire again, and now the rest of the passengers see it too.

Is it not too much to ask that the impoverished beadle be both a master of the kabbalah and a Cassandra-like figure whose warnings go unheeded? Or, similarly, that the journey to Auschwitz be punctuated by the cries of a similarly unacknowledged visionary? In fact, if one compares the events in *Night* to Wiesel's account of his wartime experiences in *All Rivers Run to the Sea,* the evidence of artistic labor can easily be discovered. The young Wiesel, who was brought up in the Hasidic tradition, did in fact dabble in Jewish mysticism, but his master was "Kalman the Kabalist," not Moishe the Beadle, who is another person entirely. The character in *Night* is a composite, and so the dialogue that Wiesel reports, and which I quoted above, must be imagined. Mrs. Schächter and her terrifying vision appear in both books, but in *All Rivers Run to the Sea* she merits just one mention, while her role in *Night* is considerably more important. Then there is all the information that appears in the memoir but did not find its way into *Night,* including the many warnings that the Jews of Sighet did have and the repeated deliberations they made about what to do—a sharp contrast to the thunderbolts in *Night.*

Does anybody, other than literary scholars, care about such variations? Do they matter? After all, they are not serious problems of fact; they are, for the most part, moments of artistic license. And that is precisely why they are important. Wiesel's decision to make the beadle a secret kabbalist sacrifices literal fact for literary effect: it simplifies the story, helping it to achieve its parable-like quality, and it adds another dimension to Moishe's tragedy. It indicates that Wiesel recognizes the memoirist's dual obligation—to the truth, certainly, but also to tell his story (as Jorge Semprun argued to his fellow prisoners while still in Buchenwald) in the most interesting, most memorable, most meaningful way possible. Like the translator who occasionally veers from the phrasing of an individual line for the sake of the work as a whole, the memoirist too must be at liberty to shape the raw materials into a work of art.

Wiesel's shaping occurs mainly in the service of the narrator's crisis of faith, which runs as a *basso continuo* beneath the entire book. It is embodied in *Night*'s central episode: the public hanging of one of the Kapos' assistants, a young boy with an angelic face, together with two other men. Here is Ruth Wisse's translation of the scene (taken from *The Modern Jewish Canon*) as it appeared in the original Yiddish manuscript:

> Both adults were already dead. The noose had choked them at once. Instantly they expired. Their extended tongues were red as fire.
>
> Only the slight Jewish child with the lost dreamy eyes was still alive. His body weighed too little. Was too light. The noose didn't "catch."
>
> The slow death of the little *meshoresl* [assistant] took thirty-five minutes. And we saw him wobbling, swaying, on the rope, with his bluish-red tongue extended, with a prayer on his grey-white lips, a prayer to God, to the Angel of Death, to take pity on him, to take his soul, liberating it from its death-throes, from the torments of the grave. When we saw him like that, the hanged child, many of us didn't want to, couldn't keep from crying.
>
> —Where is God?—the same man asked again, behind me. Something in me wanted to answer him:
>
> —Where is God? Here he is, hanging on the gallows...
>
> That evening the soup had no taste.
>
> We hid it away for the next day.

And here it is in *Night,* in Marion Wiesel's translation:

> The two men were no longer alive. Their tongues were hanging out, swollen and bluish. But the third rope was still moving: the child, too light, was still breathing...
>
> And so he remained for more than half an hour, lingering between life and death, writhing before our eyes. And we were forced to look at him at close range. He was still alive when I passed him. His tongue was still red, his eyes not yet extinguished.
>
> Behind me, I heard the same man asking:
>
> "For God's sake, where is God?"

And from within me, I heard a voice answer:
"Where He is? This is where—hanging here from this gallows…"
That evening the soup tasted of corpses.

The "improved" version is shorter, most obviously, but it also speaks from a subtly altered perspective. The voice in the first passage is communal: "When we saw him…many of us…couldn't keep from crying." The second emphasizes the singular experience of the narrator: "He was still alive when I passed him." The Holocaust happened to a whole community, obviously, but the community cannot effectively speak as a whole. It is only with the voice of an individual messenger that we can identify. Most importantly, the new version also boldly alters the final line. Wisse comments that the passage's new ending is "more credible," since "by all accounts, no one at Auschwitz could have left his soup for the next day." But her reading overlooks the fact that Wiesel has taken a straightforward description ("the soup had no taste") and substituted a literary trope ("the soup tasted of corpses"). To the best of my knowledge, even at Auschwitz, corpses were not actually used to prepare the soup. Paradoxically, a metaphor becomes more believable than an unembellished description.

It is worth noting, though, that the substance of the passage—which is not altered at all in the translation of the original Yiddish into French and then English—is a highly stylized scene constructed to maximize every bit of its shock value. As many critics have noted, the execution of the angelic young boy together with two anonymous men has Christlike overtones, which are heightened by the physical similarity between the gallows and the crucifix. But even discounting this framework, the narrator bluntly informs us of the death of God in phrasing that is strikingly similar in the two versions. The passage functions as a turning point in *Night,* after which the narrator apparently ceases to believe. Up to now, he has occasionally invoked God's presence, if only as bitter commentary. "I concurred with Job!" he remarks early on. "I was not denying [God's] existence, but I doubted His absolute justice." But soon after the hanging, the inmates celebrate Rosh Hashanah, and Eliezer feels unable to take part in the services. "Blessed be God's name?" he asks:

Why, but why would I bless Him? Every fiber in me rebelled. Because He caused thousands of children to burn in His mass graves? Because He kept six crematoria working day and night, including Sabbath and the Holy Days? Because in His great might, He had created Auschwitz, Birkenau, Buna, and so many other factories of death? How could I say to

Him: Blessed be Thou, Almighty, Master of the Universe, who chose us among all nations to be tortured day and night, to watch as our fathers, our mothers, our brothers end up in the furnaces?...

I no longer pleaded for anything. I was no longer able to lament. On the contrary, I felt very strong. I was the accuser, God the accused. My eyes had opened and I was alone, terribly alone in a world without God, without man.

In his memoirs, Wiesel writes with some annoyance that *Night* has often been read as a narrative about the loss of faith. On the contrary, he says, he remained a believer after the war (he writes with joy of resuming his Talmudic studies at a camp for displaced children in France) and continues to practice Judaism to this day. Yet what he has written in *Night* is more than an indictment of God's absence during the Holocaust, along the lines of Paul Celan's famous poem "Tenebrae," in which the Jews in the camps address God in a tone that is half menacing, half loving ("Pray, Lord, / Pray to us, / We are near") or Zvi Kolitz's story "Yosl Rakover Talks to God," which imagines an extended soliloquy directed by a Jew in the Warsaw Ghetto to a God who has "hidden his face from the world." Indeed, after this point God nearly disappears from *Night,* returning only at the very end for one last plea. Watching an elderly rabbi search for the son who has abandoned him in the desperate snowy march from Auschwitz, Eliezer prays "in spite of myself" to "this God in whom I no longer believed. Oh God, Master of the Universe, give me the strength never to do what Rabbi Eliahu's son has done." His prayer, if it is heard, is not answered.

The only real challenge to *Night*'s credibility as a memoir—I am discounting the revisionists who have leaped like hyenas on each perceived discrepancy—was brought by Alfred Kazin. In his essay "My Debt to Elie Wiesel and Primo Levi," published in 1989 in the collection *Testimony: Contemporary Writers Make the Holocaust Personal,* Kazin chronicled his reading of Holocaust literature through the lens of his close friendship and subsequent falling out with Wiesel. They first met, according to Kazin, in 1960, after he had written a review of *Night,* which prompted a letter from Wiesel. "He personified the Holocaust as no one else in New York did," Kazin writes. The aspect of the book that spoke to Kazin most deeply was what he, too, read as the narrator's religious crisis. "To the best of my knowledge," Kazin has written, "no one of this background"—he means Wiesel's Orthodox upbringing—"has left behind him so moving a record of the direct loss of faith on the part of a young boy."

Thus, *Night*'s primary value for Kazin was not as a chronicle of the Holocaust, but as a story at once more specific and more universal.

The trouble with this interpretation, at least for Kazin, was that Wiesel would soon cultivate a public persona, through his lectures at the 92nd Street Y in Manhattan and elsewhere, as a "platform idol who gave...rhetorical assurances of the Jewish tradition to secularized middle-class audiences." In the face of seemingly overwhelming textual evidence, he would no longer admit to religious crisis as playing a part in *Night* at all. In a speech given in 1981, he identified his (temporary) loss of faith as having taken place after the war; in Auschwitz, he said, he needed God. His memoirs support this claim, offering further evidence that Wiesel conducted himself in the camp as an observant Jew: he recounts putting on tefillin together with his father at Auschwitz ("A few dozen prisoners thereby sacrificed their sleep, and sometimes their rations of bread or coffee, to perform the mitzvah"). One of the stories in *Legends of Our Time*—a collection of more fanciful but possibly true tales not unlike Levi's *Moments of Reprieve*—tells of the efforts to organize a Yom Kippur service in Auschwitz, in which the story's narrator participates.

Did Wiesel's crisis of faith take place in Auschwitz, or afterward? This question leads Kazin to the infamous declaration that ended his friendship with Wiesel. "I had to conclude that Wiesel was a powerful myth-maker about his relation to God, with himself as the bearer of the myth," Kazin wrote. "The more I learned about him, the more I pursued the vast literature about Auschwitz, the less surprised I would have been to learn that the episode of the boy struggling on the rope had never happened." For if Wiesel did not in fact lose his faith while he was in the camp, then the emotional climax of the scene—the young narrator's cry against God—could not have taken place. "When he marched past the hanging child, did the young Wiesel *really* cry out against God by imagining Him hanging there on the gallows?" the critic Gary Weissman asks. "Or did Wiesel the writer invent this cry, retrospectively adding it to a scene based on actual events?"

This question is important not necessarily for what it reveals about Wiesel's faith, but because it serves to illustrate a problem that affects every form of autobiography, whether it be memoir or autobiographical novel. The critic Ellen Fine, trying to find a "third way" to classify *Night,* inadvertently points to the problem. "Essentially it is *témoignage,*" she writes, "a first-hand account of the concentration camp experience, succinctly related by the fifteen-year-old narrator, Eliezer." But *Night* is *not* actually related by the fifteen-year-old Eliezer, though it appears to be. The true narrator is the twenty-five-year-old

Elie Wiesel, who had ten years after liberation to reflect on his experiences. "Eliezer" is a semifictional construct for the purposes of the memoir, differentiated from the author whose name appears on the cover by the simple variation on the name. Eliezer is Elie Wiesel, but he also is *not* Elie Wiesel. And so Eliezer contemplates the Holocaust not necessarily as the religious teenager might actually have done (and reports having done in his memoirs), but from the post-Holocaust vantage point shared by the book's readers—a vantage point that questions how God could have allowed the Holocaust to happen.

And this, Weissman concludes, is the only way to reconcile *Night*'s apparent contradictions. Both versions—the religious and the antireligious—are true, because both people actually existed: the religious Eliezer and the crisis-afflicted Elie. *Every* memoir, by definition, is written from the standpoint of the later self. And it is hardly unexpected for the later self to have a somewhat different take on things. "The difficulty of settling on a single, authoritative testimony speaks to a larger truth: that each survivor's account of his or her experiences presents its own theme or subjective truth, that a single survivor's accounts may present contrasting themes or truths over time," Weissman writes.

Wiesel, I suspect, would agree. Another passage cut from the Yiddish version describes in detail the death of his father, which—even more than the loss of faith—is the great tragedy of *Night*. "Why not include those [lines] in this new translation?" Wiesel asks in the foreword. "Too personal, too private, perhaps; they need to remain between the lines. And yet…" He goes on to give the passage in its entirety nonetheless. The material that was cut adds nothing to the factual content of the scene: it describes his feelings, his fear of the SS guard who was beating his father and thus his reluctance to come to his father's aid, and his shame at his own fear. The final version leaves more to the reader's imagination:

> In front of the block, the SS were giving orders. An officer passed between the bunks. My father was pleading:
>
> "My son, water… I'm burning up… My insides…"
>
> "Silence over there!" barked the officer.
>
> "Eliezer," continued my father, "water…"
>
> The officer came closer and shouted to him to be silent. But my father did not hear. He continued to call me. The officer wielded his club and dealt him a violent blow to the head.
>
> I didn't move. I was afraid, my body was afraid of another blow, this time to *my* head.

My father groaned once more, I heard:
"Eliezer..."
I could see that he was still breathing—in gasps. I didn't move.

Is one version "more true" than the other? No one could say—not even, I suspect, Wiesel himself, which is precisely why he includes them both. "I mean to recount not the story of my life, but my stories," he writes in *All Rivers Run to the Sea*. "Consider this account, then, as a kind of commentary." In an essay on Rashi, the great biblical commentator, Wiesel explicitly connects the act of commentary and the act of memory. "To comment on a text"—he is referring here to ancient texts, to the Bible or the Talmud—"is to know that though I am not always capable of attaining truth, I may come closer to its source," Wiesel writes. "But how are we to know which interpretation is correct? The answer lies in the one that enriches memory. If it distorts it, the interpretation is wrong. In other words, an excess of imagination risks harming the original thought."

But if Wiesel's memoirs—and in this category I include *Night* and the two later volumes of autobiography, *All Rivers Run to the Sea* and *And the Sea Is Never Full*, as well as the numerous autobiographical essays and stories he has published over the years—function as commentary, then what is the primary source alongside which his works stand in the margins? This source, Wiesel's works have made abundantly clear, is the Holocaust itself. "Auschwitz is as important as Sinai," he has famously said. This remark, with its unsettling mix of hyperbole and blasphemy, has consistently characterized Wiesel's position on the subject of Holocaust literature over the last fifty years. It is ironic, to say the least, that a person who experienced a crisis of faith along the lines of the crisis in *Night* would go on explicitly to cast the Holocaust itself in religious terms.

Even putting aside the theological implications of such a declaration, the literary implications are also serious. Wiesel believes that, like the Torah or indeed God himself, the Holocaust is a sacred subject. It must be approached very carefully, according to established rituals and customs, so as not to insult or degrade it, even inadvertently. Few would disagree that the Holocaust must be treated with the greatest seriousness. But who determines which avenues of approach are appropriate and which are trivializing or tasteless? Who establishes the rituals and customs, and excommunicates those who fail to comply? The answer, at least with regard to the Holocaust in American culture, has often been Elie Wiesel. The targets of his often furious criticism have protested (and they are not the only ones) that he has turned the Holocaust into a religion of which he is the sole prophet, or to which he at least has privileged, priestly access. As such, he is even himself treated as a religious figure: in one of the more astonishing examples of this, during a tribute to Wiesel at the 92nd Street Y in 2008 to celebrate his eightieth birthday, he sat on stage as a singer serenaded him with a pop-ballad arrangement of the *shehecheyanu* prayer, which is normally recited to mark the start of a Jewish holiday.

If Wiesel has not exactly embraced this characterization, he has done little to contest it. Interviewed for a *New York Times* article in 1980 devoted to "the new phenomenon of public enthusiasm for remembering the Holocaust," he used religious terms to denounce the vulgarity of popular novels and movies on the subject. "I myself was afraid always of desacralizing it," he told the *Times* reporter. "We need to regain our sense of sacredness." Paradoxically, his insistence on sacralizing the Holocaust has manifested itself in the unequivocal rejection of writing that takes almost any kind of literary license with the Holocaust. In reviews and essays published over the last fifty years, Wiesel has fulminated against those writers who have been guilty, in his eyes, of "an excess of imagination," and celebrated those who, in his eyes, have adhered most closely to the historical record.

In doing so, Wiesel invariably invokes the religious trope of Auschwitz as immeasurable, incommunicable, unnamable. "The experience cannot be communicated, not *truly* communicated; one knows it only from within, where knowledge becomes an obsession," he wrote in a 1963 review of *The Terezín Requiem,* which he treated—inaccurately—as a nonfictional text. "Thus it is not surprising that authors of the modern novel, despite their perpetual quest after new themes, have been conspicuously unable to deal with the overwhelming contemporary reality of an Auschwitz: here neither the talent nor artistic sensibilities of a writer will suffice. Something else is necessary: a great audacity, much anger, even more humility." In 1968, praising Jerzy Kosinski's supposedly autobiographical novel *The Painted Bird,* he wrote that "most attempts by scientists, psychologists, moralists and even novelists to come to grips with the phenomenon of men's mass extermination by man have ended in failure. The task of the chronicler seems somehow easier. He writes not to reach conclusions and to be rewarded for them; all he asks is to be heard, to be believed." (Both of these books were published as fiction, a fact of which Wiesel was either unaware or, in the more complicated case of Kosinski, chose not to believe: he was apparently incapable of appreciating them as anything other than testimonies.) Ten years later, he raged against the television miniseries "Holocaust" for its vulgarity and inauthenticity, but also simply because it dared to impose a fictional veneer over its subject. Condemning the use of special effects to simulate the gas chamber, he wrote:

> Similar techniques are being used for war movies and historical recre-
> ations. But the Holocaust is unique, not just another event. This series
> treats the Holocaust as if it *were* just another event. Thus, I object to
> it not because it is not artistic enough but because it is not authentic
> enough. It removes us from the event instead of bringing us closer to
> it.... The witness feels here duty-bound to declare: What you have seen
> on the screen is not what happened *there*. You may think you know now
> how the victims lived and died, but you do not. Auschwitz cannot be
> explained nor can it be visualized. Whether culmination or aberration
> of history, the Holocaust transcends history. Everything about it inspires
> fear and leads to despair: The dead are in possession of a secret that we,
> the living, are neither worthy of nor capable of recovering.... A film
> about Sobibor is either not a picture or not about Sobibor....
>
> The Holocaust? The ultimate event, the ultimate mystery, never to be
> comprehended or transmitted. Only those who were there know what it
> was; the others will never know.

As late as 1989, in a *Times* article titled "Art and the Holocaust: Trivializing Memory," Wiesel was still arguing that "the cry unuttered is the loud-
est" and deploring the "exploitation" of the Holocaust—now a "fashionable
subject"—by films such as *Sophie's Choice* and a Broadway play called *Ghetto*.
The words "ghetto" and "Broadway" do ring of the absurd when used in a
single phrase, and Wiesel is not the only critic to have felt a pang of disquiet
as the Holocaust in American culture experienced its strange transformation
from unmentionable to ubiquitous. But this reasonable concern is swallowed
up by the bombast of his rhetoric. Wiesel's insistence on the absolute uniqueness of the Holocaust—not simply as a political or historical event, but as a
metaphysical event—renders it untouchable except by the initiated. "Let us
repeat it again," he wrote in "Art and the Holocaust": "Auschwitz is something
else, always something else. It is a universe outside the universe, a creation that
exists parallel to creation. Auschwitz lies on the other side of life and on the
other side of death.... Then, it defeated culture; later, it defeated art, because
just as no one could imagine Auschwitz before Auschwitz, no one can now
retell Auschwitz after Auschwitz. The truth of Auschwitz remains hidden in

its ashes. Only those who lived it in their flesh and in their minds can possibly transform their experience into knowledge."

This rhetoric, passionate though it may be, is deliberately antirational. What can it mean to say that Auschwitz is "always something else"? In sheer point of fact, it wasn't "a universe outside the universe." It may have *felt* as though it existed beyond the bounds of the world of humankind, but it was a real place with a geographic location easily discovered on the map, conceived and designed and run by human beings. And in the face of the great works of fiction and nonfiction that have come to constitute the literature of the death camps—some written by "those who lived it in their flesh and in their minds," but some written also by those, such as Cynthia Ozick, who did not—how can anyone truly believe that "no one can now retell Auschwitz after Auschwitz"?

Wiesel ends this article by exhorting his audience to read testimonies and histories, to watch documentaries, and to "stop insulting the dead." But such a doctrinaire formulation fails to take into account the considerable work of shaping and translating memory that goes into any testimony. Joshua Sobol, the author of the play *Ghetto* that Wiesel denounced, responded by pointing out the eternal difficulty of establishing authoritative accounts, noting that "there are almost no two concurring testimonies about one single important event." In *The Lost: A Search for Six of Six Million,* his recent investigation of his own family's history, the critic Daniel Mendelsohn went even further, demonstrating in painstaking detail that even for relatively insignificant events it can be impossible to sort through multiple reports to attain a single truth. As we saw above, *Night* itself deviates from the pure facts of its account for the sake of literary impact.

Another problem with a school of critical thought that assigns value to a text about the Holocaust only according to that text's correspondence with reality is that if the text turns out to be fictional, the criticism is discredited as well. For a fraudulent memoir along the lines of Misha Defonseca's tale of surviving the Holocaust with a pack of wolves, this makes sense. But what about a more ambiguous case, such as that of Jerzy Kosinski? If Kosinski, as it turned out, was not the "chronicler" Wiesel's review made him out to be, then the implication is that his book has no value—even though it was published as a novel and can be read and understood profitably, and far more credibly, as a work of fiction rather than a work of testimony.

By virtue of Wiesel's Nobel Prize, as well as his prodigious gifts as a writer and a lecturer—by the 1980s he had virtually come to symbolize the Holocaust to many Americans—his viewpoint on the fictionalization of the Holocaust has dominated the cultural discussion, even as the public appetite for films, novels, and plays about the Holocaust shows no signs of decreasing. The result has been the casting of a kind of mystic spell upon the Holocaust, in which it is continually asserted—such a thing cannot be argued, only asserted—that the uniqueness of the event resides in its deeper truth, a truth that is always by definition unattainable, "hidden in its ashes." There can be no doubt that the act of trying to put *Night* under the fact checker's lens smacks of indecency. One cannot seriously worry about whether babies were burned alive or dead at Auschwitz (one of the questions that has been raised periodically about the book) without losing something of one's own humanity. Is it not enough to know that they were burned at all? But if it feels barbaric to perform critical dissection on a book such as *Night,* the alternative is worse.

I am not thinking only of the possibilities for Holocaust fraud, although the notorious fraudulent memoirs that made their way onto the public scene in the last decade—Defonseca, Wilkomirski, and others—were able to be published precisely because editors, publishers, and critics had abdicated their responsibility. I am thinking also of the problems inherent whenever a topic is deemed taboo, closed off to critical or creative thought. There is something priestly about Wiesel's insistence in guarding the Temple against those who would desecrate it, but there is also something totalitarian about it. No book—not even Borowski's, bound in the relics of concentration-camp clothing—should be treated as a hallowed object, to be worshiped and obeyed rather than analyzed. If a novel about Auschwitz is either "not a novel or not about Auschwitz," then what are we to do with *Night?*

Such an approach, which equates questioning with denial, runs explicitly counter to the love of dialectic that Wiesel himself displays in his memoir, with its enigmatic stories inviting many possibilities for interpretation. For the purpose of a commentary, as Wiesel knows well, is to explicate—but also to invite discussion, argument, further commentary. And as even the young kabbalist in the death camps knows, the union of question and answer will take place only in eternity.

4

The Antiwitness: Piotr Rawicz

Was Boris any closer to me than Yuri? Was he any more real? My
two halves seemed to be melting away into the giant landscape that
surrounded my days.

   Can it be that what we regard as "authenticity," as "tangible truth,"
is even more false than falsehood and fiction itself? This hypothesis
may be absolutely right, for "truth" and "reality" are invested with an
arrogant and outrageous pretentiousness that is even less justifiable than
the most reckless of lies and the least consistent of fictions. It was all
very well Boris's presuming on his "legitimacy" vis-à-vis Yuri: the latter
was not without weighty arguments of his own. Their quarrel, if quarrel
there was, went on so long ago that it no longer even succeeded in
"harrowing" my inner self. Though (and this was the main question) was
there anything whatever to harrow?

                                             —from *Blood from the Sky*

Almost none of the books that we now think of as Holocaust "classics" were
immediately recognized as such. In 1947, when Primo Levi first sought to publish *If This Is a Man*, the book was rejected by Einaudi, the prestigious Italian
publishing house that would eventually become his home, and international
recognition would wait for more than a decade. The original Yiddish version
of Elie Wiesel's *Night*, which appeared in 1956 in an Argentinian series of

wartime memoirs, also met with little fanfare—the book was acknowledged as a definitive text only after Wiesel (with the encouragement of François Mauriac) pruned it down for its French publication two years later. Even Anne Frank's *Diary of a Young Girl* did not achieve widespread acclaim until its publication in English in 1952, five years after the original Dutch edition.

But no writer has been as consistently—even systematically—ignored as Piotr Rawicz. Nearly fifty years after its original publication, his novel *Blood from the Sky* (*Le Sang du Ciel*), which appeared in France in 1961, three years after *Night,* remains one of the most original works of fiction ever written about the Holocaust. Yet the critic Lawrence Langer, in his preface to a recent paperback edition of the book that brought it back into print in English, notes the strange fact that "virtually no detailed critical commentary has appeared in English or any other language" on the novel, which he deems a "masterpiece." And even Langer admits with regret that over the course of an entire career spent writing about Holocaust literature, he has never managed to "discharge [his] overdue obligation" to Rawicz. When Rawicz is remembered, it is most often as one of a group of writers that includes Tadeusz Borowski, Paul Celan, and Jerzy Kosinski: Holocaust survivors who committed suicide.

Born in Lwów (now Lviv) in 1919 into an educated family—his father was a lawyer, his mother a poet—Rawicz lived in that town until the start of the war, then spent a year in hiding before his arrest and imprisonment, first in Auschwitz and then in Leitmeritz, a camp in Czechoslovakia. He managed to conceal his Jewish origins, an effort that forms the primary drama of *Blood from the Sky,* and was imprisoned as a Ukrainian, which in the brutal hierarchy of Auschwitz meant marginally better rations and moderately less perilous circumstances. (Like Borowski, he was allowed to receive food packages.) After settling in Paris in 1947, he earned degrees in Sanskrit and Hindi; in addition to those languages, he also spoke Ukrainian, Russian, Polish, German, French, English, Yiddish, and Hebrew. Like Wiesel, with whom he became acquainted in Paris, he was a journalist; like his countryman Czesław Miłosz, he served for a time as an attaché to the Polish legation; and he worked also as a translator, chauffeur, and meat salesman. He killed himself in 1982, shortly after the death of his wife from cancer.

The main character in *Blood from the Sky,* a Holocaust survivor named Boris D., shares some of his creator's biography—the novel consists in large part of Boris's reports about his year on the run in what is now Ukraine and Poland—as well as his contemporaneous situation: he is a down-at-the-heels poet living the bohemian life in postwar Paris. (The novel takes place in 1961, the year of its publication.) "Cynicism, boredom, laziness, booze, café-haunting, sexual irresponsibility, poverty, *je m'en foutisme,* chaos, romantic idealism—all were present in the life of this survivor," writes Anthony Rudolf, an acquaintance of Rawicz's and the author of *Engraved in Flesh: Piotr Rawicz and His Novel "Blood from the Sky,"* a slim but enlightening biographical-critical study of the writer. But to call Rawicz's book an "autobiographical novel" is a serious oversimplification. Not only does the disjointed form of *Blood from the Sky* discourage any effort to understand the book as a chronicle or testimony, but the postscript on the book's last page explicitly disavows its authority: "*This book is not a historical record.* If the notion of chance (like most other notions) did not strike the author as absurd, he would gladly say that any reference to a particular period, territory, or race is purely coincidental. The events that he describes could crop up in any place, at any time, in the mind of any man, planet, mineral.…"

And this, I believe, is why Rawicz's gorgeously written, funny, bitingly intelligent book—Irving Howe called it "wantonly brilliant"—has largely failed to find a readership. Just as the brash, debonair Rawicz seems to have had little in common with the stereotype of the Holocaust survivor as frail and unremittingly serious (as embodied by Elie Wiesel), *Blood from the Sky* absolutely refuses to conform to standard notions about what a Holocaust novel should be. Despite critics' attempts to understand it as a work of testimony—the *New York Times* reviewer wrote that "'Blood from the Sky' is one more piece of evidence, one more word of confirmation, as to what happened in our time in a civilized society"—Rawicz's novel, though it tells the story of a catastrophe, is not a novel of witness. In fact, the persona of the writer that emerges from the cobbled-together sketches, poems, and reports that constitute the book is a kind of antiwitness—a man who deliberately omits or alters dates, place names, and names of people; who mistakes human heads for cabbages; who introduces another chronicler to fill in a missing piece of his story; and who even implies that he may have taken part in one of the incidents of violence on which he reports. His writing, which ranges from passages of beautifully poetic prose to choppy, awkward poems, is more than dispassionate: it refuses to pass judgment on any person, any action. Even Tadeusz Borowski, often thought of as the Holocaust's great amoralist, cannot choke back the anger that animates his stories of Auschwitz; but Rawicz describes scenes of horrifying brutality without a trace of emotion. To a reader accustomed to the moral fervor of Wiesel or the clarifying evaluations of Levi, Rawicz's tone of amoral objectivity is far more disquieting than the atrocities—many of them by now familiar—that his antihero so calmly relates.

Blood from the Sky begins not with Boris, but in the acerbic voice of the unnamed man who serves as the novel's narrator and the frame for Boris's story. The owner of a café, one day he notices a newcomer among his regular customers: "Fashioned from a dark metal, very thin and very straight, he must once have been not bad-looking at all.... His skin is dried up, and the color of tobacco ash. His hair is thick and flaxen; the whiteness of his teeth is a dead whiteness." (I quote from Peter Wiles's fine translation from the French, which originally appeared in 1964 and was brought back into print in 2003 by Yale University Press.) We learn nothing about their personal relationship other than that, after a long day and night of conversation, Boris entrusts the narrator with his notebooks, which tell of the destruction of "an average-sized town in the Ukraine" during World War II. As the story progresses, the narrator will sometimes quote the journals verbatim and sometimes paraphrase them in his own words; at times he calls attention to his editorial interventions, but usually he performs them silently. "Our customer's narrative begins in quotation marks," he writes in a footnote to the first excerpt from Boris's journal. "I hope these quotation marks will get lost as we go along."

The critic Theodore Solotaroff wrote that both Rawicz and Boris are symbolist poets, and while that designation seems a bit exaggerated for the broken snatches of Boris's verse that we see here, it does aptly describe the strangely immaterial, thoroughly antirealist tone in which Boris relates the story of the town's destruction. In the first passage from the journal, Boris describes the town as "a boat. A floating island made of crystal." As the townspeople assemble in the square for the first selection and transport, "the helmeted and unreal soldiers stood around the gently vibrating square like the angels of the Lord. No sooner had the moorings been cast off than, slowly and deliberately, the vessel got under way." When he comes upon a group of workers in the cemetery breaking down tombstones for the SS to use to pave the streets, he imagines the letters mystically flying off in "white-hot shell splinters," taking on a secret life. Soon afterward, one of the soldiers takes revenge on a woman with the last name of Goldberg, who supposedly gave him gonorrhea, by rounding up and executing all the female Goldbergs in the town: "They were made to stand in a long line, like the fragile keys of a spinet."

This exquisitely aestheticized prose coexists with passages of startling carnality, which reveal an obsession with sex more typical of the memoirs of a libertine than of a Holocaust novel. In addition to his girlfriend Naomi, with whom he goes into hiding, Boris fantasizes about nearly every woman with whom he comes into contact, and with some he does more than fantasize.

His blond hair and aristocratic appearance protecting him from suspicion, he watches from a distance as the town's Jewish citizens are ordered to assemble in the square for the first transport. "There were some quite acceptable-looking girls, whose breasts and hips were beginning to fill out," he writes. "Unripe apples that were soon to be picked. I was overcome by a feeling of jealousy at the thought of their end, of the flame that was to usurp my place and lick these breasts and hips to death." During a conversation Boris has with Dr. Hillel, the town scholar and historian, we learn in an aside that Boris has slept with the older man's wife. When the caretaker of the cemetery shows him the bodies of a group of people who had committed suicide the night before, he recognizes the corpse of the girl to whom he lost his virginity. And after he and Naomi go into hiding together, their romantic idyll is interrupted by Boris's constant desires for other women and her jealous insistence on sexual exclusivity. Her only comfort is his fear of discovery. "Would not the sign of the Covenant inscribed in my body betray me to the very first tart I picked up?" he admits ruefully. (In a rare reference to sexual practices in Auschwitz, Rudolf writes that Rawicz's own sexual ardor was not diminished in the camp, where he claimed to have had an affair with the wife of an SS officer.)

Consequently, it is Boris's penis—the "tool" of two of the book's section headings, "The Tool and the Art of Comparison" and "The Tool and the Thwarting of Comparison"—that becomes the focus of the novel's exhilaratingly farcical climax. Boris, who has been using the false papers of a Ukrainian farm hand named Yuri Goletz (one of Rawicz's sly jokes: *goletz* can mean both "have-not" and "naked man"), is arrested and subjected to the usual identity test, the removal of his pants: "The ripped trouser-fly reveals the bluish penis. On it, the sign of the Covenant is inscribed in indelible lettering, all too easy for these bustling men to read. The tool and the art of comparison. Though to what is it possible to compare this matchless moment, in which the entire universe converges and recedes and rears till it becomes a ring, a steel ring: cold and painful, this steel ring encircling Boris's tool."

He is imprisoned first with six other Jews, and witnesses their deaths one by one. Then he winds up in a cell with a group of non-Jews who mock him and force him to clean the excrement pail: "He began to love shit: a patient substance, humble and completely unaggressive." Finally, under repeated interrogation, he tells the lieutenant in charge that he is not a Pole, as he has claimed, but a Ukrainian. The lieutenant is skeptical, but accedes to Boris's request that a Ukrainian be summoned to put him to a citizenship test. (Rudolf reports that Rawicz experienced something like this in Auschwitz, even though he had a medical certificate to justify his own circumcision: "Presumably Rawicz felt that the reader would think [the certificate's] its existence was too good to be fictionally true.") The man begins by asking him the name of the greatest Ukrainian poet. "It was then that the game began to amuse Boris," the narrator tells us. Instead of supplying the obvious answer, he names a young avant-gardist. From there they are off, hotly debating minutiae of politics and cultural pride in fluent, cultivated Ukrainian. "That's no Jew," the man concludes. "Take my word for it. He couldn't be. He's trash, of course.... But he isn't a Jew. No question of that. He speaks our language too well, he knows too much about our history, our literature, our way of life." This triumphant scene has the rollicking comic pace of Philip Roth.

Pressed to explain his circumcision, Boris concocts a story of contracting from a whore a venereal disease that led to phimosis. "I cried openly in front of the doctor—I was just a kid, you know," he tells the lieutenant. " 'I don't want to look like a Jew-boy,' I told him. To which [the doctor] said: 'You needn't worry yourself on that score, sonny. Any doctor will always be able to tell that, by the time you were operated on, you were already a grown man.'" The first doctor thus summoned refuses to make the call, but the second goes along with Boris's story, pompously (and absurdly) explaining the difference between a medical "concision" and a ritual circumcision. Boris is freed.

In his memoirs Wiesel recalls asking Rawicz, "How did you experience fear over there?" The answer: "Oh, it made me laugh. The whole thing was just a farce, a farce on a cosmic scale."

There is often a moment in a Holocaust memoir or novel when the narrator experiences a specific kind of epiphany: if I survive, he or she realizes, it is for the purpose of telling my story. Think of Levi reciting Dante in Auschwitz and hearing the lines of poetry as a personal call to action: "For brutish ignorance / Your mettle was not made; you were made men, / To follow after knowledge and excellence." Boris has no such realization. His survival has no obvious meaning for him, and he doubts both his ability and his desire to communicate what he has seen to others:

So I've got away with it, thought Boris. And what good has that done me? Outside, it's cold and naked. In here, I had a home....

Perhaps one day I shall try to capture this scene. If I do, a niggardly demon will do its best to rob me of every destitute word that might serve to describe the objects and human beings surrounding me here and now, so close and so tangible—human beings with whom I don't know what to do, except love them. I shall have obstinately to snatch from this jealous demon every word that is even slightly appropriate, and it will be a harder battle than the one in which I have just gained victory. More shameful, too, like everything that serves to describe, to debase reality. Only one sin is graver: that against unreality.

Boris's writing is far from impoverished. But it does enact precisely the tension between reality and unreality that this passage describes. On the one hand, Boris feels some kind of obligation to bear witness to the town's destruction; he does, after all, commit his words to paper. But his record keeping is of an unusual kind. Whereas most memoirists take pains to record details of time and place as precisely as they can—Levi once insisted in an interview that "a testimony that has no 'where' and 'when' is not worth much"—Boris coyly leaves his undefined. Dates are omitted—we are told only that the year is "194-." Place names are abbreviated or falsified: the Polish mountain resort Zakopane, easily recognizable from Boris's description, is referred to as "O." People, too, are identified obliquely. When the SS invade the town, they are euphemistically called "Captain H.'s special brigade." ("Captain H.," one guesses, refers not to Hitler but to Reinhard Heydrich, commander of the *Einsatzgruppen*.) Leo L., the head of the ghetto's *Judenrat,* is "the king of the walled-up town." And the yellow stars that mark the inhabitants' clothes are "the hexagonal sign of our King." These metaphors uncannily echo of the Germans' falsification of their own language with duplicitous terms such as *Sonderbehandlung* (special treatment).

Boris writes in his notebook that "before the town was destroyed, Leo L. spoke of the vocation to be witness, the only one that matters." But Leo L., we have already seen, is a pompous provocateur given to outrageous statements: he has already referred to his role in the town's destruction as "a performance…in the theatrical event of a lifetime." To take his pronouncements at face value is an interpretive error akin to an unironic reading of Polonius's "to thine own self be true" speech. And Boris recognizes that, in any event, "witnessing" is hardly a matter of straightforward recounting. "At the moment, memory is letting me down," he writes soon after the liquidation. "The colors are fading. The town has died. For a second time. The memory of it has become a burdensome fetus no longer breathing."

But if memory is suspect, literature is not an obvious alternative. "The 'literary manner' is an obscenity by definition," he writes.

It is even more so by the nature of its constituent parts: process, process—the very notion is like the trek between office and home performed day in, day out by a civil servant suffering from piles.

Literature: anti-dignity exalted to a system, to a single code of behavior. The art, occasionally remunerative, of rummaging in vomit. And yet, it would appear, *navigare necesse est:* one *has* to write. So as to trick loneliness, so as to trick other people. But above all: loyal to my destiny, however disloyal my destiny may be to me, I feel bound to emphasize my similarity to an insect; now, haven't you noticed that man never so much resembles an insect as when he engages in the activity of writing…? Dissecting the world into tiny bits, covering paper with tiny scribbles that aspire to be unique: that is the posture in which the brotherhood of man and insect—hideous, if the truth be told—manifests itself in the purest form, with the utmost obscenity.

To write about atrocity is impossible. "Composition on the subject of decomposition?" Boris asks rhetorically near the start of the novel. Yet not to write about it—though to do so is absurd, obscene, repugnant, insectlike—is equally impossible. And so Boris takes a kind of middle position, which might be called that of the "antiwitness," since it seeks to thwart its own impact, to undermine its own authority. The episodes from the town's destruction that he takes it upon himself to relate—episodes of horrifying violence and bloodshed—are captured obliquely, filtered through the poet's aestheticizing consciousness. These pages must be read multiple times just to figure out the basics: who and what and how. It is as if he is seeing it all through his peripheral vision, looking and not looking at the same time.

Consider the scene at the end of the town's liquidation, in which Boris and Naomi, along with a group of women and children who seem to be among the only survivors, are hiding in a cellar beneath the workshop where Naomi had been employed. One of the little girls begins to cry, and Boris takes her in his arms: not out of compassion, but "mechanically, to keep himself from falling asleep." Soldiers discover the hiding place. A boy sticks out his tongue at them: the corporal cuts it out with a bayonet. Then he turns to the girl in Boris's arms, gouges out her eyes, and gives them to Boris, "who took them in his palm and thought: a pair of eyes, useful enough items, when all is said and done, so intricate and hard to reproduce.… They were slippery. They were trickly." Finally one of the women, whom Boris had noticed earlier for her good looks and composure, is gang-raped, though it is unclear whether she is still alive when this occurs:

> The quiet woman, the only one who at the outset hadn't seemed to believe in the magic efficacy of official documents, was stretched out and impaled. The magnitude of the rape blossomed out in the room, a multi-colored exotic flower. What is mentionable persisted—gray, unassuming, basely amenable to reason—side by side with the unmentionable. The magnitude of the rape flowed between the woman's spread-eagled legs without her making a sound. A dumb show. Like gashed statues, thought Boris, whom the amiable Corporal was inviting to share in the general merrymaking. Boris doesn't say whether he declined the invitation. At a given moment, he sensed something like a veiled threat in the kindly Corporal. As though to say: "The gentleman doesn't deign to participate in these vulgar manly festivities. That could cost the gentleman dear."

In terms of its content, this scene ranks among the most brutal in all of Holocaust literature. Yet its emotional impact is dulled and deflected by the oblique manner—the "literary manner"—in which it is written. Rawicz recounts the details of the atrocity in a meandering style that distances the reader rather than engaging his or her emotions. Boris does not ask for sympathy, or pity, or revenge. Instead, he coldly compares a woman's spread legs to damaged art ("gashed statues"), the rape to "a multicolored exotic flower." His compassion must be inferred: shortly afterward he returns with a nurse who gives the surviving children lethal injections, "distributing death like portions of gingerbread stuffed with darkness." In a review of the novel that appeared in the *New York Review of Books* in 1964, the critic Stanley Kauffmann wrote:

> What [Rawicz] has tried to do with his experience and with his knowledge of the larger experience is to pretend in a deliberate, grim way—to smile at it, to let Boris recount his life something like a twentieth-century Gil Blas [the hero of an eighteenth-century French picaresque novel], not really demanding that anyone believe what he says yet treating it as commonplace. This game with reality serves to give his subject another dimension of horror because we supply for Rawicz the missing steps of his progress to this view: viz., everyone knows what happened and no one can really comprehend it, not even those who were there; so why not

treat it as if it were only one more of the many tribulations of man? This shrugging, sometimes even light acceptance of hell makes the depth of the abyss even clearer; it gently but pitilessly illuminates the many hidden deaths—of Jews, of others, of worlds—that are contained in it. Sitting at his café table, Boris tells us as easily as he might have commented on a passing girl that two thousand years of history may have ended up in six million graves.

The book's most startling instance of antiwitnessing takes place shortly after Boris and Naomi have gone into hiding. Using his false papers, they are easily able to procure an apartment, since most Jews have already been deported. (With his trademark blend of cultivation and carnality, Boris muses that the area allotted to the ghetto had seemed to grow continually smaller, "like Balzac's magic piece of shagreen," resulting in "enforced promiscuity.") Out for a walk one evening, they accidentally trespass on army property. After a polite conversation, the lieutenant invites them back to headquarters for a drink. In the yard out back Boris notices "what looked like four or five cabbageheads, white and yellow, jutting from the ground," with a group of pigs occasionally chewing on them; a soldier comes out and urinates on one. They drink brandy and the lieutenant reads them some of his poetry. Suddenly a searchlight illuminates the scene: "I checked an instant desire to vomit. It wasn't cabbageheads that the pigs were licking and chewing. Five men were buried upright in the tiny garden adjoining the canteen...their half-devoured heads were projecting from the soil like giant mushrooms." But again there is no judgment, no emotion. "Facing a grave full of corpses, he does not recite Kaddish; he sheds no tears," Wiesel wrote in an early review of the book. His only reaction is physical: he violently smashes the windowpane with his arm before the lieutenant drags him away.

Why is Boris's account so circumscribed—on the one hand so richly imagined, on the other so emotionally stunted? One answer might be found in the example of one of the novel's strangest characters, a hunchback identified as David G. who writes his own chronicle of the last days of the ghetto hospital. Unlike Boris, David G. is a deliberate witness, painstakingly recording events and his reactions to them in a notebook, "a log of a vessel in her final hours afloat." He is also a psychopath. One entry tells of the rape of a thirteen-year-old girl, who "dared not scream" because the head nurse had ordered her not to disturb anyone. "Next morning, I took a long look at the kid's face. Pity I haven't a camera!" David writes. He trades cigarettes for the stump of a leg amputated from a former teacher of his, which he enjoys talking to and playing with: "I only parted with the leg when it began to stink too much." And he observes Boris having sex with one of the nurses in the operating room, and the nurse's tears after he leaves: she begs forgiveness from her younger sister, already deported, with whom Boris was supposedly in love. (In his own journal Boris mentions nothing about the sister, but this background helps to explain his statement that "the few occasions on which [the nurse] lay on her back for me...were more harrowing than grief.") The selections from David's journal end with a kind of perverse credo: "The only form of constructive action that I acknowledge and am capable of: I spit on everything. Therefore I *also* spit on spittle, my own and everyone else's. And I spit on the spitters. Without such pertinacity, such iron pertinacity, it would be hard to get through these times. I *intend* to get through them." If this kind of sociopathic behavior is necessary to "get through these times," perhaps it is better to look away from the cabbage heads, to avoid seeing too much.

But the trouble with any assumptions we make about Boris is that everything we know and hear about him is filtered through the persona of the unnamed narrator, the café owner we met on the book's first page, who occasionally steps in to remind us of his presence but is usually content to sit back and allow us to imagine that Boris is telling his story in his own words. In fact, the narrator is a distinct person with his own agenda and a skeptical attitude toward both Boris himself and the task at hand. "It was not without faint repugnance that I handled Boris's papers," he tells us near the end of the book's first section. "That kind of intimate journal is like dirty linen, a stranger's linen." Worse, the book as it is given to him is a mess, which he feels obliged to clean up:

> Too many different threads, too many snippety themes (misconceived, for the most part) got tangled up in a narrative in which I would have preferred, goodness knows, to see greater unity. I don't have it on my conscience, therefore, that I decided to discard everything that hadn't a direct bearing on the story that Boris had spun to me in the course of that one and only night.... To hell with the endless procession of a failure's "states of mind." But cutting is easier than judging: in this great sea of words, what had and what hadn't a bearing on the precious story?... The task confronting me was clearly no sinecure: the notes—even those I had been able to isolate after removing the pseudo-lyrical bits—were extremely muddled.... That character Boris had played a dirty trick on me. And yet, little by little I fell victim to the temptation to salvage the

remains of a story which wasn't one, or wasn't quite.... It was in a spirit of unfeigned humility that I stuck at my labors and now offer the fruits of them. I have quoted from the manuscript wherever I was unable to do otherwise. I have summarized as often as seemed possible, but first and foremost: I have *cut*. And if I fancy I have earned the right to any gratitude whatsoever from any reader whatsoever—and I am in doubt as to that—it will all be due to this wholesale amputating.

Unfortunately, we have no way of assessing the narrator's alterations. What are all these cuts that he has made? Perhaps it is his fault, and not Boris's, that the story is full of strange gaps: we don't witness the moment of Boris's arrest, nor do we find out what happened to Naomi. (Rawicz's companion, named Anka, remained in hiding and sent him packages in Auschwitz. After the war they married, though they were estranged at the time of her death, just a few weeks before his suicide.) If he really tried to remove all the "pseudo-lyrical bits," why did he leave in so much of Boris's bad poetry? And what we are told about his literary judgment does little to add to our confidence: "When speaking of himself, Boris used sometimes the first and sometimes the third person," the narrator muses. "Did this wavering betoken a hidden need to objectivize his own existence, a need generally experienced by those whose existence is giving them the slip?" This obtuse reading, based on amateur psychology, is a parody of literary criticism.

But the most important question seems to be why the narrator at once distances himself from the text and deliberately reinserts himself into it, resurfacing occasionally to remind us that the story is actually Boris's. This technique is unusual in novels about the Holocaust, which usually take great pains to affirm the authority of the speaker and his or her grasp of the truth. Even those writers who do not—such as W. G. Sebald, who often allows the characters in his stories to assume the narrative voice—are self-conscious about the ethical problems involved in appropriating another person's story. But Rawicz's narrator encourages the slippage, starting from the book's first line: "I'm scared of your cops, of your summonses, of your justice, of just plain you," he tells us. This is ostensibly his rationale for his coyness about the "tool" of the section heading—"You'll get no strong language out of me." But it soon becomes clear that there is something suspicious in the narrator's background as well. For some reason his papers are not in order, and he feels isolated from the ordinary world: "Ambiguity—strained and creaking ambiguity—is the one remaining bridge which occasionally allows him to steal, in the evenings, into the encampment of the human."

Is the narrator a survivor as well? There is no way to prove this, but it would explain certain puzzlements in the text, including why Boris chose him as the recipient of his story and Boris's assumption early in the book that he is familiar with the techniques of interrogation by electric current. If the narrator is a survivor, then the book becomes a kind of double testimony, in which the narrator, unwilling or unable to tell his own story, uses Boris as his mouthpiece. Thus he feels at liberty to alter the text as he wishes, because he sees it as serving his own purposes as well as Boris's. This becomes even clearer in the book's strange "Coda," in which Boris's story abruptly ends—or at least this segment of it does—and the narrator has begun to fantasize about another of his customers, hoping someday to hear his story as well. He finishes by asking for payment: "I don't wear a hat. I don't even own a hat. Nonetheless, I remove it from my bony head and humbly prepare to pass it around. If you haven't a copper to spare, ladies and gentlemen, at least let me have a nice dry Gauloise."

But such speculation is antithetical to the spirit of Rawicz's book, expressed most clearly by its haunting postscript: "The events that he describes could crop up in any place, at any time, in the mind of any man, planet, mineral…" Rather than asserting, as Rawicz's contemporary Wiesel had already begun to do, that the Holocaust was a unique event that explicitly *could not* be compared to any other, *Blood from the Sky*—with its dueling narrators, its "lost" quotation marks, its undefined place names and dates, its opaque imagery—suggests exactly the opposite. Arguing against Adorno's statement about poetry after Auschwitz in a preface to the French edition of Danilo Kiš's story collection *Hourglass (Peščanile)*, Rawicz drew an analogy between the Holocaust and Jewish catastrophe throughout history, writing that the Holocaust constitutes "the repetition of an archetypal and metahistorical event," the destruction of the temple in Jerusalem—which the prophet Jeremiah expressed "in the language of poetry, doubtless the most—the *only*—adequate language." What would art be, Rawicz asks, without human suffering?

At the same time, however, a successful work of fiction—as *Blood from the Sky* certainly is—must be grounded in the particular as well as the universal. "The book purports to tell a story, even a true story, but this hardly makes it even a fictional historical record, despite its mediated links with [Rawicz's] own life," Rudolf writes. "To attempt a literary telling is not to avoid explanatory structures, but it is to foreground the personal, the desperately personal, the personally desperate, while honoring the reader who will take on board…the way of telling." Testimony, even the most meticulously observed and exquisitely written testimony, inherently and by definition asserts the supremacy of the survivor—and in doing so, it effectively shuts the reader out. Look and listen, the survivor tells us; it is my experience, and only my experience, that matters. Literature, as Rudolf suggests, honors the reader by inviting him or her to empathize imaginatively, to engage with and accept the story on a deeper psychic level than is experienced by the reader of history.

It is precisely this aspect of literary experience that has so troubled the critics of Holocaust literature, and it is this aspect that Rawicz's novel so brilliantly embodies: the tension between the desire to commit imaginatively to the story and the fear of usurpation, of overstepping the bounds of propriety, of disturbing the rest of the dead. But if it is not barbaric to write a work of literature after Auschwitz, then neither is it barbaric to read one. Piotr Rawicz offers one of the first models for how it can be done.

5

The Bird Painter: Jerzy Kosinski

"I've been thinking," he said, leaning against the wall, "and so have some
of my editors: Would you consider writing a book for us? Something
on your special subject.... Sir, I'm thinking: it would be only fair
and it would certainly be to the country's advantage to promote your
philosophy more widely.... Right here and now I think I could promise
you a six-figure advance against royalties and a very agreeable royalty and
reprint clause. The contract could be drawn up and signed in a day or
two, and you could have the book for us, let's say, in about a year or two."

"I can't write," said Chance.

Stiegler smiled deprecatingly. "Of course—but who can, nowadays?
It's no problem. We can provide you with our best editors and research
assistants. I can't even write a simple postcard to my children. So what?"

—from *Being There*

When Elie Wiesel and Jerzy Kosinski first met, it was 1965. Wiesel, in his mid-
thirties, was working as a journalist, and *The New York Times* had assigned him
to review *The Painted Bird,* Kosinski's first novel—a nightmarish tale about
an unnamed six-year-old boy sent by his parents at the start of World War II
to live in the countryside. Forced after his caretaker's sudden death to wander
from village to village, he is treated with outrageous brutality by the peasants
he encounters. Kosinski, five years younger than Wiesel, was intent on making

his name as a writer, and Wiesel found him "young, nervous, impatient, eager to dazzle and disconcert." As Wiesel recounts the story in *And the Sea Is Never Full,* his second volume of memoirs, he asked Kosinski: "Is your book based on fact?" Kosinski answered yes. "Are you Jewish?" Wiesel asked next. Kosinski answered no. Amazed that a non-Jew had "lived through all these atrocities," Wiesel decided that this made him "even more deserving," and added "a few compliments" to his already positive review.

Every story told about Jerzy Kosinski seems to be a combination of truth and lies, and this one is no exception. Kosinski was lying about not being Jewish, as Wiesel would soon learn. After his review was published, he began to receive angry letters from Polish Jews, castigating him for being sympathetic to the self-hating Kosinski and claiming that the latter's book was "nothing but a collection of mad rantings." Wiesel asked Kosinski again if he was Jewish; again Kosinski denied it, claiming that the letters came from his "enemies." The following year, when *The Painted Bird* appeared in France, Piotr Rawicz, who happened to be a friend of Wiesel's, reviewed it for *Le Monde.* "Is Jerzy Jewish?" Wiesel asked him. "Of course he is," Rawicz replied. But Kosinski would not admit it until Rawicz, in a bizarre reenactment of a scene from his own novel, threatened to force him to expose his penis.

Kosinski's answer to Wiesel's first question was also a lie. *The Painted Bird* may have been technically "based on fact," as Wiesel cannily phrases it. Kosinski's own preferred formulation, in the official blurb that he wrote for the book's jacket, was that the novel "draws deeply upon a childhood spent, by the casual chances of war, in the remotest villages of Eastern Europe." But, as is now well known, the events of Kosinski's life, as he portrayed them in the book, were heavily fictionalized, beginning with the fundamental premise: he was not abandoned by his parents, but spent the war together with them in hiding, sheltered by peasants (who were, more often than not, sympathetic to the family) in various villages. To be sure, Kosinski's descriptions of the book's contents had always been cagey; in a self-published pamphlet called *Notes of the Author on "The Painted Bird,"* which he distributed to reviewers and friends, he wrote that to call the book nonfiction "may be convenient for classification, but is not easily justified." But *The Painted Bird* was almost universally *perceived* as autobiographical—not least because the flamboyant Kosinski, who soon after his immigration became New York society's "resident European intellectual" (in the words of his biographer James Park Sloan), for years had been entertaining crowds at cocktail parties with wild stories that were supposedly about his childhood.

In 1982, Kosinski—by then the author of eight novels, including *Being There,* a best seller that was made into a successful film starring Peter Sellers—suffered a double discrediting. Kosinski had always claimed to have written his books in English, and he was often praised for his great facility in the language, which he had learned only as an adult, after he came to America. Now, writing in the *Village Voice,* the reporters Geoffrey Stokes and Eliot Fremont-Smith not only revealed the truth about his wartime experiences, but also alleged that Kosinski had employed a legion of assistants who had helped him to write his novels. Sworn to secrecy and forbidden to remove anything—even notes—from Kosinski's apartment, these assistants claimed to have performed various types of editorial work: everything from translating chapters of *The Painted Bird* from the original Polish to rewriting the bulk of later manuscripts. Some of them would later come to their employer's defense, saying that Stokes and Fremont-Smith had misrepresented their statements. But Kosinski never recovered his prestige after this incident. When he committed suicide, nearly ten years later, many of his obituaries blamed his demise on the decline of his career.

A reader who comes to *The Painted Bird* without preconceived notions about its literal truth can still appreciate it as a novel, as some critics managed to do even at the time. And if Kosinski's theoretical writings can be treated as sincere—a big "if," to be sure, considering the slipperiness of his rhetoric and the caginess of his public persona—he seems to have intended the book as fiction. Nonetheless, *The Painted Bird,* once a mainstay of high school and college syllabi, has disappeared almost entirely from the Holocaust canon, tainted by the stigma of fraud. Most recent works of criticism about Holocaust literature do not mention it at all.

Did Kosinski commit a literary crime, and if so, what exactly was it? His dependence on others for the production of his prose was "unorthodox," as Sloan tactfully puts it, but not entirely without precedent: other writers, including Balzac (as Kosinski himself was fond of pointing out), have employed line editors. And in an age that has seen the proliferation of false memoirs about everything from addiction recovery to true love at Buchenwald, the fact that *The Painted Bird* was published *as a novel* is a mark of the book's integrity. That's not to downplay Kosinski's misrepresentations: his remarks about the book ranged from the outright lie that "every incident is true" to hazier statements about the inherent falseness of memory, which he once referred to— not indefensibly—as "the automatic process of editing." In a comment typical of the confusion surrounding the book's reception, the editors of the *New York Times Book Review* wrote that Kosinski "does not call his book autobiography, although everything in it happened."

The Painted Bird is an accomplished novel, an often beautiful novel, and certainly a significant novel in the canon of Holocaust fiction. But it can be understood as an autobiographical novel only in the most theoretical sense. And yet if Kosinski misrepresented his book, he also misrepresented his life. The crime of which he was most guilty, it seems, was the failure to set up and adhere to a clear boundary between fiction and reality *in his own mind.* Kosinski may have lived to tell stories—everyone who knew him remembers what an extraordinary storyteller he was—but in a certain way he also lived his stories. "Whatever help he might have employed" for the actual writing of his texts, his biographer concludes, "he was clearly the author of the true and original text—the text of Jerzy Kosinski." Unfortunately, the distinction was often lost not only on him, but also on his friends, his critics, and his readers.

The Painted Bird takes its title from a character named Lekh, a master of the prank that becomes the book's emblematic act of cruelty. Unusually skilled at trapping birds, he paints his captives before releasing them, then watches as the rest of the flock, failing to recognize their former comrades, brutally attack them. According to Sloan, the custom in Poland of painting birds dates back to medieval times; he writes that Kosinski based the character in his book on a teenager he knew in one of the villages. I have been unable to discover any evidence of this custom, however, and it seems just as plausible that Kosinski might have invented it. But if Kosinski did take the metaphor from real life, he made a crucial alteration. The real-life Lekh supposedly used lime wash to mute the birds' colors. The character in the novel, however, paints them in "rainbow hues...more dappled and vivid than a bouquet of wildflowers."

The novel's protagonist—and, correspondingly, Kosinski himself—has often been identified as a "painted bird" in human form. (The *Times* wrote that "Mr. Kosinski—like the Painted Bird of his story—wandered, starting aged 6, through wartime Poland.") Abused and cast out by his flock, he is condemned to roam the countryside alone, his encounters with others resulting only in more brutality. Most obviously, the novel can be read as a parable about the cruelty of human beings toward those who are perceived as different, and as a caution against the dangers of trying to pass as something one is not. Yet, as Sloan points out, "The painter of birds is...an artist of sorts, although an evil artist, weaving the lives of helpless others into his 'plots.'" Kosinski may have seen his childhood self as a kind of painted bird, rejected by both Jews and Gentiles in his futile attempts to blend in. But as an adult he transformed himself into a bird painter, combining fact and fiction in his own life and the lives of others in ways that were in turns amusing, illuminating, and excruciating.

As a teenager, Kosinski was obsessed with a Polish pulp novel by Tadeusz Dołęga-Mostowicz called *The Career of Nikodem Dyzma*. In the novel, a postal clerk from the provinces, arriving in Warsaw to seek his fortune, crashes a party at a fancy hotel, reprimands a boorish official for bumping into him, and inadvertently becomes the hero of the evening. His mishaps grow more and more providential, until finally, having become the lover of a rich and powerful woman, he is proposed as a candidate for prime minister. According to Sloan, Kosinski told his childhood friend Stanisław Pomorski that he intended to take the story of Nikodem Dyzma as a model for his future—a "life script." (Nikodem happened to be Kosinski's actual middle name.) When his novel *Being There* was published—in which a simpleminded gardener stumbles into the role of adulated businessman—some critics noticed the similarities between its plot and that of *Nikodem Dyzma* and accused Kosinski of plagiarism. But this was no straightforward case of one book imitating another. "It might be most accurately charged that it was [Kosinski's] life that drew unduly upon the Dołęga-Mostowicz text," Sloan notes dryly. Stephen Schiff, in an admiring *Vanity Fair* profile of Kosinski that attempted to rehabilitate him several years after the scandal, went even further, calling Kosinski "some sort of daft conceptual artist, his life a blueprint for his work, and the work incomprehensible without an in-depth knowledge of his life."

Sloan describes Kosinski's method—literary and extraliterary—as follows: throughout his life, he would "appropriate an episode first as an autobiographical 'fact' before rendering it in the form of fiction"—either in a novel or in one of the many tales that won him fame as a storyteller. Pomorski, similarly, described three steps in the production of a "Kosinski story": "First, something happened. Second, something happened and Kosinski was involved in it. Third, Kosinski was the chief character in what happened." Sloan wonders whether Kosinski knew the truth and embellished it consciously, or whether he actually lost his ability "to distinguish between the real and the products of his imagination." And what was the connection with his art? Did Kosinski need to believe in his stories, even to inhabit them, in order to tell them so compellingly?

But a look at Kosinski's theoretical writings shows that it is misguided—not to say impossible—to insist on a strict division between truth and untruth. It's not that he was unable to distinguish between fact and fiction. Rather, he simply preferred not to, insisting on the essential overlap of imagination and reality. At times he seems to have relished the exquisite limbo of the in-between state; in other cases, he struggled to clarify his motives. "As an actor playing Hamlet is neither Hamlet nor merely an actor, but, rather, an actor as Hamlet, so is a fictive event neither an actual event nor totally a created fiction with no base in experience; *it is an event as fiction,*" he wrote in the pamphlet that accompanied *The Painted Bird*. Kosinski's phrasing can be circular and vague, but what is clear is that this stance was a conscious artistic choice.

Indeed, Kosinski seems to have envisioned his life as a form of performance art. His motto, he asserted proudly, was *Larvatus prodeo:* "I go forth in disguise." He delighted in practical jokes, many of which involved costumes or other forms of concealment: a favorite game was to hide behind the sofa cushions during a party and then jump out, startling the other guests. Kosinski also liked to dress up in military-style uniforms that he had custom-tailored, relishing the deferential treatment they invariably inspired. His pranks are all variations on a single template: in each, he offers deceptive or partial information about himself and then watches in amusement at his onlookers' misperceptions. "It is the witness who deceives himself, allowing his eyes to give my new character credibility and authenticity," a character in his novel *Cockpit* comments with regard to a similar prank. "I do not fool him; he either accepts or rejects my altered truth." Kosinski would speak of his work in similar terms: "A book, like a culture, says to its reader: My dear, I'm yours. You are free to do with me what you will."

Sloan traces the creation of *The Painted Bird* back to 1958, when Kosinski, newly arrived in New York from Poland, made the acquaintance of Mira Michałowska, the wife of a Polish diplomat. She invited him to her home for lunch, but after she told him that her household included a dog as well as children, he asked if they could meet at a restaurant, alluding to his "terrible experiences" during the war involving children and dogs. Over weekly lunches at Schrafft's, he told her many of the stories that would find their way into the novel, which she listened to enthusiastically.

But a look at Kosinski's childhood shows that the creation of his personal mythology started early on. He was born in 1933 in Łódź, an industrial city in central Poland known for its textile industry; the family was originally called Lewinkopf, an identifiably Jewish name. In autumn 1939 Jerzy's father acquired papers bearing the Gentile name Kosinski and moved the family to the town of Sandomierz in southeastern Poland. The Lewinkopfs would take on their new identity gradually. Though they boarded with a Gentile family named Lipinski, the house was in a Jewish neighborhood, and the Lewinkopfs socialized with the Jewish community. But Jerzy did not fit in with the other children. He told them that he was a Pole and didn't play with Jews, and that his name was Kosinski, not Lewinkopf. Sloan sees this as evidence of Kosinski's training as a "seven-year-old undercover agent," and notes that Jerzy's mother told him not to play with Jewish children so as to avoid picking up their recognizable accent. But it could also be an early sign of his lifelong preoccupation with games involving identity and metamorphosis. Later, after the family had adopted its new name, he told a Polish girl that his real name was Lewinkopf and he was a Jew from Łódź. When her parents confronted the Kosinskis, he swore she had made it all up. Another child might have been legitimately confused; with Kosinski, one suspects the boundary-pushing was deliberate.

By March 1941, when the Lewinkopfs/Kosinskis left the Lipinski house, Jews were required to wear the Star of David, and the Nazi roundups had reached eastern Poland. (The house was incorporated into the Sandomierz ghetto the following year, and all the Lipinskis' Jewish tenants perished.) The family moved several times before briefly settling, in August 1942, in an isolated cottage belonging to a peasant woman named Marianna Pasiowa. Physically, at least, she seems to have been the inspiration for the hunchbacked Marta in *The Painted Bird,* "old and always bent over, as though she wanted to break herself in half but could not." At the start of the novel, Marta is the boy's foster mother, alternately benevolent and hostile; she strokes his hair and encourages him to play, but accuses him of trying to cast spells on her with his Gypsy eyes. After she drops dead in her chair one night, the boy accidentally sets the hut on fire, which marks the start of his homeless wanderings. In reality, Sloan writes, Pasiowa belonged to an underground railroad that helped Jews escape from Sandomierz. She hid a Jewish baby in a hole dug into the side of a hill near her cottage, and fed it with cow's milk when its mother could not leave the ghetto to nurse it. (In a detail emblematic of the historically conflicted relationship between Polish Jews and Polish Catholics, Sloan notes that during the war Jews were hidden in the presbytery of the local cathedral, which happened to be decorated with a fresco depicting the ritual murder of a Christian child by Jews.)

Around this time, the Lewinkopf/Kosinski family acquired two additional members: a Polish nanny named Katarzyna, together with her charge, a blond, blue-eyed toddler named Henio, apparently the son of Jewish parents unable to escape Sandomierz. Kosinski seems to have incorporated a number of details from Henio's life into *The Painted Bird:* here was a little boy who truly had been separated from his parents and entrusted to strangers. A local priest arranged a home for the Kosinskis with the family of farmer Andrzej Warchoł, in a nearby village called Dąbrowa Rzeczycka. Henio wore three layers of trousers to protect his penis from exposure, and Jerzy's hair was cut short to camouflage his curls, but the Kosinskis lived comfortably in a private apartment, and even hired a local woman to work as their maid. They decorated their apartment with Christian icons, attended church (where Jerzy received his first communion and served as an altar boy), and celebrated Christmas with a local family. Once, while ice skating on the lake, a group of older boys tried to force Jerzy to display his penis, but Warchoł's son scared them away.

I do not intend to diminish the hardships that the Kosinskis experienced during these years. At any moment they could have been exposed; they must not have had much food; they lived in uncomfortably close quarters and at daily risk of discovery. And the episodes of anti-Semitism that Sloan describes, in which village children taunt Jerzy and Henio by shouting, "*Jude, raus!*," must have terrorized them. Meanwhile, their native city, Łódź, became the site of the largest ghetto in Europe. Of the extended Lewinkopf family, who numbered more than sixty in 1938, every member but one (aside from the Kosinskis) perished. No one disputes Kosinski's legitimacy as a Holocaust survivor.

But the discrepancies between the circumstances in which the Kosinski family actually lived during the war and the boy's experiences in *The Painted Bird* will be obvious to anyone who has read the novel. Most dramatically, the boy in the book is on his own; in reality, Jerzy spent the war with his parents, who seem to have protected him to the best of their ability. To be sure, the seeds of some of the book's episodes can be discerned in Kosinski's childhood. The entire village of Dąbrowa Rzeczycka actually did gather one day to see a giant catfish, but the fantastical ending of that story (in which the boy floats down the river on the fish's giant bladder as if it were a raft) is entirely Kosinski's. He was indeed friendly with a local girl named Ewka, but the grotesque incestuous relationships of the character by that name in the novel seems to be his invention. The Kalmyks (a legendarily violent Asiatic tribe) did rampage through the region, raping and pillaging in neighboring towns, but all the villagers fled to the forest and were spared. And so on.

The most extreme alteration involves the famous episode of the dropped missal, the dramatic peak of the novel. Called on to replace a sick altar boy, the book's protagonist is charged with the task of transferring the large, heavy missal from one side of the altar to the other. He staggers under its weight and drops it. The enraged congregation, shouting "Gypsy vampire!," drags him outside and throws him into a manure pit. "Its brown, wrinkled surface steamed with fetor like horrible skin on the surface of a cup of hot buckwheat soup," Kosinski writes. "Over this surface swarmed a myriad of small white caterpillars, about as long as a fingernail. Above circled clouds of flies, buzz-ing monotonously, with beautiful blue and violet bodies glittering in the sun, colliding, falling toward the pit for a moment, and soaring into the air again." When he emerges from the foulness, retching, he has been struck dumb. He remains mute until the end of the novel.

Kosinski really did once drop a missal, but he picked it up immediately and was not punished. The furious peasants, the cries of "Vampire!," the steaming pit of excrement, the muteness—all were made up. Sloan seizes the opportu-nity to psychologize, speculating that in Kosinski's inner life, "the dropping of the missal was clearly a devastating and pivotal event.... Cast in the role of pre-adolescent anthropologist, he was forced to figure out an alien culture and pass a test upon which his survival, and the survival of his family, might depend. When the missal dropped from his hands, it seemed to him that he had failed the test." But could it really have seemed that way to the ten-year-old Kosinski? It seems at least equally likely that the grown man—far from his native land and anyone there who might contradict his story, anxious to impress, and in thrall to the idea of the fluidity of narrative—called up from memory a fairly anodyne incident, recognized its symbolic potential, and transformed it into a moment of high drama. Or perhaps he had once heard a story about a boy flung into a manure pit? *First, something happened. Second, something happened and Kosin-ski was involved in it. Third, Kosinski was the chief character in what happened.*

Even as Houghton Mifflin was preparing *The Painted Bird* for publication, editors at the house were unsure how to classify the book. Dorothy de San-tillana, Kosinski's editor, had heard him telling his stories at a party. Assum-ing that they were autobiographical, she encouraged him to write them down. But some of her colleagues, upon reading the manuscript, had taken it to be a novel. Santillana asked Kosinski to clarify: "It is my understanding that, fic-tional as the material may sound, it is straight autobiography," she wrote to him. In his response, Kosinski cultivated the tone of vagueness that he would later elevate into his artistic credo. He told her that it was a literary work, not an "autobiographical survey." It represented "the slow unfreezing of a mind," in which "foregrounds lose definition, and backgrounds emerge from the shad-ows." But he did not categorically deny that the events in the book had actually happened—nor would he ever.

Kosinski seems to have believed that it was not his responsibility to make such a denial. His book was his book, and he could not be blamed for the way people read it. Even if he sent it forth in disguise, was it his fault if readers misunderstood it? And what was he supposed to call it, anyway? "Expanded fact is not fiction; enriched memory is not simple invention," he wrote in the *Notes* pamphlet. "To the publisher the area between is traditionally no-man's-land." It is worth pointing out that this frontier is not quite so unexplored as Kosinski claimed. In an essay that appeared a few years ago in the *New York Review of Books,* Timothy Garton Ash examined this question with regard to the work of Ryszard Kapuściński, the celebrated Polish journalist and travel writer who began writing at around the same time as Kosinski, noting that his books include some "haunting claims that would certainly not survive the attentions of a fact-checker at *The New Yorker.*" Garton Ash likens the boundary between "the literature of fact and the literature of fiction," in Kapuscinski's work and elsewhere, to an "open, unmarked" African border crossing: "Some very fine writers stray across it quite casually, as one does when traveling in the Masai Mara—no border posts, same shrubland, same dust, same lions, but suddenly you are in Tanzania, not Kenya."

A look back at the first reviews of *The Painted Bird*—it did not get many— shows that critics largely picked up on the book's blurring of categories. Charles Poore, reviewing it in the daily *New York Times,* noted that the boy's experience "may in part be [Kosinski's] own," but chose to read the novel as a universal comment on injustice and barbarity. "The nightmare world of *The Painted Bird* is a timeless corner of Goya's 'Disasters of War' changed to another land and people," Poore wrote. "It has happened before. It can happen again. Indeed, it may be happening right now." (It is worth noticing that there is very little about Kosinski's narrative that is specific to the Holocaust. In fact, were it not for the novel's opening passage, which identifies it as beginning "in the first weeks of World War II" and set in "the most backward parts of Eastern Europe," there would be almost no way to tell when or where the book takes place.) Richard Kluger, writing in *Harper's,* called the book a memoir and assumed the truth of certain of its elements (most notably the sadism of the peasants, which would eventually come back to haunt Kosinski), yet at the same time intuitively recognized the fictional aspect of the book's construction: he referred to the boy as "Kosinski's young narrator" rather than as Kosinski himself. "It is a staggering book, literally incredible, yet this catalogue of depravity is detailed with such control and economy that we feel instinctively it is true," Kluger concluded.

And for Kosinski it *was* true—but in the sense that all great art is true, because it reveals something essential about humanity. "Every incident is true," he brazenly told a reporter for the *New York Times,* and then hedged: "The bricks are real, but the wall is mine." According to this definition, truth in literature means any character or incident that *feels* true—anything that could happen, or could have happened. In a reminiscence about his friendship with André Wat (son of the poet Aleksander), Kosinski remembers Wat's advice to him as a writer: "Think of what you could have seen if you had not seen what you saw. Think of what you saw during your wanderings...and, if you can, turn this into an essential state of a child's endangerment." (This piece is included in a volume called *Passing By,* a padded compilation of brief articles and other ephemera that Kosinski's widow published posthumously, much of which has a distinctly defensive ring to it.)

Of course, such advice is hardly original or controversial. It is the method of all realist fiction: to create an imaginary person or place or incident that feels connected in its particulars to the world we know and yet simultaneously rises above it to achieve an "essential state." But since people in Kosinski's fiction are capable of nearly anything—copulating with goats, knifing their neighbors at the dinner table, tossing children into pits of manure—then nearly everything falls into the novelist's domain. Throughout his career, Kosinski would insist that his interest in extreme behavior had nothing to do with perversion or depravity. He believed, rather, that only at moments of extremity do people express their true nature. "I see myself as an adversary novelist whose role is to confront—not to escape from—life's threatening encounters," he once insisted to an interviewer. "There is nothing in all my novels that couldn't take place in these United States in the very city block in which so many of us live." If this sounds hyperbolic—I do not believe anyone on my block has ever been impaled on a stake and then left to bleed to death, as in one of *The Painted Bird*'s gorier episodes—it nonetheless contains an element of truth: think of the sadistic kidnappings and murders periodically discovered in small towns or peaceful suburbs, the news of which is invariably greeted with shock. The criminals of *The Painted Bird* are not Nazis or other authority figures—they are the farmers down the road. The book's obsession is not the extraordinary brutalities that were specific to the Holocaust, but the everyday sadism of ordinary people. The *Times* review of *The Painted Bird* was headlined: "Things Like These Happen to People We Know."

If "things like these" can happen, then does it follow that "things like these" could have happened to the novelist? Most writers would hesitate to go this far. But Kosinski, it should by now be clear, welcomed the extreme in all aspects of his life. An essay called "Death in Cannes," published in 1986, illustrates the slippage between novelist and character. The essay is based on a true event (so reports Sloan, anyway): Kosinski's friend Jacques Monod, having decided to discontinue the medical treatment that was artificially prolonging his life, asked Kosinski to document with photographs the last few days before his death. Kosinski calls the piece that he writes about the experience "autofiction," which he defines as "a literary genre... generous enough to let the author adopt the nature of his fictional protagonist—not the other way around." This "fictional protagonist" is a writer identified as "JK," the author of novels easily recognizable as Kosinski's.

Why does Kosinski insist on identifying himself with the fictional character rather than identifying the fictional character with himself? The first option expands possibility; the second cancels it out. A reader who assumes a biographical source for everything in a novel, no matter how obvious such sources may appear or how tantalizingly the novelist might tease the reader with them (as Philip Roth has done with his alter ego Nathan Zuckerman), denies himself the act of imagination that is—or ought to be—the most fundamental aspect of the reading experience. Kosinski mocked this approach in a 1982 interview. "Thank goodness novelists die, because their biographies die with them," he said. "So then you just read their books. You read *The Kreutzer Sonata* by Tolstoy and you no longer say, 'Oh, Tolstoy knew this musician and this musician was making a pass at Tolstoy's wife.'" Here Kosinski is right: it cheapens and diminishes a work like *The Kreutzer Sonata* to understand it as a mere report on happenings in Tolstoy's life. That novella is an examination of love and jealousy; it is not a report on life among the upper class in Russia during the late nineteenth century. It contains details that help to identify it as belonging to a certain period, and certain facts about Russian society can be extrapolated from them, but no one would confuse it with a work of history or social science.

It is precisely this sort of confusion, however, that occurs as a matter of course regarding works of literature about the Holocaust. And there is no better example of the pernicious effects of this approach than the reception of *The Painted Bird*. The trouble began with Elie Wiesel's review of the book in the *New York Times Book Review,* in which he brazenly identified it as *not* a novel. "Most attempts by scientists, psychologists, moralists and even novelists to come to grips with the phenomenon of men's mass extermination by man have ended in failure," Wiesel wrote. "The task of the chronicler seems somehow easier. He writes not to reach conclusions and be rewarded for them; all he asks is to be heard, to be believed. For he knows what to say and what to omit, when to commit blasphemy with word or prayer, and also when to remain silent. His purpose then is not to bring forth new grandiloquent ideas or to exercise death or guilt, but simply to bear witness on behalf of himself and of those whose voices can no longer be heard." It was as precisely such a chronicle, Wiesel wrote, that Kosinski's book "achieves its unusual power."

Remember that, according to Wiesel's account, Kosinski told him that the book was autobiographical—though remember also that his exact words (as Wiesel later remembered them) were that it was "based on fact." Even so, it is astonishing that Wiesel—or anyone else, for that matter—could have accepted *The Painted Bird* as a literal testimonial of the Holocaust. Even putting aside the extreme brutality of some of the episodes, it is simply not credible that a single person, especially a boy of that age, could have witnessed so much. His view—through a crack in the floorboards, from behind the barn, and so forth—is too good; the detail in the episodes is too distinct. A real seven- or eight-year-old would have occasionally covered his eyes in horror—even one as apparently intrepid as the young Jerzy Kosinski. But the boy in the novel was not the young Jerzy Kosinski. Rather, as Kosinski would tell one of his assistants, the boy was his "fictive self." The character is not identified with the novelist; the novelist identifies himself with the character.[1]

Now, more than forty years after the publication of *The Painted Bird*, it is no longer controversial to argue that memory itself is always a variety of fiction, because of the imaginative work our minds inevitably perform when we try to reconstruct past events. Even in the mid-1960s, Kosinski was hardly the first writer to assert the intermingling of fact and fiction in the human consciousness. Think of Rawicz and the complicated frames he places around the chronicle in *Blood from the Sky*—a chronicle that, for all we know, may have as little basis in biographical fact as Kosinski's. (To the best of my knowledge, no one ever asked Rawicz if he actually looked out the window of an army headquarters and saw human heads planted in the garden like cabbages.) But Kosinski, always pushing the boundaries, carried the postmodernist commonplace to an extreme. Not only memory, but also life itself becomes a variety of fiction. "Since our minds conceive of and empathize with created situations according to fixed patterns, certain fairly constant fictive realities—everything

---

1. Kosinski was not alone in this. The trend became more popular in the 1960s, but one of its most famous practitioners was the turn-of-the-century Portuguese writer Fernando Pessoa, famous for using multiple "heteronyms" as distinct alter egos who wrote various of his books. José Saramago's 1986 novel *The Year of the Death of Ricardo Reis* imagined the biography of one of these heteronyms. "Is there a way in which all of us are fictional characters, parented by life and written by ourselves?" the critic James Wood has remarked about this novel.

drawn from the depths of our memories, or dredged up from our subconscious, or wrought from our creative abilities—will distort the hard edge of solid fact," he wrote in an article published in 1981, the year before the *Village Voice* controversy exploded. "For we fit the facts of social experiences into molds which simplify, shape and give acceptable emotional clarity to them. The social event becomes to a degree a fiction."

A novel derives meaning primarily from what it tells us about the human condition: "Things like these happen to people we know." A memoir, conversely, derives meaning primarily from what it tells us about a human being: the memoirist tells us, in effect, "This happened to me." Often, of course, the form takes on a more universal dimension: part of the reason we value certain memoirs is because their authors are archetypes, emblematic of a certain moment in history. Frank McCourt's experience as a young Irish boy immigrating to the United States is taken to be representative of the vast number of Irish immigrants, just as Primo Levi, one prisoner among thousands, is imagined to speak for them all. And so the writer who is caught fabricating under these circumstances betrays not only the trust of his or her reader, but also the silent group of victims for whom he or she was supposedly speaking. To say in retrospect that such a book was true because of its fidelity to the writer's interior world, as the writer calling himself Binjamin Wilkomirski and other Holocaust fabulists have done, is in effect to reclassify it as a work of fiction. While such a justification may be plausible on purely literary grounds, a book cannot simultaneously function as a novel and as a memoir, because the reader's investment in the two forms is significantly different.

We can recognize, along with Kosinski, that no memoir is entirely factual (because the act of memory is itself a kind of imagining), just as we recognize that no novel is ever entirely fictional (because every character is in some way a composite, pieced together from bits and pieces of the novelist's experience with actual people). But an autobiographical novel works on both levels, relying at once on the authority it takes from the facts of its author's life and the literary quality of the imagined world it creates. And the two sides are very rarely in perfect balance. In the case of Borowski, Levi, and Wiesel, the weight tips toward autobiography. For Rawicz, Kosinski, and later Imre Kertész, it tips—sometimes very strongly—toward fiction.

Because of the fundamental instability of the form, it is up to the author to give the reader a clear signal as to how his book is to be read—either through clues in the text or by means of the book's physical apparatus. What such a book cannot do is simply say, "My dear, I'm yours. You are free to do with me what you will." As the career of Jerzy Kosinski shows, to do so is to invite misunderstanding and even disaster.

Kosinski's novel *Being There,* an exquisite fable that lends itself to a nearly infinite variety of interpretations, is the story of a simpleminded man—perhaps somehow mentally deficient—who goes by the single name of Chance. Orphaned at an early age, he has been all his life the ward of a wealthy patron, who gives him room and board in exchange for his services tending the garden. He has no contact with the outside world or even with the other inhabitants of the house; when he is not in the garden, he stays in his room, watching television. When his patron dies, Chance, for the first time in his life, must fend for himself. Almost as soon as he steps through the garden gate, he is hit by a car chauffeuring the wife of an invalid financier, who offers him medical care in her own home. Through a series of misunderstandings, "Chance the gardener" is perceived to be a businessman named "Chauncey Gardiner." He sits in on a meeting between the financier and the U.S. president and makes a remark that the president understands as financial advice; soon he appears as a commentator on national television and is sought by every reporter and diplomat in town.

Chance plays no role in his own misperception. He encourages no one. The only words he speaks are about his own experiences in the garden. It is his listeners who operate under mistaken assumptions, understanding metaphorically what he means literally: "the garden" somehow becomes the world financial system, and Chance's platitudes about all things having a season and the importance of nurturing roots are taken as economic optimism during a time of recession. When he refuses to comment to reporters, they interpret his silence as discretion. Meeting a Russian diplomat, he laughs because the man's language sounds funny to him; the diplomat believes he is laughing at a joke and assumes that he speaks fluent Russian. To be sure, not everyone is so gullible. But Chance's naysayers are far outweighed by his powerful supporters.

Being There, and the hit film that it inspired, has been read as a political satire, a commentary on the American culture of celebrity, a philosophical meditation ("being there" is a literal translation of Heidegger's *Dasein*). Some critics read it as a plagiarism of *The Career of Nikodem Dyzma,* not realizing that Kosinski had deliberately taken that novel as a kind of personal training manual. But it also can be understood as a version—heavily fictionalized, to be sure—of the trajectory by which Kosinski became a spokesman for survivors of the Holocaust.

Like Chance the gardener, Kosinski appeared on the American scene with no history, no papers, no family. To explain himself and where he came from, he offered only his stories: stories which he knew to be largely fictional, but which were perceived as literal descriptions of what had happened to him. Chance spoke of gardens and people heard finance; Kosinski spoke of depravity and people heard the Holocaust. In a commentary on *The Painted Bird* published in the second edition, which appeared in 1976, Kosinski gave his own, typically disingenuous version of the book's reception:

> Because I saw myself solely as a storyteller, the first edition of *The Painted Bird* carried only minimal information about me and I refused to give any interviews. Yet this very stand placed me in a position of conflict. Well-intentioned writers, critics, and readers sought facts to back up their claims that the novel was autobiographical. They wanted to cast me in the role of spokesman for my generation, especially for those who had survived the war; but for me survival was an individual action that earned the survivor the right to speak only for himself. Facts about my life and my origins, I felt, should not be used to test the book's authenticity, any more than they should be used to encourage readers to read *The Painted Bird*.

Unlike Chance, Kosinski did plenty of talking, and the things he said were often misleading—sometimes playfully, sometimes not. But he offered sufficient clues that a person paying attention ought to have been able to see through the smokescreen he put up around his novel. "The patterns we create unwittingly to help along our own thinking and identifying...are our individual little fictions," he wrote in the pamphlet he would offer alongside *The Painted Bird*. "For we fit experiences into molds which simplify, shape, and give them an acceptable emotional clarity. *The remembered event becomes a fiction, a structure made to accommodate certain feelings*" (italics in the original). No one can accuse Kosinski of concealing his intent here. And yet—thanks not least to Wiesel's certification of it in the *New York Times*—the book was accepted as an authentic testimony, and its author as a witness, pure and simple. In fact, the book's blurring of genres made it ideal as a screen on which a naive public, overly eager for a direct connection to the horrors of the war, could project its own desires for a particular kind of authenticity. "I'm a connoisseur of [Holocaust] survivors and have studied them as writers, actors, doctors, cops," Barbara Gelb wrote in an astonishingly credulous profile of Kosinski, published in the *New York Times Magazine*. "And after I'd listened, enthralled, for several hours, I knew that Kosinski was not only a vintage raconteur, but, probably, the ultimate survivor."

The role of Holocaust spokesman fit Kosinski poorly. He stunned an audience in Israel by refusing to condemn the Poles as anti-Semites and attacking Claude Lanzmann's *Shoah* as "totally unfair, as biased a movie as I have ever seen." His insistence that he owed his life to Polish peasants provoked an angry shouting match among his listeners in Tel Aviv, who not only believed that Poles had thrown Kosinski into a pit of manure but who also may have themselves suffered at the hands of Polish peasants. (Of course, only Kosinski knew how greatly distorted his own accounts of life among the peasants were.) In an article published in 1990 in the *Boston Globe,* he criticized the American Jewish community for its "persecution complex": "Attempts to erect dignified, soul-stirring and unforgettable monuments…have regrettably evolved into what can only be termed a second Holocaust," he wrote. By eulogizing "Holocaustica," he argued, Jews had failed to sufficiently emphasize Jewish contributions to world culture or to preserve important Jewish sites in Europe. He also promoted a plan to rebuild the Jewish section of Kraków so as to turn the city into "the site of a New Jerusalem drawing Jewish tourists from around the world." Jewish leaders scoffed at this idea, but Kosinski was ahead of his time. Within a few years of his death, Kraków's former Jewish quarter had indeed become a tourist destination, spurred largely by the efforts of the Lauder Foundation to rebuild the old synagogues and by tourists chasing down the sites in *Schindler's List.*

"Am I to go through life defined always as a survivor of the Holocaust?" Kosinski complained to his Israeli audience. To be sure, he had his own reasons for wanting to downplay that aspect of his background as more and more evidence of his deceptions was coming to light. But the validity of his complaint ought to be acknowledged. The critics who searched for the sources of his stories, he felt, were like the reader of *The Kreutzer Sonata* who thinks the story is about a musician who made a pass at Tolstoy's wife. He was right, of course, that there is a vulgarity in this kind of reading, just as Primo Levi was right to insist angrily on his own identity as a writer first and a survivor second. But if Kosinski was going to make his readers join him on the seesaw, they in turn were justified in forcing it to tip one way or the other. Even a child as young as the boy in *The Painted Bird* knows the difference between being told a story and being told a lie. It is the intent that matters, and while it may no longer be fashionable to imagine that we can know an author's intent, there are some cases in which it is clearer than in others. In the end, the convolutions of literary theory surrounding Kosinski's novel can feel like another of his practical jokes. Perhaps the reader ought to have known better, like the party guests who might have noticed that the sofa cushions looked a little lumpy. But that does not justify the prank.

In one of Kosinski's essays, he entertained a fantasy of pure fiction: a writer and a reader, alone in a room. It had become his habit during his travels, he wrote, to spend some time visiting hospitals or nursing homes—"any refuge for those whom the world has discarded." He would introduce himself to the person on duty and ask to be escorted to the bedside of an incurably ill person. There, he would sit and read a story, either one of his own or someone else's. The story, he wrote,

> takes my listener along the trail of life, the trail painful, often surprising, but never as painful or surprising as life in this room. Our visions unleashed, my listener and I now travel with the freedom unmatched by any spaceship over the mutable landscape of time lived, or left behind, or still to come, of revengeful wars, of nature that freely gave and fiercely took back of man's greed and man's mercy, of the strategies of love and deceit, of joy and despair.... No longer solitary, my listener is now like me, a fugitive, a displaced person in an uncharted landscape, an émigré to the frontier beyond the very scope of life's transit; with life about to end, an inner journey has only begun.

There is something almost unbearably poignant about the image of Kosinski in a darkened hospital room, reading aloud to the dying. Despite his highly relativistic understanding of fiction and memory, he nonetheless clung to a vision of literature as salvific, capable of restoring life. "A novelist is the supreme spiritual entertainer," he once said. "And this is true in every moment of his life and in every moment of his performance."

6

Child of Auschwitz: Imre Kertész

I was stupid enough to encourage him to write it down.

"You don't know what you're talking about," he responded.

I suppose I really didn't know.

"It's fine the way it is," he continued, "shapeless and bloody, like a placenta. But once I write it down, it becomes a story. Discerning editor that you are, how would you assess a story like that?"

I held my tongue.

"Come on, now," he urged, "out with it."

"I don't know," I said.

"The hell you don't," he fumed. "Look here, I submit to you a piece concerning how, with the cooperation of a bunch of thoroughly decent people, a child is born in Auschwitz. The Kapos lay down their clubs and whips, and, moved to the core, they lift the wailing infant on high. Tears rise to the eyes of the SS guard."

"If you put it like that, then of course..."

"Huh?" he urged. "Huh?"

"Well...kitsch," I said. "But it can also be written in other ways," I added hastily.

"It can't. Kitsch is kitsch."

"But it's what happened," I protested.

That's precisely the problem, he explained. It happened, yet it's still not true.

—from *Liquidation*

The scene appears nearly verbatim in two of Imre Kertész's novels. It takes place at a New Year's Eve party in Budapest, sometime during the 1980s. The guests, a group of dissident intellectuals, are playing a game that one of them later calls "*Lager* poker." "A simple game, simple rules," explains a philosopher. "The players sit around the table and each person says *where they have been*. Only the place-name, nothing else. That was the basis for determining the value of the chips. As best I remember, two Kistarcsas were worth one Fő; Street...one Mauthausen, one and a half Recsks....We had no money, we were only able to play with the values that life had dealt us." The players dispute some of the hands, but they all agree on the royal flush. Auschwitz is "untrumpable."

Auschwitz is untrumpable in all of Kertész's work, the first principle around which his fictional universe revolves. Born into a Jewish family in Budapest in 1929, he was deported to the camp in 1944 and then transferred to Buchenwald, where he remained until the end of the war. *Fatelessness* (*Sorstalanság*), nominally based on his camp experience (though he has balked at calling it autobiographical) and published in 1975, was his first novel, thirteen years in the writing. *A kudarc* (Fiasco, translated into German, Spanish, Hebrew, and other languages, but not English), *Kaddish for an Unborn Child,* and *Liquidation* are, each in its own way, its sequels.

The questions raised in the aftermath of Auschwitz have ranged from "How can one write poetry?" (as Adorno is often paraphrased) to "How can one eat lunch?" (the facetious retort of Mark Strand)—questions about the legitimacy of aesthetic representation of catastrophe that lead to even larger questions about the difficulty of continuing to live in a world where such horrors have occurred. Kertész's answer to these questions, which forms a constant connecting his four major novels—he is the author also of two enigmatic novellas as well as a miscellany of other prose—is unapologetically bleak. There is no disconnection between the world before Auschwitz and the world after Auschwitz; Auschwitz is, and has always been, the way we live now. "Auschwitz has been hanging around in the air since long ago, who knows, perhaps for centuries, like dark fruit ripening in the sparkling rays of innumerable disgraces, waiting for the moment when it may at last drop on mankind's head," says the narrator of *Kaddish,* a writer and translator identified as B., who shares certain common characteristics with Kertész but is not identical to him. In his Nobel lecture, Kertész made the point even more explicitly. "What I discovered in Auschwitz is the human condition, the end point of a great adventure, where the European traveler arrived after his two-thousand-year-old moral and cultural history," he said.

B., who appears also in *Liquidation,* has a distinctive tattoo—a letter and four numbers on his thigh rather than his arm—which testifies that he was among the very few children born in Auschwitz. Kertész was already a teenager at the time of his imprisonment, but metaphorically he, too, is a child of the camps, in that they form the basis—"ground zero," as he has said—for the way he perceives the world. Since Auschwitz has no beginning, it also has no end. His life's work, B. explains at one point, is "in its essence digging, the continued digging of the grave that others had begun to dig for me in the air and then, simply because they did not have time to finish...they thrust the tool in my hand and left me standing there to finish, as best I could, the work that they had begun." "My ballpoint pen is my spade," he says later. "I write only because I have to write, and I have to write because I am whistled up every day to drive the spade deeper." (He is alluding to a line in Paul Celan's "Todesfuge," a quotation from which serves as the book's epigraph.)

Yet of all the survivors who have gone on to write Holocaust fiction, Kertész has been the most emphatic about distancing his books from testimony. In an interview, he once referred to *Fatelessness* as a "pure novel," adding: "It does not inform anyone." The protagonist (his name, mentioned only once in the novel, is György Köves) seems to be modeled on the young Kertész, and their experiences have the same rough outline. But Kertész has never been comfortable with calling the book an "autobiographical novel," as critics tend to do. In *Dossier K.*—a strange hybrid of a book that Kertész claims came about when, editing the transcripts of interviews that a friend had done with him, he decided to rewrite them all—he draws a sharp distinction between fiction and autobiography, claiming that there is no such thing as an autobiographical novel. "Such a genre absolutely does not exist," he writes.

> [A book] is either an autobiography or a novel. If the question is one of autobiography, then you conjure the past, you take pains to adhere as precisely as possible to your memories, and it is of great importance that you describe everything the way it really happened—in other words, that you add nothing to the facts. A good autobiography is like a document: the image of an epoch, which one can "lean upon." In a novel, however, the deciding factor is not the facts, but rather only what one adds to them.

But what exactly does the novelist add? And isn't Kertész being disingenuous when he asserts such a sharp distinction? He does not actually mean that a novel cannot be autobiographical. Just a few pages later, he writes that he treats his life as "raw material" for his novels: "That's how I think of it, anyway, and thus I free myself from all constraints." Raw material cannot stand on its own; it is intended to be shaped into something else. (Of course, autobiographers do this with their own raw material too.) What he seems to be saying, rather, is that the adjective "autobiographical" is useless in describing a novel. A novel is a novel, and its relationship (or lack thereof) to the writer's life ought to be of no significance either to the writer or to the reader.

Put another way, the essence of Kertész's statement is that he wants to be considered as a writer—not as a Holocaust writer. But, as Primo Levi discovered, if such a pure form of literary criticism could exist under any circumstances, in the context of the Holocaust it has proved impossible. And for Kertész there is a double dilemma, because his novels have focused almost exclusively on the Holocaust. Is it possible to write about the Holocaust without being a Holocaust writer? Kertész's work after *Fatelessness* is in large part an attempt to resolve this identity question: a double helix of texts, sometimes widening, sometimes narrowing, that rewrite each other in a virtually endless loop.

Kertész appreciates the potential falseness of documentation—and, correspondingly, the value of literature—better than most. As he recounts in his Nobel lecture, the director of the Buchenwald Memorial Center, upon hearing about his prize, sent him a copy of the camp's daily report for February 18, 1945, which records the death of prisoner 64,921: "Imre Kertész, factory worker, born in 1927." All the information in this report is incorrect: his age (increased by two years so that he would be classified as an adult), his occupation (he said he was a worker rather than a student so as to appear more useful), and, of course, the fact of his death. Yet it comes from an authoritative, official Nazi document—precisely the sort of document that scholars have often considered to be the most dependable source of information about the Holocaust.

Literature, needless to say, can be just as unreliable. But it has the advantage of being able to be always self-conscious about its own unreliability. And Kertész's fiction, more than most, is exquisitely attuned to the difficulties of pinning something—anything—down, the slipperiness of even the most basic facts. Consider the immediately contradictory first lines of *Fatelessness:* "I didn't go to school today," the narrator says. "Or rather, I did go, but only to ask my class teacher's permission to take the day off." Here Kertész sets the tone of ironic pseudoprecision that is one of the hallmarks of his work. Did the boy go to school or did he not go to school? Well, each is true, in its own way. The greater question is whether an opening like this one inclines us to trust the narrator or to distrust him. On the one hand, he is trying so hard to give an accurate account that he contradicts himself in the very pursuit of truth. But it also reminds us that no matter how hard he tries, there can still be two sides to the truth, multiple versions of any story, and the version he knows may not be the most accurate. Beneath these layers we strike the bedrock of the writer's prerogative: his quasi-godlike power to present the universe as he wills, his total freedom to say whatever he likes about whatever he likes. A quotation from Beckett serves as the epigraph to *Liquidation,* but it comments as well on the preceding novels: "Then I went back into the house and wrote, It is midnight. The rain is beating on the windows. It was not midnight. It was not raining."

It has often been said, by George Steiner among others, that the German language was one of the casualties of World War II. In his book *The Language of the Third Reich,* the philologist Victor Klemperer (who would later win fame for his superb diary of the war years) enumerates many of the ways in which the Nazis used language to disrupt the entire fabric of the nation. Rather than coining new terms, they adopted words already in common use and subtly altered their meanings, turning the language itself into an instrument of propaganda. Some of these are familiar: the depersonalization of the Jews as "vermin," rather than "men" (as members of the German army were always called), to be "exterminated" or "liquidated" rather than killed. The Jews' possessions were not "confiscated," but rather "placed in safekeeping," and goods passed on when their original owners were deported were said to be "inherited." In their advertisements, business owners were not allowed to speak of having "the most highly trained staff," but rather "trained" or "highly trained"; superlatives were reserved for the use of the government. And in Wehrmacht dispatches the figures for German casualties were given precisely (if unverifiably), but the numbers of enemy dead were always "unimaginable" or "countless."

"Words can be like tiny doses of arsenic: they are swallowed unnoticed, appear to have no effect, and then after a little time the toxic reaction sets in," Klemperer writes. "If someone replaces the words 'heroic' and 'virtuous' with 'fanatical' for long enough, he will come to believe that a fanatic really is a virtuous hero, and that no one can be a hero without fanaticism." But the contrary can also be true. Many survivors have written of the shock of discovering the real meaning of the word *Sonderbehandlung* (special treatment). To call it by its true name—"extermination by gas"—would spoil the surprise, as it were: a surprise that functioned at the time as an instrument of terror and has since been put to good use in Holocaust literature as dramatic irony. Think of Borowski's story "This Way for the Gas, Ladies and Gentlemen": the title derives its grim humor from the fact that this is precisely what *cannot* be said.

What sets Kertész apart from virtually all other writers of Holocaust fiction is his embrace of exactly this sort of dramatic irony, a tone he maintains without faltering throughout the entirety of *Fatelessness*. But in contrast to the stories of Borowski, in which the narrator is consciously ironic, fully aware of the real meanings behind his words, the fourteen-year-old boy in Kertész's novel is innocent of the true implications. He relates the book's events in a casual, direct, understated tone, frequently interjecting filler phrases such as "by the way" and "I should mention." The contrast between the words themselves and the reality continually bubbling underneath them gives the novel a lack of affect that at times can be almost comedic but finally ends in devastation.

The novel begins on the day that the narrator's father has been called up for labor service, and the boy observes, barely comprehending, as his father turns over his store to a Gentile and receives anxious relatives to bid him goodbye. He is more interested in Annamarie, the girl who lives next door, who is "already starting to round out under her yellow star." During an air raid, when a bomb goes off nearby, she spontaneously throws her arms around his neck, leading to his first kiss. Aside from his youth, part of the reason why the narrator is unable to appreciate the gravity of the situation is that until now he has hardly even identified himself as a Jew. (Kertész has often spoken of his own family's high level of assimilation; his grandfather, born Adolf Klein, Hungarianized the family name.) The Köves family is so distanced from traditional Judaism that the father's last supper at home consists of pork. "Awhile ago we took little notice of the neighbors, but now it has turned out that we are of the same race, which calls for some exchanging of views of an evening on the matter of our mutual prospects," the boy comments. Until now he has been satisfied to believe that any "differentness" of the Jews is external, as superficial as the yellow star. But Annamarie is horrified by the thought: "If our own qualities had nothing to do with it, then it was all pure chance, and if she could be someone else than the person she was forced to be, then 'the whole thing has no sense,' and that notion, in her opinion, is 'unbearable.'" His confusion about whether any meaning can be found in his fate will persist until the last pages of the novel.

Soon the narrator is assigned to work at a refinery, in a group of around twenty boys his age. With the job comes the perk of identification papers that allow him to travel outside the city, and he believes himself to be out of danger.

But one day all the boys are rounded up on the bus on the way to work. By that evening they have been transferred to a brickyard that is serving temporarily as a deportation site, filled with families carrying luggage. There, men from the *Judenrat* offer them the chance to volunteer for work in Germany. The boys talk it over and decide that this sounds like a good plan: "What I could look forward to from working…was above all orderliness, employment, new impressions, and a bit of fun—all in all, a more sensible lifestyle more to my liking than the one here in Hungary, just as was promised and as we boys, quite naturally, pictured it when we talked amongst ourselves, though alongside that it crossed my mind that this might also be a way of getting to see a bit of the world." As they are herded into the stables for the night, he has the sudden desire to laugh, "in part out of astonishment and confusion, a sense of having been dropped slap in the middle of some crazy play in which I was not entirely acquainted with my role."

The first cracks in the façade of his innocence appear soon after the boys board the cattle cars. The gruesomeness of the train journey, familiar in all its horrifying detail from the work of writers such as Levi and Wiesel, is visible only in pieces, filtered through the narrator's determined combination of naïveté and optimism as he still tries to convince himself that nothing is wrong. When an old woman in a neighboring car dies, the boys tell each other that she must have been ill. The only sign of any change in him is his uncertainty when they reach their destination, marked with the sign "Auschwitz-Birkenau." "I was glad, very naturally," he says, "though in a different way, I sensed, than I would have been glad yesterday, say, or still more the day before that."

The scene that follows is one of the most extraordinary in Holocaust fiction. In his Nobel lecture, Kertész explained his method:

> The hero of my novel does not live his own time in the concentration camps, for neither his time nor his language, not even his own person, is really his. He doesn't remember; he exists. So he has to languish, poor boy, in the dreary trap of linearity, and cannot shake off the painful details. Instead of a spectacular series of great and tragic moments, he has to live through everything, which is oppressive and offers little variety, like life itself.
>
> But the method led to remarkable insights. Linearity demanded that each situation that arose be completely filled out. It did not allow me,

say, to skip cavalierly over twenty minutes of time, if only because those twenty minutes were there before me, like a gaping, terrifying black hole, like a mass grave. I am speaking of the twenty minutes spent on the arrival platform of the Birkenau extermination camp—the time it took people clambering down from the train to reach the officer doing the selecting. I more or less remembered the twenty minutes, but the novel demanded that I distrust my memory. No matter how many survivors' accounts, reminiscences and confessions I had read, they all agreed that everything proceeded all too quickly and unnoticeably. The doors of the railroad cars were flung open, they heard shouts, the barking of dogs, men and women were abruptly separated, and in the midst of the hubbub, they found themselves in front of an officer. He cast a fleeting glance at them, pointed to something with his outstretched arm, and before they knew it they were wearing prison clothes.

I remembered these twenty minutes differently. Turning to authentic sources, I first read Tadeusz Borowski's stark, unsparing and self-tormenting narratives, among them the story entitled "This Way for the Gas, Ladies and Gentlemen." Later, I came upon a series of photographs of human cargo arriving at the Birkenau railroad platform—photographs taken by an SS soldier and found by American soldiers in a former SS barracks in the already liberated camp at Dachau. I looked at these photographs in utter amazement. I saw lovely, smiling women and bright-eyed young men, all of them well-intentioned, eager to cooperate. Now I understood how and why those humiliating twenty minutes of idleness and helplessness faded from their memories.

Not only does Kertész not trust his own memory, but notice which "authentic source" he consults first: a work of fiction! It is autobiographical fiction, to be sure, but it is fiction, as Kertész recognizes (he calls it a "story"). He recognizes the survivor accounts, despite their unanimity, as deceptive, because the survivors' memories are (perhaps inevitably) distorted by their knowledge of what came afterward. But unlike Borowski, whose narrator is only too well informed about the situation, Kertész forces his reader to perceive the events through the filter of his narrator's ignorance. His rhetorical strategy does not allow him to shape the narrative according to his knowledge of the future; he adheres unswervingly to his narrator's tone of naïveté. And so the boy is amazed when Jewish prisoners arrive to unload the cattle cars: "Their faces did not exactly inspire confidence either: jug ears, prominent noses, sunken, beady eyes with a crafty gleam. Quite like Jews in every respect. I found them suspect and altogether foreign-looking." Also to his amazement (remember how little he knows of Jewish culture), he discovers that Jews speak languages other than Hebrew. These men are frantically whispering to the newcomers in a language he can recognize only as a bastard German:

> They all started to get very curious about our ages. We told them, "*Vier-zehn*" or "*Funfzehn*"…They immediately raised huge protestations, with hands, heads, their entire bodies: "*Zestsayn!*"…"*Willst di arbeiten?*"—Did I want to work, he asked, the somehow blank stare of his deep-set, drawn eyes boring into mine. "*Natürlich*," I told him…At this, he not only grabbed me by the arm with a tough, bony, yellow hand but gave it a good shake, saying then in that case "*Zestsayn!*…*vershtayst di? Zestsayn!*" I could see he was exasperated, on top of which the thing, as I saw it, was evidently very important for him, and since we boys had by then swiftly conferred on this, I somewhat cheerfully agreed: all right, I'll be sixteen, then.

As the scene continues, the gulf between the narrator's innocence and the reader's expectations can only grow deeper. He sees the watchtowers, and believes them to be blinds for game shooting. As he passes his selection by Josef Mengele, he takes pride at the doctor's satisfaction with him: "I sensed that he must have taken a shine to me." Now the boys are led into the camp itself to shower, and he is delighted to see what appears to be a soccer field[1] and even vegetable patches, as well as "some oddly shaped buildings indeed, long, flat…with some sort of apparatus for ventilation or lighting protruding from the roof." Before the shower their hair is clipped and shaved; afterwards they are given prisoners' clothing. "The other boys had also all finished by then: we just looked at one another, not knowing whether to laugh or be dumbstruck."

But slowly the information begins to mount, and the boys realize that it does not add up. Particularly unsatisfactory is the explanation the narrator hears from another prisoner regarding the crematoria: they are said to be used for burning the bodies of prisoners who die from disease, but as he counts at least three crematoria, he begins to wonder what sort of outbreak could produce so many dead. "I can state that even before dusk fell on that first day I fully understood just about everything, by and large," he says.

---

1. In *Diary of a Galley Slave*, Kertész writes that even though he remembered that there was a soccer field at Birkenau, he wouldn't have dared to put it in his fiction if Borowski hadn't done so first.

There across the way, at that very moment, fellow passengers from our train were burning.... They too had proceeded from the station to the baths. They too had been informed about the hooks, the numbers, and the washing procedure, just the same as us. The barbers were also there, so it was alleged, and the bars of soap were handed out in just the same way. Then they too had entered the bathroom itself, with the same pipes and showerheads, so I heard, only out of these came, not water, but gas.... All along, I hear, everyone is very civil toward them, swaddling them with solicitude and lovingkindness, and the children play football and sing, while the place where they are suffocated to death lies in a very picturesque area, with lawns, groves of trees, and flower beds, which is why, in the end, it all somehow roused in me a sense of certain jokes, a kind of student prank.... Of course, I was well aware that it was not altogether a joke, looked at from another angle, as I was in a position to convince myself of the outcome, if I may put it that way, with my own eyes and, above all, my increasingly queasy stomach; nevertheless that was my impression, and fundamentally—or at least so I imagined—that must have been pretty much the way it happened.

At least so I imagined. Our narrator is *there;* he speaks, or so the illusion goes, from the *anus mundi* itself. "Caught in the dreary trap of linearity," he lives the experience rather than remembering it. But even so he is forced to imagine the fates of those who were selected for the gas, because this is something that he cannot see—as no one could. And this is precisely why the book Kertész writes must be a novel. He cannot write it as autobiography, as testimony, in which (as he put it in *Dossier K.*) he would be obligated to "adhere as precisely as possible" to his memory, to describe "the way it really happened." Instead, though he feels he must be faithful to his memory, his account tries to do no more than imagine "pretty much the way it happened." And this is why, though Kertész knew Auschwitz and Buchenwald as real places, in the novel he must recreate them afresh as a fictional universe. "Fiction creates a world, while in autobiography one remembers something that already was," he wrote also in *Dossier K.* "In the novel I had to create Auschwitz anew for myself, to bring it to life."

The novel proceeds slowly, episodically. The boy remains in Auschwitz for only three days before he is transferred to Buchenwald and then to Zeitz, a satellite of that camp. At first, he manages to keep up his tone of ironic detachment: "I too soon came to like Buchenwald," he tells us, noting the camp's relatively better rations and more comfortable sleeping conditions. At Zeitz he meets a man named Bandi Citrom, one of the classic "organizers" of the camps, who looks him up and down and observes, "It's obvious that you must have been tied to Mummy's apron strings up till now." Citrom gives him advice on how to get by in the camp, telling him to wash regularly, ration out his food, and avoid the *Muselmänner*, since "you lost any will to live just looking at them." And at first the narrator experiences a strange eagerness to please, to be seen as a "good prisoner."

But gradually conditions in the camp deteriorate; the half loaves the prisoners once received daily become thirds and fourths. As his hunger mounts, the boy discovers that "it took that little bit more effort to walk, somehow everything started to become harder." Without realizing it, he is becoming a *Muselmann*. He pines for home, though with his trademark lack of sentimentality, he imagines not the happiest days but rather an ordinary one, a "rotten day, with an early rising, school, anxiety, a lousy lunch, the many opportunities they had offered back then that I had missed, rejected, or indeed completely overlooked.... Now, here in the concentration camp, I set them all right." He recalls with chagrin "dishes that I had been fussy about, had picked at then put aside, simply because I didn't like them, and right at the present moment I regarded that as an irreparable omission."

Soon he develops a knee injury and is sent to the infirmary, which any reader of Holocaust literature will recognize as a death sentence. (Remember the mordant chapter title from *We Were in Auschwitz:* "I Don't Recommend Getting Sick.") Eventually he loses the will even to fend off the lice feeding on his open wound: "I gave up and just watched the gluttony, the teeming, the voracity, the appetite, the unconcealed happiness; in a manner of speaking, it was as though it were vaguely familiar to me from somewhere.... To some extent, and taking everything into account, I could see it their way." When the boy who shares his bunk dies, he is so far removed from normal human feeling that he breaches the final taboo:

I suspect he must have had a fever as heat was pouring steadily from his persistently shivering body, from which I was able to take agreeable profit. I was less enchanted with all his tossing and turning during the night, which, to be sure, did not always pay adequate consideration to my wounds. I told him as well: Hey! Cut it out, ease up there, and in the end he heeded the advice. I only saw why the next morning, when my repeated attempts to rouse him for coffee were futile. All the same, I hastily passed his mess tin to the orderly along with my own since, just as I was about to report the case, he snappily asked me for it. I later also accepted his bread ration on his behalf, and likewise his soup that evening, and so on for awhile, until one day he began to go really strange, which was when I felt obliged to say something, as I could not carry on stowing him in my bed, after all.

Soon the narrator is sent back to Buchenwald with a group of prisoners about to die. His transformation into a *Muselmann* is now complete; a person can come no closer to death without crossing over the border. "My body was here," he says. "I had precise cognizance of everything about it, it was just that I myself somehow no longer inhabited it." Nearly unconscious, he is cast into a pile of "debris" from the "freight consignment." But as the bodies are tossed one by one into a handcart, something inside him reawakens, though it happens instinctively, so unconsciously that he reports the scene as if he were observing it, not even aware that it is happening to him:

A snatch of speech that I was barely able to make out came to my attention, and in that hoarse whispering I recognized even less readily a voice that had once—I could not help recollecting—been so strident: "I p...pro...test," it muttered....And I immediately heard another voice....It was a pleasant, masculine-sounding, friendly voice, slightly foreign, the Lager vernacular of the German attesting, so I sensed, more to a degree of surprise, a certain amazement, than any malice: "*Was? Du willst noch leben?*" ["What? You still want to live?"] he asked, and right then I too found it odd, since it could not be warranted and, on the whole, was fairly irrational. I resolved then that I, for my part, was going to be more sensible. By then, however, they were already leaning over me, and I was forced to blink because a hand was fumbling near my eyes before I too was dumped into the middle of a load on a smaller handcart.

Still not understanding what has happened, the narrator is certain that he is about to die, and he is bothered by only one thing: that he doesn't know "how they did it here: was it with gas, as at Auschwitz, or maybe by means of some medicine, which I had also heard about." And yet, as it soon becomes clear that this will not be his fate, at least not yet, he is filled with a kind of joy:

Here and there, more suspect plumes of smoke mingled with more benign vapors, while a familiar-sounding clatter drifted up faintly my way from somewhere, like bells in dreams, and as I gazed down across the scene, I caught sight of a procession of bearers, poles on shoulders, groaning under the weight of steaming cauldrons, and from far off I recognized, there could be no doubting it, a whiff of turnip soup in the acrid air. A pity, because it must have been that spectacle, that aroma, which cut through my numbness to trigger an emotion, the growing waves of which were able to squeeze, even from my dried-out eyes, a few warmer drops amid the dankness that was soaking my face. Despite all deliberation, sense, insight, and sober reason, I could not fail to recognize within myself the furtive and yet—ashamed as it might be, so to say, of its irrationality—increasingly insistent voice of some muffled craving of sorts: I would like to live a little bit longer in this beautiful concentration camp.

This scene takes place shortly before liberation. Returning penniless to Budapest, the narrator is nearly thrown off the streetcar for not having a ticket, but another man, recognizing him as a camp survivor, intercedes. This man insists on hearing an account of "the hell of the camps," but the narrator objects to his metaphor: he is unacquainted with hell, he says, and can give an account only of the camp. Yet when he tries, his interlocutor chokes up, insisting that "it's impossible to imagine it." "So, that must be why they prefer to talk about hell instead," the boy realizes. In his book *The Survivor,* published a year after *Fatelessness,* Terrence Des Pres criticized the comparison of hell and the concentration camps by critics such as George Steiner, who had written that the camps were "*Hell made immanent* . . . the deliberate enactment of a long, precise imagining." The invocation of this archetype is misleading, Des Pres writes, because it encourages us to project a mistaken symbology onto the camps, to see "the SS as satanic monsters and the prisoners as condemned souls." But it is wrong also, as Kertész suggests here, because it offers the imagination an easy way out, an escape from the specifics of the torture in the camps to the generalities of an image familiar from centuries of literature and art.

The man says that he is a journalist, and urges the boy to collaborate on a series of articles: "public opinion has to be mobilized." After he leaves the tram, the boy tosses away the slip of paper containing the man's phone number, without comment. Yet later, after he has ascertained that little remains of his family—his father has died in Mauthausen, and his stepmother has remarried—the conversation comes back to him.

Suddenly something the journalist had said came to mind: there are only given situations and the new givens inherent in them. I too had lived through a given fate. It had not been my own fate, but I had lived through it, and I simply couldn't understand why they couldn't get it into their heads that I now needed to start doing something with that fate, needed to connect it to somewhere or something; after all, I could no longer be satisfied with the notion that it had all been a mistake, blind fortune, some kind of blunder, let alone that it had not even happened.... We can never start a new life, only ever carry on the old one. I took the steps, no one else, and I declared that I had been true to my given fate through-out.... If, on the other hand... if there is such a thing as freedom, then there is no fate; that is to say—and I paused, but only long enough to catch my breath—that is to say, then we ourselves are fate.

This, remember, was the essence of the disagreement the narrator had with Annamarie at the start of the novel. Was the fate of the Jews "pure chance," based on superficial differences, and if so, what kind of meaning can be ascribed to it? Now he no longer believes this, but the other option is equally unbear-able: like Levi, he finds it hideous to think that his survival *could* have any meaning, since he knows that it was only by chance that he lived while others died. There is even an explicit example of this always-implicit knowledge in a scene towards the end of his imprisonment, when he is back in the infirmary at Buchenwald, and a nurse arbitrarily switches the label on his bed so that he will be spared instead of another boy. Of the original group of seventeen boys picked up with him, he reports in *Dossier K.,* he was the only one to survive: "It's not easy to be an exception." The only way to live is to accept that he is "neither the cause nor the effect of anything," since both of those options imply some sort of responsibility for what has taken place. "They should try to see, I almost pleaded, that I could not swallow that idiotic bitterness, that I should merely be innocent." He must simply exist.

It feels ludicrous to ask of a novel as powerful as *Fatelessness* the perennial ques-tion: is it true? As Kertész said, it is a "pure novel.... It does not inform any-one." By this, presumably, he means that it contains no concrete information about the camps—the meals, the living conditions, the infirmary—that can-not be gotten elsewhere. One does not read *Fatelessness*—as, for example, one might read Levi's *Auschwitz Report*—for information about the caloric value of the soup at Buchenwald.

But this begs an important question about Holocaust literature. The implicit comparison Kertész makes is to testimony, which presumably does inform. But in fact it is the rare testimony that provides new information, information that cannot be found elsewhere. This is especially true now, when the Holocaust has become the best-researched and most thoroughly documented genocide in history. But it was true even in the 1950s and 60s, as we know from the chorus of critics insisting on their own prior knowledge of the events. Remember how François Mauriac characterized *Night* as a book "coming as it does after so many others and describing an abomination such as we might have thought no longer had any secrets for us." In his 1964 review of Rawicz's *Blood from the Sky,* Theodore Solotaroff wrote that "by now there has been a glut of books and articles, reminiscences and diaries, documentary histories and objective analyses that tell us everything we need to know about life in the ghettoes and prisons and death camps; no survivor need feel compelled to assume the burdens of testimony to the degradation, torture, and murder that reiterate endlessly through these accounts and finally dull and deaden consciousness of their import." Kertész himself has expressed scorn for the oral histories and video testimonies of "trained survivors" (as he calls them) collected by organizations such as the Spielberg Foundation. "You have 500 old ladies who say the same thing," he says. " 'We were deported, put in a wagon, we were thirsty, we were hungry, dogs were barking, they were yelling....' We know that."

What testimony does tell us, however, is that the narrator was *there.* That is its primary value: not that the information in it is new, but that the narrator witnessed it himself. About a topic on which we do imagine that we already know "everything there is to know," this is the surest way to make it new. This is why the appetite for testimony about the Holocaust has continued unchecked even as the decades wind on. And it is a consolation that fiction denies us. No matter how closely events in a novel appear to adhere to those in its author's life, no matter how trustworthy we find the author or narrator, we can never be certain of an episode's truth-value. This is a stumbling block for the most literal-minded readers of Holocaust literature, but it has been a boon to those writers who are fascinated by the particular epistemological problems that literature presents, and who recognize the potential of the Holocaust as a crucible for such experiments. W. G. Sebald, a master exploiter of the uncertainty that arises from the contradiction between the fictional and nonfictional universes, calls this feeling vertigo. Kertész, similarly, has spoken of *Fatelessness* as if it were *Alice in Wonderland*. "Starting already with the first sentences you can sense that you have entered into a strange, self-determined world, in which anything possible can happen. And as the story progresses, the reader's sense of being lost becomes stronger and stronger; he feels more and more as if the earth were sliding away beneath his feet."

Kertész accomplishes this through his distinctive rhetorical strategy: his adherence to "the dreary trap of linearity," the slow unfolding of the book's episodes, the stubborn refusal to impose a false coherence based on retrospective knowledge. The structure of the book thus reinforces its own conclusion of "fatelessness," because no greater meaning is to be found in these episodes— they allow the narrator no grand conclusion about why he was able to survive the camps or even why he was put on earth. In so doing, Kertész anticipates the complaint that his own characters would later make about the futility of writing stories about the Holocaust. As B. says in *Liquidation,* "It's fine the way it is, shapeless and bloody, like a placenta. But once I write it down, it becomes a story."

This is the looming curiosity about Kertész's strange career: the fact that after writing perhaps the greatest novel yet to be written about the Holocaust, he has devoted the rest of his work to questioning his own project, even attempting to unwrite it. In *A kudarc* (Fiasco), published in 1988—thirteen years after *Fatelessness*—a middle-aged writer, who refers to himself as "the Old Man," rediscovers a diary written by his younger self, describing the difficulties of publishing his first novel. This book was followed almost immediately by *Kaddish for an Unborn Child* (1990), a hundred-page monologue spoken by B., the writer and translator born in Auschwitz, in response to an apparently innocent question put to him by a new acquaintance: does he have a child? A simple "no," the first word of the book, would not suffice; he is overcome by "an overwhelming compulsion to speak," and from his fog of words the story of his marriage and divorce slowly emerges. Readers have invariably assumed this story to be autobiographical, since the tone of the novel is extremely personal and idiosyncratic. But such a reading overlooks the obvious differences between B. and his author. It overlooks also Kertész's complete lack of interest in adhering to the details of autobiography when fiction allows him the freedom to make of them whatever he likes.

Kaddish is the story of the failed romance between B., whose life remains utterly dominated by the wretched circumstances of his birth, and Judith, a young doctor who is the child of Holocaust survivors. Her mother died early on, B. tells us, of "some disease brought back from Auschwitz," which manifested in skin eruptions; Judith, consequently, has become a dermatologist. But B. argues that "the disease my wife's mother had suffered was, in reality,

Auschwitz itself, and there is no cure for Auschwitz, no one will ever recover from the disease of Auschwitz." Judith, too, will live always under "the mark of Auschwitz," or so he believes.

Until she met B., Judith had resisted all "Jewish matters," which made her feel, she says, as if she were grinding her face into mud. But she is attracted to B. precisely because of his history: she approaches him at a party after reading one of his articles, wanting to discuss it, and "talk about it we did until we talked ourselves into bed." Loving B. makes Judith feel that she has come closer to her parents and their experiences, and thus has attained some kind of mastery over her past. As a sign that they have truly moved on, "so that *together* we might extricate ourselves from the swamp and leave it behind forever, like the bad memory of an illness," she wants to have a child with him. But this B. refuses to do. He cannot bring a child into the world after Auschwitz, because "how can one compel a living being to be a Jew"? With unbearable sadness, he tells her that "what happened to me, my childhood, must never happen to another child."

And for B. there is no escaping that this is precisely what would happen, because there is no such thing as the world after Auschwitz; Auschwitz is a constant state of being. At the party where they met, people were discussing "a modish book of that period" that presented the theory that "there is no explanation for Auschwitz," a statement that B. finds dangerously naive. "To my amazement, this gathering of, after all, for the most part hardheaded people accepted, analyzed and debated this simplistic statement, scrutinizing it this way and that, with eyes blinking slyly or hesitantly or uncomprehendingly from behind their masks, as if this declaration to nip all declarations in the bud was actually declaring something, though you do not have to be a Wittgenstein to notice that in the point of linguistic logic alone it is flawed and reflects at most certain desires, a false or frankly infantile morality and sundry suppressed complexes but apart from that has no declarative value whatsoever," he says. "There would be no explanation precisely for an absence of Auschwitz." In contrast to the narrator of *Fatelessness,* who does make a genuine choice for life in the most unpromising circumstances—"I would like to live a little bit longer in this beautiful concentration camp"—B. leads what he calls a "subtenant life," feeling as if "the Germans might return at any moment." He calls it "not quite living, and indisputably not quite a life, rather it was just being alive, yes, *surviving.*" Judith rejects this, declaring in the end that "she had simply wanted to live." Later she will happily marry a man who is not Jewish and go on to bear him two children.

But Judith cannot really escape either, as we discover in *Liquidation,* large parts of which literally rewrite its predecessor. Now B. has committed suicide (another act that distinguishes him from his creator), leaving a man named Kingbitter, his friend and editor, in charge of his papers. His archive yields a few novellas and scattered other pieces, as well as a play called *Liquidation*—the first scene of which eerily forecasts the way in which the writer's friends will discuss his affairs after his death. But Kingbitter senses a gap: "Something is missing. The synoptic work, the book. He would not have gone without that; you don't impute that kind of dilettantism to a true writer."

On one level, *Liquidation* functions as a classic literary detective story, following Kingbitter as he makes the rounds of B.'s intimates seeking the lost masterpiece. The trail leads first to Sarah, B.'s lover at the end of his life, and then back to Judith, B.'s ex-wife. She denies to Kingbitter that such a book existed, but later, in a dramatic monologue addressed to Adam, her current husband, she admits that she burned it. The book she burned was "an Auschwitz-tinged love story," in which the woman wants a child and the man cannot forgive her for it. "Because of Auschwitz," he tells her, it is forbidden to bring a child into the world. The letter accompanying the manuscript that B. left her, asking her to burn it, describes it as "a private letter from the hereafter that no one has written and that is addressed to no one."

Of course, the so-called missing masterpiece sounds suspiciously like *Kaddish for an Unborn Child,* the very existence of which contradicts Judith's story. This is but one of the games Kertész plays with fiction and reality in this short work. Not since Kafka or Beckett—both clear influences (the epigraph from Beckett's *Molloy* is no surprise)—has a writer packed so much literary metaphysics into so tight a space. We see Kingbitter the character in the play speaking a line of dialogue, and the same line repeated immediately afterward as interior monologue in the novel. At one point Kingbitter, functioning now as the novel's narrator, admits to dramatizing the dialogues, "even quite inadvertently... they were no doubt a lot duller and simpler."

"The play's raison d'être is a novel," B. writes in a note to the play ("Liquidation") within the novel (*Liquidation*). "Its reality is thus another work." Kertész is exaggerating for effect, of course. But he has also spoken of all art as a form of exaggeration. "The narrator exaggerates, and because it's a novel we're talking about, all the characters have to be distorted into exaggeration," he tells the interlocutor of *Dossier K.*—who, remember, may or may not be fictional. "If you really think about it, art is nothing other than exaggeration and distortion." Here Kertész sounds suspiciously like Thomas Bernhard, that other "exaggeration artist," an obvious stylistic influence; *Kaddish* in particular has the run-on sentences and hysterical pitch characteristic of Bernhard's monologues in novels such as *Correction* or *Extinction*.

After a generation of postmodernism, this kind of sleight of hand has come to feel unremarkable. But what are the implications when the Holocaust is the subject of "exaggeration and distortion"? Elie Wiesel, as we have already seen, has argued that there is no ethical way to engage in such exercises in fictionalization; the only way he can admire writers such as Rawicz and Kosinski (both of whom could reasonably be said to exaggerate and distort) is by refusing to admit the imaginative aspects of their work. B., too, seems to argue that fiction about the Holocaust is inherently suspect. "Look here," he tells Kingbitter in response to the latter's encouraging him to write down the story of his birth. "I submit to you a piece concerning how, with the cooperation of a bunch of thoroughly decent people, a child is born in Auschwitz. The Kapos lay down their clubs and whips, and, moved to the core, they lift the wailing infant on high. Tears rise to the eyes of the SS guard." Kingbitter rather lamely offers the rejoinder that "it can also be written in other ways." "It can't," B. says. "Kitsch is kitsch.... It happened, yet it's still not true. An exception, an anecdote. A speck of grit gets into the corpse-mincing machine."

It happened, yet it's still not true. For B., the character in this novel, to transform the story of his birth—"bloody, like a placenta"—into a neat, symmetrical narrative is tantamount to denying it. The very act of telling the story must falsify it, because to tell it implies that it has some kind of internal logic. And so the story is literally "untellable," as Kingbitter will conclude, because no way of telling it can adequately represent its irrationality. Literature is simply too pleasant. Kingbitter, as a professional editor, knows this as well as anyone: he speaks seductively of the pleasures of reading, "a narcotic which pleasantly blurs the merciless outlines of the life that holds sway over us."

The problem is not just literary representation—it arises in any artistic reconstruction of the Holocaust. Judith, describing a visit to Auschwitz with a group of colleagues, is struck by the feeling that she is herself an actor in a production, a participant complicit in a contrived scenario. "Everything that I was already well acquainted with from the photographs was there," she says. "The inscription over the gate, the barbed-wire fences stretched between the recurved concrete posts, the single-story stone buildings—everything with an air of implausibility, like a copy.... I was haunted by a sense of walking around an outdoor folk museum. I was struck by the mischievous notion that an extra dressed in striped prison clothes might pop up at any moment." Like so many visitors to concentration camps, she is disturbed by the contrast between the surroundings and the everyday behavior of her travelling companions. "Someone asked if it was permitted to light a cigarette. The general hum of conversation never let up for a single moment." At the hotel, a member of the group discovers that her purse is missing: "The receptionist enlightened her that Auschwitz was teeming with pickpockets, who took advantage of the visitors' deeply emotional state and attendant inattentiveness."

Is the writer of Holocaust literature a kind of pickpocket at Auschwitz, a purveyor of kitsch who preys on his readers' emotions or lazily relies on the force of his subject matter to camouflage his own artistic deficiencies? Or can it "also be written in other ways"? Kertész, perennially searching for different ways to tell the same story, would seem to concur with the latter. But the fundamental uncertainty that permeates all his work comes from the desire to maintain both positions at the same time. For Imre Kertész, to write a true story about Auschwitz, and to keep it true in the telling, requires the spinning of myriad layers, ever shifting, ever unresolved, ever untrue.

Part Two

Those Who Came After

7

A Story for You: Thomas Keneally, Steven Spielberg

As the film ran and reached the scenes of the liquidation of the ghetto, I was, in a way, gasping for breath. The people I watched on the screen were in a terrible flux of history, in a mincer, a shredder of dreams and attachments.... The performances in the Schindler film were such as to make me forget that I had once broken bread, or the seals on bottles of rough Bulgarian wine, with these folk.... It was not until the lights came up that I remembered where we were, that we were in a Washington cinema toward noon on an overcast Monday, with my daughter whispering, "Wasn't that great?"

—Keneally, from *Searching for Schindler*

Schindler's List began in a Beverly Hills luggage shop. As Thomas Keneally tells the story in *Searching for Schindler*, his memoir about his book and the blockbuster movie it inspired, he was en route home to Australia from a book tour in the United States when his briefcase broke. Shopping for a new one, he happened into a store owned by Leopold Pfefferberg, a Jewish immigrant from Kraków. Keneally introduced himself as a writer, and Pfefferberg ushered him into the back room. "I know a wonderful story," Pfefferberg told him. "It is not a story for Jews but for everyone. A story of humanity man to man.... It's a story for you, Thomas."

Pfefferberg, who died in 2001, was one of the now-famous "Schindler Jews," the thousand-plus prisoners whose lives Austrian businessman Oskar

Schindler managed to save by spiriting them out of Płaszów, a labor camp near Kraków, to Brinnlitz, his own factory-camp in what is now the Czech Republic, where the food was generous, the beatings were rare, and the work consisted mainly of waiting for the war to end. "I was saved, and my wife was saved, by a Nazi," Pfefferberg told Keneally. "So although he's a Nazi, to me he's Jesus Christ." A persistent but charming man—to sweeten his often presumptuous requests, Pfefferberg addressed every woman as "darling" and was as generous with his compliments as Schindler was with his cognac—over the years he had become a "de facto archivist" of the Schindler story, amassing two filing cabinets' worth of documentation: newspaper clippings, speeches, and testimonials from other Schindler Jews.

Keneally was enraptured by the material. First of all, there was the ambiguous hero at the center of the story, a "young, hulking, genial but not quite respectable ethnic German" who came to Kraków at the start of the war in search of business opportunities. As Pfefferberg described him, Schindler was "all-drinking, all-black-marketeering, all-screwing." While some have been troubled by the contradictions inherent in Schindler's character, Keneally saw them as the entire point—the twist that made the tale of Schindler's rescue effort, in Pfefferberg's words, "a wonderful story." "Paradox is beloved of novelists," Keneally writes in his memoir. If Oskar Schindler had simply been a saint, his story would have been of human interest, but not of psychological interest. But the unashamedly decadent, womanizing, self-indulgent Schindler was an unlikely candidate for heroism, and the tension that animates Keneally's book comes from the question that the writer chooses to leave unanswered: what made him do it?

The other "wonderful aspect of the material," Keneally continues, is that "Oskar and his Jews reduced the Holocaust to an understandable, almost personal scale."

He had been there, in Kraków and then in Brinnlitz, for every stage of the process—for the confiscation of Jewish property and business, for the creation and liquidation of the ghettos, and the building of labor camps, *Arbeitslager*, to contain labor forces. The *Vernichtungslager*, the destruction camps, had cast their shadow over him and, for a time, subsumed three hundred of his women. It was apparent at once that if one looked at the Holocaust using Oskar as a lens, one got an idea of the whole machinery at work on an intimate scale and, of course, of how that machinery made its impact on people with names and faces.

It would be impossible to write a book—fiction or nonfiction—that captured the scope of the Holocaust as a whole; the writer and survivor Aharon Appelfeld has compared doing so to looking directly into the sun. As a practical matter, a writer, no matter what his or her subject, needs a "lens"—a single character whose experience runs through a cross-section of a larger scenario. This is the standard, normally uncontroversial novelistic method. *Les Misérables,* to give one example, tells us the story not of the French Revolution, but the stories of a handful of characters whose sufferings we get to know intimately, and in so doing it tells us some possible stories of the French Revolution.

The complaints about this method seem only to arise regarding books about the Holocaust. Such complaints are familiar: that to focus on a single character—especially one such as Schindler, whose story is exceptional, not at all emblematic of the Holocaust as a whole—will inevitably render a distorted perspective. "This is a movie about World War II in which all the Jews live," *Village Voice* critic J. Hoberman mordantly remarked about the film. "The selection is 'life,' the Nazi turns out to be a good guy, and human nature is revealed to be sunny and bright." No matter how closely Keneally, and Spielberg after him, labored to get all their details correct—and both of them did, as we will see, though in different ways—Schindler's story can never be an authentically representative story of the Holocaust, for the simple reason that there were no other Schindlers. But despite these inherent problems, the fact remains that there may be no better way to write a novel, or a novelistic work (since Keneally's book cannot properly be called a novel), about the Holocaust, as long as the teller recognizes that he is telling "a" story and not "the" story—a fact of which novelists are usually well aware.

Finally—and this seems to have been the crucial factor in Keneally's decision to undertake the task of writing this book—the mass of documents that Pfefferberg presented to the writer conferred upon him the aura of authenticity that so often seems to be indispensable to the Holocaust narrative. When Keneally walked into the luggage shop, it was 1980. The surge of interest in fictional representations of the Holocaust—two decades later the writer Melvin Jules Bukiet would estimate, with only moderate hyperbole, that one-tenth of the novels found in any bookshop had something to do with the subject—had not yet occurred. Fiction about the Holocaust was still largely taboo. The miniseries *Holocaust* had been shown on American television only two years earlier—to great acclaim, but also to harsh criticism, most notably from Elie Wiesel, who objected to the way fiction and fact were combined in this "docudrama" ("How is the uninformed viewer to distinguish the one from the other?") and angrily declared that the Holocaust is "the ultimate event, the ultimate mystery, never to be comprehended or transmitted [by art]." As a non-Jewish Australian, Keneally was concerned that he was unqualified to write a book about the Holocaust, which he first learned about as a child, watching newsreel footage at the movies in May 1945. He was not personally acquainted with many Jews, and Pfefferberg was the first Holocaust survivor he ever met.

But Pfefferberg's vast archive gave Keneally the authority he needed to take on the task. And its greatest prize was the document that would become enshrined in public fantasy: the famed list itself, drawn up, according to the version presented in the movie, by Schindler and his secretary Itzhak Stern over the course of a single fevered night, its cosmic significance distilled into the film's tagline: "The list is life." By the time Keneally's plane landed in Sydney, he was so excited to share the story with his wife and daughters that he could not even wait to get home, and opened up his trove of papers in a coffee shop at the airport. They were fascinated by the list, Keneally wrote: "its bureaucratic form, the fact that there were names on it belonging to people I had now met and spoken to at length."

"I know a wonderful story," Pfefferberg had said. "It is not a story for Jews but for everyone. A story of humanity man to man.... It's a story for you, Thomas." But there are some inconsistencies in the story—as Pfefferberg told it; as Keneally investigated and recorded it; as Spielberg adapted it. Perhaps the greatest is that there was no single "Schindler's list" as it appears in the movie, typed by Stern and flashed on the screen—or as it appears in Keneally's memoir, presented to his incredulous family over coffee. There were, rather, a number of different versions created under different circumstances. The scene in the movie was invented by Spielberg and his screenwriter, Steve Zaillian, who used Keneally's book as a starting point but deviated from it in a number of ways both significant and less significant.

Another crucial alteration involves the character "Itzhak Stern." There was no such person as the Stern who appears in the film, the sober accountant who becomes Oskar Schindler's business confidant and eventually his trusted friend. The character is a composite of several people who worked for Schindler, including the real Stern and another secretary named Mietek Pemper, who also served as a personal assistant to Commandant Amon Goeth at Płaszów, and who claims to have typed some of the list himself. In his own memoir, which appeared in English as *The Road to Rescue: The Untold Story of Schindler's List,* Pemper argues that no single person could have kept in his head (as the film presents Stern doing) all the information required for the list: "sequential number, inmate number, first name, family name, date of birth, and profession. Errors could not occur. Quite a few pages had to be reissued and revised several times." Spielberg's version also leaves out the uncomfortable fact—documented in Keneally's book—that the list was "manipulated" by a high-level prisoner named Marcel Goldberg, a clerk at Płaszów who demanded bribes in exchange for crossing out some names and substituting others. And after all that, Pemper reports in his memoir, the list got lost while the prisoners were en route from Płaszów to Gross-Rosen, the concentration camp near Brinnlitz where the male prisoners were sent first for processing. Keneally knows this, because he describes the way the list was drawn up again at Gross-Rosen under the supervision of Goldberg, who continued to accept bribes for alterations. "The problem," he wrote in *Schindler*, "is that the list is remembered with an intensity which, by its very heat, blurs." (The episode at Gross-Rosen is omitted from the film entirely.)

Already we can see that there are multiple versions of the Schindler story that alternately diverge and converge, often overlapping but sometimes not. First there is the version promoted by Pfefferberg and supported by his archive: a version based on eyewitness testimony, from Pfefferberg himself and from other Schindler Jews, and backed up by empirical sources such as newspaper clippings and contemporaneous documentation. This version, we can assume, is largely true, but colored by Pfefferberg's voluble personality, his penchant for drama, and his own subjective position; it also omits the experiences of Schindler Jews who chose, for whatever reason, not to publicize their stories. This was the version on which Keneally based his book, a hybrid of uncertain genre, sometimes called a "documentary novel," sometimes a "nonfiction novel" (the term Keneally seems to prefer), sometimes simply a novel. When it was awarded the Booker Prize for 1982, which was announced just a day after its publication date, the question of how to categorize the book was hotly debated in the British press, since the Booker was (and is) a prize designated for a work of fiction. If Keneally's book was not fictional—as he insisted it was not—did it merit the Booker?

And then there is Spielberg's film, unquestionably a work of fiction, but itself excruciatingly concerned with questions of fidelity and authenticity. This is a director who went to such pains to reproduce the physical surroundings of the Kraków Ghetto and the concentration camp Płaszów (neither of which any longer exists) that his film was praised in an academic journal for its "quasi-documentary value in plausibly recreating scenes" for which there are no records in film, such as the liquidation of the ghetto. When I lived in Kraków during the mid-nineties, at the beginning of the boom in Jewish tourism to Poland, the filming locations had become pilgrimage sites for Jewish visitors, second only to Auschwitz. (Much of the movie was filmed in Kazimierz, the old Jewish quarter, where many of the pre-war buildings still stand; the ghetto was largely razed and rebuilt after the war.) Spielberg's film may well have been too effective in its evocation of verisimilitude—so effective that not only its viewers but also its director confused it with reality.

Keneally's book—the cover of which displays a graphic of the famed list, with one hand reaching down across it to clasp another, as if in a gesture of rescue—embodies the confusion of categories that has played out so often in the literature of the Holocaust. The publisher categorizes it as a novel, with the label "Fiction/Judaica." But Keneally insists on its nonfictional bona fides from the start. *Schindler's Ark* (the book's original British title) is dedicated "to the memory of Oskar Schindler, and to Leopold Pfefferberg, who by zeal and persistence caused this book to be written." In an author's note, Keneally outlines his research: interviews with fifty "Schindler survivors"; a visit, together with Pfefferberg, to Kraków, Płaszów, and Auschwitz; "documentary and other information" from Schindler's associates during and after the war; testimonies from the Schindler Jews deposited at Yad Vashem. "To use the texture and devices of a novel to tell a true story is a course that has frequently been followed in modern writing," Keneally writes. "It is the one I chose to follow here—both because the novelist's craft is the only one I can lay claim to, and because the novel's techniques seem suited for a character of such ambiguity and magnitude as Oskar. I have attempted, however, to avoid all fiction, since fiction would debase the record, and to distinguish between reality and the myths which are likely to attach themselves to a man of Oskar's stature." He goes on to explain that though he has sometimes made "reasonable constructs" of dialogue, most conversations, "and all events," are based on the records of eyewitnesses. Mostly, he writes in his memoir, he tried to avoid dialogue altogether.

By "a course that has frequently been followed in modern writing," Keneally alludes to the form of the "nonfiction novel" pioneered in the mid-1960s by Truman Capote with *In Cold Blood,* a suspenseful, richly written account of the murder of a Kansas family, the search for their killers, and the trial that ensued. In an interview with George Plimpton in 1966, just after his book was published, Capote argued that the factor distinguishing his vision of the nonfiction novel—"a narrative form that employed all the techniques of fictional art but was nevertheless immaculately factual"—from ordinary journalism was the quality of imagination that the novelist brings to his work. "Of course a properly done piece of narrative reporting requires imagination!—and a good deal of special technical equipment that is usually beyond the resources—and I don't doubt the interests—of most fictional writers," Capote said, adding that such a writer must also have "a 20/20 eye for visual detail." But above all, he continued, "the reporter must be able to empathize with personalities outside his usual imaginative range, mentalities unlike his own, kinds of people he would never have written about had he not been forced to by encountering them inside the journalistic situation." Most contemporary fiction, he complained, amounts to little more than navel gazing; the nonfiction novelist has a unique opportunity to step outside himself, to imaginatively inhabit another character who just happens to have been a real person.

Some aspects of Capote's description suit *Schindler's Ark* well, particularly his emphasis on "the techniques of fictional art." Keneally's book is not styled as a work of history: it begins *in medias res,* with a dramatic scene of Schindler attending a dinner party at Goeth's villa, and throughout it is heavy in atmospheric detail and dynamic action. Reviewing the book for *The New York Times,* Paul Zweig wrote that "its voices are thick with living tissue; its scenes are so vivid they appear to result from a kind of ventriloquism." But what separates Keneally from Capote and other American practitioners of this form such as Gay Talese—also famous for his total immersion in the lives of his subjects—is that they were dealing with topics drawn from contemporary life, with subjects who in most cases were still alive. For *Thy Neighbor's Wife,* his study of American sexual mores, Talese spent years observing pornographers, prostitutes, and other key players in the sexual revolution, traveling to communes in California and at one point running his own massage parlor in New York. Capote never met the Clutters, of course—he came to their story after seeing a brief news item about the murders—but he spent months in Kansas among their friends and neighbors, and became intimately acquainted with the killers. For these writers, their personal experiences and relationships with their characters form the backbone of their highly subjective works; documentation plays a supporting role. Not so for Keneally, who arrived on the scene six years after Schindler's death, and nearly forty years after the crucial events had taken place. Yes, he was able to meet many of the Schindler Jews, but for his account of Schindler in action he was entirely dependent on the recollections of others.

Capote's book takes a strong position regarding capital punishment, but the argument arises out of the narrative, not the other way around. The moral to be extracted from the work is secondary to the main business: the author's imaginative realization of his characters and his desire to tell a good story. The opposite is true of *Schindler's Ark*. Keneally is convinced of Schindler's heroism from the start—naturally, otherwise why would he have written the book? The moral is the entire point. "This is the story of the pragmatic triumph of good over evil, a triumph in eminently measurable, statistical, unsubtle terms," he writes in the prologue, adding wryly: "It is a risky enterprise to have to write of virtue." Keneally does not try to animate Schindler as a person, to figure out what motivated him to do his extraordinary deeds—a fact for which many reviewers, taking the book at face value as a "novel," would criticize him. As A. N. Wilson would conclude in his review, "The story is so important to [Keneally] that he has shrunk from the task of turning it into a novel." His aim was not to fictionalize Schindler; it was to memorialize him.

So is it, then, a "documentary novel"? Despite Keneally's emphasis on documentation, *Schindler's Ark* has little stylistically in common with a work such as Anatoly Kuznetsov's *Babi Yar,* generally considered the exemplar of the Holocaust documentary novel. Kuznetsov's book, subtitled "A Document in the Form of a Novel" and begun when he was fourteen years old, is essentially his memoir of the German occupation of Kiev and its aftermath, supplemented by some testimonies by other survivors. But though Kuznetsov's perspective and style are drastically different from Keneally's, the two writers' purposes are largely the same, and they use strikingly similar terms to describe their projects. "The word 'documentary' in the subtitle of this novel means that I am presenting only authenticated facts and documents and that here you will find not the slightest literary invention—that is, not 'how it might have happened' or 'how it should have been,'" Kuznetsov wrote in his preface. In an interview, he called the book "not a novel in the conventional sense, but a photographically accurate picture of actual events." Keneally's claims for his own book are necessarily less confident—since he was not there himself, he cannot assert the same level of accuracy—but establishing its grip on reality is no less crucial to him. "Basically, nothing has been invented," he told an interviewer at the time of its publication—a claim that includes a hedge but is nevertheless a clear statement of his priorities.

So then why call it a novel at all? In *Searching for Schindler,* Keneally explains that the decision was made mainly for commercial reasons. If the book carried the sole designation "Judaica," he worried, it would get "stuck in that section against the back wall of most American bookstores" and would be unlikely to be bought by non-Jews. (Remember Pfefferberg: *It is not a story for Jews but for everyone.*) Anyway, he continues, "I felt that in *Schindler* I had written as a novelist, with a novelist's narrative pace and graphicness, though not in the sense of a fictionalizer....I was convinced at the time that this 'documentary novel' qualified as fiction, though...at the extreme end of the [category]." He might make the same decision again, he says, but he "would certainly not defend [it] to the death." His only regret, he says, is that deniers would later use the classification "to undermine the book's clear faith in the Holocaust's reality."

How Keneally could believe that a book that he himself claimed contained no fictional elements could nonetheless "qualify as fiction" may forever remain a mystery. Today the label of "nonfiction novel" has fallen out of use, and it is no longer unusual to find nonfiction that borrows techniques from the art of the novel, by writers ranging from John McPhee to Adrian Nicole LeBlanc. *Schindler's Ark,* published now, would likely be called "narrative nonfiction" or "narrative journalism." If the circumstances had been different at the time of its publication, the matter might have been pursued no further, and the question of the book's genre allowed to remain open. We might accept, as we must for so many works of literature about the Holocaust, that "if there is a line between fact and fiction, it may by necessity be a winding border that tends to bind these two categories as much as it separates them, allowing each side to dissolve occasionally into the other," as James E. Young has written.

But the question of whether or not *Schindler's Ark* was fictional was of crucial importance to British reviewers of the book, who immediately leaped on the incongruity that a book with demonstrably nonfictional content had won the Booker. And their assessment of the book's quality depended on its category. As a nonfiction narrative, most reviewers judged, the book was excellent. Considered as a novel, however, it was not very good. D. J. Enright summed up the paradox in his *Times Literary Supplement* review: "*Schindler's Ark* deserves to have won the Booker Prize—as long as it isn't *really* a novel."

Schindler's story, the British critics largely agreed, was too simplistic, too obvious, to work as a novel. Enright pounced on the almost impossible symmetry revolving around the famous Talmudic saying "He who saves one life, saves the world entire." In Keneally's version, Itzhak Stern quotes this to Schindler in their first conversation; the saying then reappears, as viewers of the film know, as the inscription in the gold ring that Schindler's Jews make for him as a parting gift. "It seems too neat to be true," Enright wrote. "But since no self-respecting writer of fiction would indulge in so arrant an improbability, it can only be true." (Spielberg, apparently agreeing, dropped the first reference from the film version.) One wonders what Enright would have made of the final real-life twist, which Keneally was either unaware of or chose to omit from his book: that Schindler, in one of his more down-at-the-heels postwar moments, sold the ring to buy schnapps.

The story was "too good" in another way as well, Enright argued. Keneally had taken pains to emphasize the tensions in Oskar's character: to make him too saintly would have smoothed out the edges, but would not have been true to life, and more importantly would have robbed Keneally of his "novelistic paradox." But despite this, the story is a fundamentally uplifting one, and so it flies in the face of conventional Holocaust narrative, in which, to reverse Hoberman's formulation, the Nazi normally does not turn out to be a good guy and the vast majority of the Jews die. "Given the circumstances, we would not want to hear about it if it were totally fictitious, of course, for that would only be the cruel, mocking triumph of a money-making lie," Enright wrote. The happy ending of Schindler's story is permissible only because it is true. If it were fictitious, then Keneally becomes a manipulator of emotions, a cynical sower of false hopes.

On the subject of Keneally's (and later Spielberg's) choice to leave Schindler's motives undefined, critics came down on both sides. Efraim Sicher, in his book *The Holocaust Novel,* is untroubled by the fact that Keneally leaves the reader "to guess the imponderable propensity for good," praising "the admirable skill with which Keneally has constructed a novel that is structured on the unanswerable mystery of what made Schindler do it. The evidence for his excessive generosity and impetuous gestures, combined with shrewd business acumen and self-interest, is certainly not sufficient explanation for an exceptional career of rescue." Writing in the *London Review of Books,* Robert Taubman concurred. "A good novel might be expected to help us to understand more about human nature than it did before. *Schindler's Ark* is all the better because it doesn't.... [Keneally] respects the old tradition of storytelling that doesn't explain or interpret or coerce but trusts the story itself." The Oxford professor John Carey, who chaired the Booker committee, was quoted in British newspapers as praising Keneally's "restraint."

But others found the lack of development in Schindler's character a sign that Keneally had defaulted on his novelistic obligations. Wilson, in *Encounter,* argued that Keneally's conception of Schindler was that of a "very competent journalist" rather than a novelist, and called the book "a highly competent, workaday piece of reportage." "Presented with the bare outline of Schindler's career and character," Wilson continued, "the reader finds it too odd to be fully comprehensible. He remains a two-dimensional character because Keneally describes him so realistically. Had he been a character in a Graham Greene fiction, Schindler might have seemed more real." Despite his admiration for the book, Enright basically agrees, wondering what a writer such as Günter Grass or Heinrich Böll might have made out of similar material.

In his memoir, Keneally continues to defend the way he presented Schindler's character. In his consultations with Spielberg on the film, he says, "we revisited the issue of where in Oskar altruism ended and opportunism began. I made the claim that it was actually important that the question could not be answered, that the abiding attraction of Schindler's character was wrapped up in the very conundrum." But as it turned out, Spielberg would agree only up to a point. The film version, unsurprisingly, emphasizes the extremes: Spielberg's Schindler, pre-conversion, is even more opportunistic and less self-aware than Keneally's; post-conversion, he is very nearly a saint. As Daniel Mark Vogel puts it, Spielberg transformed "a book about an extraordinary man whose goodness is finally inexplicable into a film about the understandable conversion to heroism of an ethically ordinary (albeit unusually glamorous) man." By refusing to show Schindler as committed to rescue from the beginning, Spielberg gives us "the vicarious experience of choosing goodness...to recapitulate within our own hearts and minds the transforming experience that his Schindler (unlike Keneally's) undergoes." Film, of course, specializes in vicarious experiences; but *Schindler's List* goes further than most.

The climactic scene in *Schindler's List*—the scene in Schindler's office in which he and Stern together draw up "the list"—begins with the two men having what might have been their final conversation. Schindler tells Stern that the Płaszów camp is to be liquidated, all its inhabitants sent to Auschwitz. Don't worry, Schindler says, "you will receive special treatment." He has chosen the wrong phrase. "The directives coming in from Berlin mention 'special treatment' more and more often," Stern replies. "I'd like to think that's not what you mean." Always short-fused, Schindler is exasperated. "*Preferential* treatment, all right? Do I have to invent a whole new language?" he asks. Stern considers the question seriously: "I think so."

This phrase must be deliberate. (The entire scene, we remember, was created for the screenplay, since the film's Stern is a composite of various real-life characters, and the frantic night of list-making never happened.) The drive to "invent a whole new language" was nearly universal among writers in the aftermath of the Holocaust, who were convinced that not only the German language (corrupted by such euphemisms as "special treatment"), but also a more general sense of morality and human capability, had been broken and needed to be re-created from the ground up. And Spielberg, too, when he finally turned to *Schindler's List* (the rights to which he held for ten years before he set himself to the task of adapting it for the screen), felt he had to create a filmic language that was entirely new to him. All he had learned and put to use so spectacularly over the course of his career was useless, he has repeatedly said, for the task of depicting the Holocaust. "My first choice was to get rid of all the tools…basically the mainstays in my arsenal of filmic weapons, like a camera crane," he says in an interview for the documentary *Imaginary Witness: Hollywood and the Holocaust*. "Everything that had to do with slickness and beauty, I got rid of all those devices." He chose to shoot the film in black and white, he says, because using color would "beautify the Holocaust." And he claims that he deliberately tried to avoid making references to other films, perhaps to give *Schindler's List* a kind of purity, a sense of being *sui generis*.[1] His goal, he said in an interview with *Newsweek*, was no less than to "bear witness" to the Holocaust.

Spielberg's most striking decision—one that Hoberman, one of the few critics to review the film negatively, calls its own kind of "special effect"—was to film as much of the movie as possible on location in Poland, at the actual sites where the events of the story had taken place: the enamelware factory, Schindler's apartment, locations inside both the former ghetto and the old Jewish quarter, Goeth's villa. The major exceptions were the concentration camps. The Płaszów camp was destroyed at the end of the war; on the site there now stands only an abstract memorial sculpture atop a hill. Spielberg constructed an extraordinarily realistic replica of the camp in a quarry nearby, complete with streets paved with fake tombstones. And he was permitted to film outside the gates of Auschwitz, but not within the camp itself. He came up with an ingenious circumvention: since the famous gate at Birkenau looks the same from either side, he built a replica of the camp outside the gate. For the scene in which the women destined for Schindler's factory arrive at Auschwitz, he had a train back up through the gate. The train could then be filmed emerging

---

1. Various scholars have observed that, despite this claim, *Schindler's List* is deeply indebted to its cinematic predecessors, from film noir to *Shoah*. "I think he recycled every little slip of film that was made before to produce this film. It presents what we seem to know—because we have seen so many of the images—as a higher depiction of reality. And, therefore, the whole film has a kind of authoritarian quality to it" (Gertrud Koch).

from the gate into the replica, as if in a mirror image, with viewers none the wiser as to which direction it was actually headed.

These details demonstrate how far Spielberg was willing to go to create the illusion of authenticity—but they also show that he defined authenticity in his own peculiar way. For him, what mattered was that the film *feel* authentic, even if creating such an atmosphere required diverging from the actual facts of what happened. Though Keneally writes in his memoir of seeing pages from his book lined up on Spielberg's monitor during shooting, a comparison of virtually any scene in the film with its counterpart in the book (assuming such a counterpart even exists) reveals Spielberg's departures, omissions, elaborations. Schindler's story might have been "too neat" for the British press, but for Hollywood the ironies were piled on. Take the scene in Płaszów when a woman engineer runs up to Goeth to tell him that the foundation of a structure being built is unsound. Goeth listens to her speech with a look of amused contempt; when she finishes, he tells one of his underlings to shoot her. As she is hauled off, he says to the rest of the workers, "Now do it over the way she said." The story of the engineer's shooting comes directly from the book, but the last line—the twist that reveals the depth of Goeth's perversity—is Spielberg's invention. Also invented from whole cloth is the sequence in which Goeth briefly experiments with trying to be a better person: "I pardon you," he says, with visible effort, to a prisoner who has failed to clean his bathtub adequately. But he can master his impulses only briefly.

It is easy to understand why Spielberg made these changes: they introduce some complexity into the character of Goeth, who would otherwise come across as a one-dimensional ogre. (No matter that on all accounts, particularly Pemper's, this is the way he actually was.) In contrast, the changes to the character of Schindler work to reduce his complexity. In an early scene in the film, Schindler rushes to the railway station and forces the guards to pull Stern—picked up for having inadequate papers—off a train bound, presumably, for Auschwitz. As they walk off together, Schindler berates Stern for his carelessness: had he arrived a moment later, he says, "Where would I be?" This comment shows that Schindler cares nothing for Stern personally; his only concern is for his business, which he cannot manage without his accountant. Stern's incredulous glance at his boss reflects the audience's shock at Schindler's callousness: forget Schindler, where would *Stern* have been? But in the book Keneally depicts this episode as one of the first steps in Schindler's conversion, writing that "what his curtness covered was dismay at those crowds at Prokocim [the train station] who, for want of a blue sticker, stood waiting for the new and decisive symbol of their status, the cattle car." For Keneally, the seed has already been planted; but Spielberg heightens the emotional impact of Schindler's eventual conversion by emphasizing how complete an about-face it was.

Also radically simplified in the film is the question of Schindler's womanizing. All the Schindler Jews seem to have accepted that Schindler's infidelity was an incorrigible aspect of his character—part of the roguishness that made him uniquely able to perpetrate such a large-scale deception of the SS. Pfefferberg told Keneally that he and another worker once stumbled in on Schindler cavorting with a female SS guard in a rooftop water tank—serving as impromptu swimming pool—in Brinnlitz. "Sexual shame was, to him, a concept something like existentialism, very worthy but hard to grasp," Keneally writes. In the film, however, Schindler's conversion to sainthood is entire. Early on, he sends his wife, Emilie, home to Austria so that he can continue to enjoy the company of his various mistresses in Kraków. After bringing the Jews to Brinnlitz, he seeks out Emilie in a church and promises her that he will be faithful from now on.

Other added scenes offer rare moments of humor: Schindler, after interviewing secretary after secretary in his office, each more beautiful and less competent than the last, sighs to Stern afterwards, "They're all so...qualified." And of course the scene at the end of the film of Schindler's farewell speech, in which he weeps for not having been able to save more Jews, was entirely invented. This was obvious to nearly every critic who reviewed the movie, as the scene was universally condemned for its jarring incongruity. But if we can accept that Keneally's book is several steps removed from total veracity, the film is in another category entirely.

These departures from the record do not seem to have troubled Spielberg's belief in the authenticity of his film. Seduced by his own creation, he has gone so far as to suggest that there was a mystical dimension to his experience of making it. "I can't tell you the shots I did on 'Schindler's List' or why I put the camera in a certain place," he said in the *Newsweek* interview. "I re-created these events, and then I experienced them as any witness or victim would have. It wasn't like a movie." This mood of total absorption infected the cast and crew as well. During the filming of the selection scene at Auschwitz, Spielberg said, he asked the camera man if he had gotten a particularly difficult shot. "I don't know, I wasn't looking," the man confessed. An Israeli actress born in Terezín was overcome during the shooting of the shower scene and had to be carried off the set. In his memoir, Keneally, who was present on the set for some of the filming, remarks that the actors often socialized together after work, but many of them were afraid to approach Ralph Fiennes (who played Goeth), even out of character. A survivor visiting the set was terrified of him as well.

In his illuminating book *Fantasies of Witnessing: Postwar Efforts to Experience the Holocaust,* Gary Weissman explores the desire—paradoxical, even shameful, but nonetheless omnipresent—among members of the post-Holocaust generations to "witness the Holocaust as if one were really there." I have already mentioned some possible reasons for this, foremost among them the assertion that the Holocaust is inaccessible to representation or interpretation by anyone other than survivors and, correspondingly, the delegitimation of fiction as a valid means of understanding it. Proponents of this position, particularly Elie Wiesel and Claude Lanzmann, were particularly vocal in the years immediately preceding *Schindler's List* (the film came out in 1993). "A novel about Auschwitz is not a novel, or else it is not about Auschwitz," Wiesel famously declared. Lanzmann, whose nine-and-a-half-hour documentary *Shoah* has often been regarded as the diametrical opposite of *Schindler's List,* has written that the Holocaust is "unique in the sense that it erects around itself, in a circle of flames, a boundary which cannot be breached because a certain absolute degree of horror is intransmissible: to pretend it can be done is to make oneself guilty of the most serious sort of transgression."

In this way, *Schindler's List* was perfectly calibrated to its cultural moment. Because of film's transporting qualities, viewers of Holocaust films can become convinced that the act of watching a movie about the Holocaust is tantamount to bearing witness to the events: as we know, this was Spielberg's intention from the start. Unlike Keneally's book, Weissmann writes, which incorporates various devices to remind the reader of its "contrived relation to actual events," Spielberg's film and its "elaborate re-creations…aim at a documentary-like verisimilitude that *discourages* viewers from making this distinction." Leon Wieseltier, writing in *The New Republic,* made this point even more powerfully, observing that "the film is designed to look like a restored print of itself." By virtue of its somberly elegant style and its peculiar sort of verisimilitude, *Schindler's List* appeared to offer its viewers something they had always thought was every bit as impossible as dinosaurs coming back to life: the opportunity to "witness the Holocaust as if they had really been there."

Spielberg's blockbusters have always shown him to be a master illusionist. And so when he brought all his formidable talents to bear on creating an illusion of the Holocaust, it is no wonder that the results were enthralling.

Even the audiences most accustomed to skepticism—journalists and critics—
fell under Spielberg's spell. (Wieseltier, marveling at the adulation of Spielberg
in *Schindler*'s wake, noted the "collapse of criticism" that the movie engendered.) Confusion between film and reality dominates the journalism about
the movie. In an article about the making of the film, *The New York Times*'s
Jane Perlez described a scene from the movie as if it were real ("a Nazi commandant and his servile lieutenants feast on fruit and drink punch from a
crystal bowl while hundreds of terrified Jews—penned in stifling cattle cars—
beseech their captors for water") and then revealed, in the next line, that what
she has described is a re-creation. Perlez later "falls for her own trick," Weissman writes, succumbing to a linguistic confusion between "the site where this
horror unfolded" and "this scene [from the film]."

But it's not her trick, it's Spielberg's. And the confusion he creates between
fiction and reality is the essence of filmmaking itself. All films—at least, all
realist films—create the illusion of reality. If the subject being treated is the
arrival of an extraterrestrial or a theme park full of dinosaurs, the ethics are
unproblematic: we are prepared to celebrate the director's skill in achieving
verisimilitude despite everything we empirically know about the improbability of the events on the screen. But when the subject is the Holocaust, the
question of representation presents the eternally inescapable moral quandary.
On the one hand, a convincing portrayal can go far in achieving pedagogical
purposes, educating audiences who might not otherwise have been familiar
with the events. On the other hand, there are all the usual problems that go
along with the representation in film of any historical event, including the
necessity of oversimplifying complex issues and the fundamentally manipu-
lative quality of the medium. Not to mention the fear that fictionalizing the
events can provide fodder for Holocaust deniers, who will point to inconsistencies between film and reality as "proof" that certain things did not occur.
If Schindler and Stern did not actually draw up a list of Jews to be saved over
the course of a nicotine-fueled night, who is to say that the rescue operation
took place at all?

This argument is prima facie ridiculous. The variety and the depth of the
empirical evidence are so overwhelming that deniers can only be understood
as willful distortionists or so immersed in fantasy as to be mentally ill. But the
fact that the specter of denial is continually raised highlights the fraught relationship that the Holocaust has with its own historical truth. It is arguable that
no genocide, with the exception of that of the Armenians, has been called into
doubt so frequently and so aggressively by deniers. And so there is always the

slight hint of worry that to question anything having to do with the Holocaust can have the inadvertent result of casting doubt on a basic historical reality. What could more effectively dispel such doubts than giving people the ability to witness the Holocaust for themselves?

Doubtless this is no small part of why critics responded so ecstatically to *Schindler's List*. For just as reviewers of Keneally's book were inclined to judge it favorably only if they believed that it was nonfiction, reviewers of the film championed it primarily for its testimonial value, largely accepting the notion that the film itself could "bear witness." It was not enough, as nearly all the reviews show, to say that the movie was an accomplished work of art. In fact, most critics—following the literary scholars who deemed Holocaust memoirs to be "beyond criticism"—found it insufficient or inappropriate to judge the film purely on aesthetic grounds. If *Schindler's List* was successful, it was successful *in spite of* the brilliance of its actors, the beauty of its cinematography, and the power of its narrative. It was successful because it offered the "fantasy of witnessing" that Spielberg had intended. Janet Maslin, in a review headlined "Imagining the Holocaust to Remember It," wrote that Spielberg "presents the subject as if discovering it anew" and that he "has made sure that neither he nor the Holocaust will ever be thought of in the same way again." Rhapsodic in *The New Yorker,* Terrence Rafferty wrote that "Spielberg uses the resources of film so powerfully that we, in the audience, feel a profound transformation in our relation to the historical drama that we're witnessing." Is "the historical drama" the film (which we *watch,* not "witness") or the events themselves? Rafferty seems to mean the latter, going on to make an extraordinary statement about the Kraków ghetto liquidation scenes. "In this turbulent and almost unbearably vivid fifteen-minute sequence, the Holocaust, fifty years removed from our contemporary consciousness, suddenly becomes overwhelmingly immediate, undeniable," he writes. "Spielberg...creates images that have the force of intimate experience, the terrible clarity of your own most indelible memories."

But ultimately the only thing that is "undeniable" about *Schindler's List* is that it is a fiction film. And paradoxically, it may be the fact that it *is* a fiction film that makes its illusion so convincing. Documentary footage, for all its power, can come nowhere close to evoking the kind of emotional involvement that Spielberg does in his quasi-documentary scenes, just as a straightforward nonfictional book such as *The Destruction of the European Jews* lacks the emotional impact of a novelistic work such as Wiesel's *Night*. Similarly, Lanzmann's *Shoah*—which explicitly rejects any possibility of visually representing the

Holocaust, and consists solely of interviews with survivors, perpetrators, and bystanders—has a much wider focus and cast of characters than *Schindler's List,* with its emphasis on one exemplary yet exceptional story. As such, *Shoah* has been praised by many critics and scholars for its creation of an essentially new genre that avoids the treacle inevitably associated with Hollywood drama. But its insistence on the inaccessibility of the events of the Holocaust—we are shown fields and railroad tracks overgrown with weeds and asked to imagine the concentration camp that was once there—can only emphasize the viewer's distance from the events. This is, obviously, a more truthful and realistic representation of fact than *Schindler's List:* we *are* distant from the events; they *are* accessible to us only through the mediation of witnesses. But in *Shoah* we feel only the presence of the witnesses; watching *Schindler,* rightly or wrongly, we feel that we ourselves are in the thick of it. This does not mean that we know what it was like to have been there, that we experienced the events "as any victim or witness would have," as Spielberg claims he did; or that a fiction film can have the documentary power to render the Holocaust "undeniable," as Rafferty wrote. (Was the facticity of the Holocaust still up for debate in 1993?) But if Spielberg's illusion renders indelible the sadism of Goeth (whose name few viewers of the film were likely to know beforehand) or the terror of daily persecution, it is hard to find fault with that.

Does it matter that Spielberg's re-creation inevitably deviates from reality? Hoberman cites a survivor who recalled that everywhere in the Kraków ghetto during liquidation one could see corpses hanging from lampposts and trees, and says that knowing this detail, for him, "demolished Spielberg's re-creation." Those who learn of the violence in the ghetto only from Spielberg's film will not imagine these hanging bodies; they will see instead a terrified woman seeking shelter for herself and her child; Ralph Fiennes as Goeth, delivering his "Today is history" speech; a little girl in a red coat. But there is no single "reality," as the film itself takes pains to remind us. We see the ghetto scenes from multiple perspectives: the SS on the street; Schindler on his horse on a hill above; Stern looking out his window. We see less than the surviving witnesses saw, but we also see more.

There are a few moments in the film when one wonders whether Spielberg is making an oblique case for the value of fictionalizing. After all, this is a film in which people stay alive by telling fictions—to others and to themselves. A history professor represents himself as a metal polisher in order to be considered an essential worker. "Just *pretend,* for Christ's sake," snaps Schindler early in the movie to Stern, who is refusing to play the game of social niceties with his boss. Schindler's entire operation was based on the fiction that the materials he produced were essential to the war effort, and the countless stories he had to tell, to Goeth and others in the Nazi command, to get them to let him do what he wanted, such as his insistence to the SS at Auschwitz that even the children from his transport were skilled workers whose tiny fingers were perfectly suited for polishing the insides of metal casings. During wartime as perhaps at no other time, fiction is necessary in order to survive.

The film's final moments are an uncanny blur of fiction and fact. In a scene that serves as a sort of coda, the real-life Schindler Jews are shown paying their respects at Schindler's grave in Jerusalem. As they slowly approach to lay down a stone, their names appear at the bottom of the screen, names with which we are now familiar: Leopold Pfefferberg, Helen Hirsch, Henry Rosner. The Schindler Jews are elderly, and many of them need help navigating the ground around the grave or bending down to place their stones. And each is escorted by the actor who plays him or her in the film. So the now-aged Danka Dresner appears together with the familiar face of Anna Mucha, a teenaged Polish actress in round glasses and a braid down her back. Helen Hirsch is tenderly helped along by Embeth Davidtz. The widow of Itzhak Stern is holding the arm of Ben Kingsley, almost unrecognizable behind dark sunglasses.

This sequence, even on repeated viewings, is almost unbearably moving. Fiction and fact are literally brought together by the pairing of actor and subject. And the emotional impact of this juxtaposition is amplified by the names that appear on the screen—yet another version of the list. Does the name "Danka Dresner" or "Helen Hirsch" refer to the character played by the actor or to the survivor, the real-life person? Or to both simultaneously? The two have become, in effect, inseparable.

8

The Ghost Writer: Wolfgang Koeppen

The novel...draws on current events, in particular recent political events, but only as a catalyst for the imagination of the author. Personalities, places, and events that occur in the story are nowhere identical with their equivalents in reality. References to living persons are neither made nor intended in what is a purely fictional narrative. The scope of the book lies beyond any connections with individuals, organizations, and events of the present time; which is to say, the novel has its own poetic truthfulness.

—preface to *The Hothouse*

Among the many survivors who wrote testimonies immediately after the war was a man named Jakob Littner. A stamp dealer whose family originally came from Poland, he had been living in Munich for more than twenty-five years when, in October 1938, the Nazis passed a decree expelling all Jews of Polish nationality. After passing through Prague and numerous towns in Poland, he wound up, together with a few relatives, living for nine months in a hole beneath the cellar of a house on the outskirts of Zbaracz (now Zbaraz), a town in what was then Poland and is now Ukraine. Freed by Soviet soldiers in March 1944, he arrived back in Munich in August 1945, where he began to write his memoirs. Within about two months he had produced a manuscript of 183 typewritten pages, titled *Mein Weg durch die Nacht: Ein Dokument des Rassenhasses* (My journey through the night: A document of racial hatred).

Littner, like most survivors, did not write for his own pleasure: he intended to publish his testimony. To this end, he submitted his manuscript to the Munich publishing house Kurt Desch Verlag, which asked the writer Rudolf Schneider-Schelde to evaluate it. Rather mercilessly, Schneider-Schelde called the book a "sentimental-pathetic-uplifting report of experiences" that was "without the least worth, either literarily or in the way of ideas, and in terms of content offer[ed] nothing new." It might be possible to publish it in installments in a newsweekly, but only if it was rewritten first. It was "essential," Schneider-Schelde concluded, that the book be revised "both stylistically and structurally."

Somehow the manuscript found its way to a man named Herbert Kluger, who was running a tiny publishing firm out of his apartment. (He would bring out a total of eight books.) According to a contract signed in April 1947, Kluger agreed to publish the book, but only if Littner first provided five thousand Reichsmarks to cover the "literary adaptation," as well as production and printing costs. In other words, it was basically a vanity deal. Two months later, Littner and his wife emigrated to America, leaving the manuscript in Kluger's hands.

Meanwhile, the writer Wolfgang Koeppen had also made his way to Munich. Born in 1906, Koeppen had published two novels to quiet acclaim in the 1930s, and spent the war years writing "unfilmable" documentaries for the German government, which he later called his (admittedly limited) form of resistance. In 1944, fearing that Nazi colleagues would betray his stonewalling, he went underground. By war's end he was eager to pick up where he had left off, but conditions were dire. Cigarettes were the common unit of currency, he wrote in the foreword to the book he would publish shortly after the war, and he was inept at black-marketeering. But "I had survived Hitler and the war," he wrote, and "for me that was a miracle. I hoped to find my way back to myself, to be able to write again the way I had once tried to do. With the freedom of the free writer." In the meantime, Kluger, an old friend of his from Berlin, engaged him for editorial assistance.

In an interview with the German-Jewish literacy critic Marcel Reich-Ranicki in 1985, Koeppen gave one version of what happened next. Though he did not name names, it seems clear that the book he refers to in this conversation was Littner's. Kluger wanted to publish the manuscript, Koeppen said, but others had advised him that the book could not appear in its original form. The publisher "turned to me," Koeppen said; he read the manuscript and "agreed that the whole thing was somewhat primitive." So Kluger commissioned him to do an "editorial and literary adaptation." He interpreted this assignment liberally, rewriting the entire manuscript, expanding it or abridging it where he saw fit. The result of Koeppen's handiwork was a "distinct text, completely altered, which took from the original its outline and individual passages and fragments," the critic Albert Estermann has written.

But in the foreword to an edition of the book published to a firestorm of publicity in 1992, Koeppen gave a very different version of the story of its creation. After describing the dismal conditions in Munich during those years, he wrote that one day his friend Herbert Kluger, a survivor of the bombing of Berlin, received a visitor who had returned

> from one of the German hells. Once a respected citizen of his town, a world-renowned stamp dealer, then hauled off as a Jew, tormented in ghettos and extermination camps, who had stood at death's door and had gazed upon bodies in mass graves. All this was still near.
>
> Returning to his own city, destroyed by the bombs of its liberators, he believed he saw murderers. He wanted to scream, but it choked him. He wanted to speak and gazed into faces that had sanctioned it all....
>
> The Jew told the new publisher that his God had protected him. The publisher listened, he noted places and dates. The escaped man sought a writer. The publisher reported the unbelievable to me. I had dreamed of it. The publisher asked me, "Do you want to write it?"
>
> The mistreated man wanted to get out, he emigrated to America. He promised me an honorarium of two care packages each month.
>
> I ate from American cans and wrote the story of a German Jew's sufferings. And so it became my story.

The book that Koeppen wrote takes the fragmented form of a diary. After surviving *Kristallnacht* and a near deportation to Poland, the nameless narrator—a nonreligious German Jew—flees Germany. He stays briefly in Prague, then makes his way east, ending up in Zbaracz. There he and his companion Janina, who will become his wife, spend the remainder of the war: first in the Zbaracz ghetto, hiding during SS raids in a crevice that he digs out beneath the floor; and then, after the ghetto's liquidation, in the airless cellar of a Polish man's house. The narrator is sustained through his ordeals by his faith in God and by the efforts of a German woman he calls Christa, formerly his business partner, who continually sends money and even undertakes the long and treacherous journey to visit him in the ghetto. The book ends with the liberation of the narrator and Janina by the Russians.

When this slender, deftly written book first appeared in Munich in 1948, in the version published by Kluger, it carried the title *Aufzeichnungen aus einem Erdloch* (Notes from a hole in the ground). The author was identified as Jakob Littner; Koeppen's name appeared nowhere in the book. But the experience of writing it did seem to help Koeppen find his way back to himself, and in the early 1950s, in quick succession, he published a trilogy of novels sharply critical of the efforts under way to rebuild Germany, writing baldly about the reverberations of Nazism into postwar German society and culture. Not surprisingly, neither critics nor readers, in thrall to the *Wirtschaftswunder,* were especially welcoming of Koeppen's indictments of West Germany. Despite Koeppen's assertions that the characters and events were fictional, the novels were perceived by many as a personal attack. A review of *The Hothouse,* the trilogy's centerpiece, carried the headline "Not to be touched with a barge pole." A Bonn bookstore canceled a scheduled reading by Koeppen when the police said they would be unable to guarantee his safety. And Koeppen fell silent again. Between 1954 and 1992, he would publish a brief quasi memoir about his youth, travel books, and various essays and reviews, but no more fiction.

And then, three years after the fall of the Berlin Wall, the Jüdische Verlag, a ninety-year-old publisher of books on Jewish topics that had just been acquired by the venerable German house Suhrkamp, published what it said was a new novel by Koeppen. The book was called *Jakob Littners Aufzeichnungen aus einem Erdloch* (Jakob Littner's notes from a hole in the ground). But aside from the foreword, in which Koeppen gave his dubious version of how the book came to exist, and a note inside the front cover advising that the book was "an unaltered reprint of the first edition of 'Jakob Littner, Notes from a Hole in the Ground, Munich, Kluger, 1948,'" there was no explanation of what, exactly, it was. Complicating matters was the fact that Littner's book—or the book thought to be Littner's—had already been reprinted in 1985 under the guise of a memoir and had been received as a factual account. Now the reading public was being asked to accept, as the book's dust jacket trumpeted, that the novelist Wolfgang Koeppen was the true author of a book that had been believed to be an authentic Holocaust memoir and was now reclassified as a novel.

No wonder the German press reacted largely with confusion. Since the only explanation of the book's provenance was the vague and inaccurate history Koeppen offered in his foreword, no one knew that there had existed an original text that Koeppen had adapted into literary form—a bit of information that Koeppen, after his interview with Reich-Ranicki, never again volunteered. Some critics continued to understand the book as an essentially true memoir that Koeppen had merely ghostwritten; they resorted to standard tropes of Holocaust literary criticism, praising the book for its "documentary value" and Koeppen's straightforward prose as appropriate to a subject that touches on the "limits of language." Those who believed that Littner was a fictional character constructed by Koeppen found the book thematically more troubling, particularly its conciliatory conclusion, in which Littner declares that he "hates nobody" and that "only God can judge that which is entirely lacking in humanity." Some were convinced by this call for mutual forgiveness: one reviewer even claimed that Koeppen, through the writing process, had assimilated the suffering of a Jew to such a degree that his identity merged with that of the victim. (*I ate from American cans and wrote the story of a German Jew's sufferings. And so it became my story.*) But others found the implications of such a position ethically questionable. Writing in *Die Zeit,* the critic Eberhard Falcke argued that Littner was one of numerous fictional Jewish characters created to "indulge the wishful thinking of the German public." Falcke accused Koeppen of putting "words from a German hand into a Jewish mouth," and he described the statement of forgiveness as a "monstrosity." Its implications in 1948, Falcke argued, were by no means subtle: if "only God can judge" the perpetrators, then the Nuremberg Trials were meaningless, since no Nazi could ever be brought to justice by a human court.

In Falcke's eyes, one of the most damning elements was a letter that had recently come to light that Littner had written to his publisher soon after the book's publication, in which Littner angrily disavowed the book. "This is not my book; I find in it neither myself nor my family," he wrote. Why did Kluger and Koeppen keep this letter secret? Falcke wondered. He concluded that theirs was an act of usurpation, pure and simple. But their ability to carry out such an act was abetted by Littner's absence as an author. *Aufzeichnungen aus einem Erdloch* became Koeppen's story "not only through an act of narrative appropriation and identification, but for another reason: there was no detailed account by Littner and none was requested," Falcke wrote. "All that existed were some notes the publisher had taken down after his conversations with Littner. This is how the book, which was presented to the public as a factual account, was produced." The fact that Falcke finally judged the novel to be "a good and moving work" did not take the sting out of his criticism.

Koeppen's own comments were hardly clarifying. In one interview he said that in the first edition "Jakob Littner" had been his "pseudonym"; in another, he claimed that the "notes" Littner had given him constituted no more than "three scraps of paper." In short time it was reported that a man named Jakob Littner, a stamp dealer, had indeed lived in Munich before and after the war, and had emigrated to New York in 1947. Koeppen died in 1996 without saying anything further about the book.

In 1995, Reinhard Zachau, a professor of German at the University of the South in Tennessee, came upon *Jakob Littners Aufzeichnungen aus einem Erdloch*. He was so taken with Koeppen's novel that he contacted Suhrkamp to inquire about translating it into English. But he became suspicious when the publisher said the book had to be published exactly as it was, without the addition of notes or an introduction. Zachau had heard that a real person named Jakob Littner had existed, and he decided to do some research on his own.

In the Ship Passenger Arrival Records at the National Archives in Washington, he discovered an entry for Jakob Littner, "age 64, citizen of Hungary, accompanied by Janina, 47." The Littners had arrived in New York on July 17, 1947. After months of research in the archives of the Joint Distribution Committee, YIVO, and other Jewish organizations, Zachau managed to locate a distant relative of Littner's named Kurt Grübler, a retired mechanical draftsman living in Rockville, Maryland. Grübler was writing a family history, and Littner's stepson had given him the original manuscript of Littner's memoir: the 183-page testimony, typed on onionskin paper and bound in Munich in 1945, that Littner had called *Mein Weg durch die Nacht*.

With Zachau's discovery of this original manuscript, and the subsequent publication of lengthy excerpts from it in the German studies quarterly *Colloquium Germanica* in 1999, it became obvious that Koeppen's version of the creation of *Jakob Littners Aufzeichnungen aus einem Erdloch* had been far from honest. Of course, at this point it is impossible to know exactly what transpired between Koeppen and Littner. But a comparison of *Mein Weg durch die Nacht*—which has since been published in a complete German edition— and *Jakob Littners Aufzeichnungen* indeed demonstrates that Koeppen, as he had told Reich-Ranicki, worked from Littner's typescript, not from the "three scraps of paper" that he later said he had received from Herbert Kluger. Koeppen's novel follows the general story line of Littner's manuscript, but he made considerable formal adjustments, changed the names of some characters, deleted various people and events, and added a variety of scenes and details apparently of his own invention. It may be that Littner provided Koeppen, either orally or in writing, with additional details not found in the original manuscript, but no evidence of this has come to light. Thus we may assume that any discrepancies between the original manuscript and Koeppen's version of it are the products of Koeppen's imagination.

As the previous chapters have shown, the past few decades have seen a number of controversial instances in which Holocaust memoirs or so-called autobiographical novels that purported to be authentic turned out to be fiction: Jerzy Kosinski's *The Painted Bird,* Binjamin Wilkomirski's *Fragments,* and various others. But *Jakob Littners Aufzeichnungen aus einem Erdloch* appears to be the first case in which a text believed to be fiction turned out to be based on fact. The reaction in Germany was measured. Though it was generally acknowledged that Koeppen and the Jüdische Verlag ought to have been more transparent about the genesis of the book, critics also recognized that *Jakob Littners Aufzeichnungen* and *Mein Weg durch die Nacht* were vastly different books. In an interview with *Der Spiegel,* Roland Ulrich, Koeppen's archivist, said that though Koeppen had based his work on Littner's typescript, he had "doubtless given the book literary polish. That remains his great achievement." Ulrich lamented the omission of Littner's name in the book's republication as an unnecessary stain on Koeppen's reputation. "Why did Koeppen so forcefully obliterate the traces of the original text and its author?" Ulrich asked "Neither the book nor his reputation would have suffered if he had stuck to the truth." Writing in the *Frankfurter Allgemeine Zeitung,* Hans-Peter Riese reached a similar conclusion: "Koeppen made Littner's personal report more literary, and raised it to the level of the general.... Koeppen and his publishers did not need to fear this truth. It changes nothing about the literary standing of Koeppen's adaptation."

The American reception was considerably less nuanced. In the aftermath of the Wilkomirski fraud, it was all too easy for critics and writers to seize upon any sort of falsification regarding the Holocaust as morally reprehensible. In the rush to judge Koeppen, the facts of the matter were often mischaracterized. Continuum, which published the English version of Littner's manuscript (it appeared as *Journey through the Night: Jakob Littner's Holocaust Memoir*), released a statement claiming that "while there have been several Holocaust 'memoirs' that have been unmasked as fictions, this is perhaps the first time that a Holocaust 'novel' turns out to be a fabrication based minutely on a genuine Holocaust memoir." Of course, this was not exactly what had happened: it is unfair to describe a work of fiction as a "fabrication," and Koeppen's book was based loosely at best on Littner's memoir. (The German critics tended to use the word *Bearbeitung,* or adaptation, to describe Koeppen's book, which acknowledges his creative contribution while recognizing the novel's basis in another work.) In an inaccuracy-riddled article in the *New York Times* head-lined "Holocaust Memoir is Reissued, No Longer Designated Fiction," Ralph Blumenthal confused the two books, making it sound as if *Jakob Littners Aufzeichnungen* had been designated as nonfiction rather than the original manuscript, and writing that "Koeppen appropriated Littner's memoir after assisting its first brief publication in Germany."

Paradoxically, those who recognized the extent of Koeppen's changes casti-gated him posthumously for his temerity in tampering with the holy writ of a Holocaust testimonial. "You'd think by 1992 it would have been axiomatic not to alter a Holocaust memoir," Phil McCombs wrote in a lengthy piece about the Koeppen-Littner affair in the *Washington Post*. "This is sacred ground. Every detail, nuance, memory—no matter how terrible, or banal—is pre-cious." In an article accompanying the excerpts from the original manuscript in *Colloquium Germanica,* Zachau enumerated some of the ways in which Koeppen had deviated from the original text, and speculated on the various psychological motivations behind them. Koeppen's guilt as a German after the war, Zachau argued, had led him to place far more emphasis on the roles of "'good' Germans" than Littner had in the original.

While savaging Koeppen, these critics reserved their highest praise for Littner's relative Kurt Grübler, who would soon make his own contribu-tion to the steadily growing stack of Littner-related texts with the publica-tion of *Journey through the Night: Jakob Littner's Holocaust Memoir*. This book, which includes Grübler's translation of Littner's original manuscript augmented by a few footnotes, as well as copies of family photographs and documents, was presented as the final word on the Koeppen-Littner affair. "It is now possible to classify Koeppen's text as an elaborate fictionaliza-tion of authentic events where the dividing line between truth and fantasy remains blurred (see Wilkomirski)," Zachau wrote in his foreword to *Jour-ney through the Night*. "Kurt Grübler provides a more detailed account not only of Littner's experiences, but also of the bigger picture. The host of docu-ments, relating to the Littner family, greatly enhances the historical objectiv-ity of this book." McCombs went further: "Littner's often arch and flowery language, pious musings, plunges and flights of emotion—all the rich and flawed human material that Koeppen cut—has [*sic*] been restored in a loose but faithful translation by Grübler, whose notes and research are carefully set apart from the original text....Littner's book, as he wrote it, is so powerful that it shakes you to your foundation and cannot be read without weeping. It is reality—there's no need for fancy writing."

But Koeppen's critics raise far more questions than they answer. First, the comparison to Wilkomirski is utterly false. Koeppen never claimed that the events in *Jakob Littners Aufzeichnungen aus einem Erdloch* had happened to him; he said only—and honestly—that he had fictionalized events that had happened to Littner. And if Koeppen's book is indeed an "elaborate fictionalization," why was he wrong to call it a novel? His purpose, after all, was to write an artistically coherent text, not a news report. The resurfacing of the original manuscript ought to have been a boon for Koeppen's reputation—after all, it shows just how much imaginative work he performed.

And neither Zachau nor McCombs commented on the fact that Littner's 183-page typescript—which amounted to 147 book pages in the 1948 version, even considering Koeppen's additions, deletions, and rewritings—had shrunk to just 108 book pages in Grübler's translation. Or that Littner's original title (My journey through the night) had been shortened to simply *Journey through the Night*. Or that some interesting details seemed to have been left out—and others added. If *Jakob Littners Aufzeichnungen* does not represent "Littner's book, as he wrote it" (which Koeppen, incidentally, never claimed that it did), neither does *Journey through the Night*. The urge to tamper with the "sacred ground" of the Holocaust memoir, it seems, was hard for more than one writer to resist.

In an introduction to his translation of *The Hothouse,* widely considered Koeppen's masterpiece, Michael Hofmann ruefully writes that Littner's manuscript "has been used as a stick with which to beat Koeppen for his own reissued work. This is, I think, unfair. Koeppen's version of the story may not be—could not be—authentic, but sentence for sentence and page for page, it is incontestably the better book: it begins with the titles." If one judges *Jakob Littners Aufzeichnungen* based on its consistency with Littner's original manuscript, then of course it does not hold up. How could it? Fidelity to historical fact was not the point. But whether or not one believes that it is a crime to alter a Holocaust testimony, if the books are evaluated on purely literary grounds—as a novel ought to be evaluated—Hofmann is clearly right.

Jakob Littners Aufzeichnungen is tighter and more streamlined than Littner's rambling report. Koeppen stripped out most of the subplots and the secondary characters, and he gave Littner's thoughts greater complexity. But his most significant change was structural: he took Littner's lengthy report and broke it up into sections of just a paragraph or two, shifting between past and present tense, to give it the feel of a diary. All in all, Koeppen allowed hardly a line of Littner's manuscript to pass unaltered into his version.

Aside from some contextual material, Koeppen's additions come mainly in the form of minor fictionalizations of the underlying factual matter. The following passages give a good sense of his method (all citations from both texts are in my own translation).

Here is Littner:

One day in October 1938, at five o'clock in the morning, a uniformed police officer appeared in my apartment, got me out of bed, and said, after he had checked my personal data, "I must arrest you."

And here is Koeppen:

It was still dark when there was a ringing at my door. I woke and saw that it was only five. I knew right away that something terrible was about to happen. There is an old rumor that says people are "picked up" around this time of day....I ran to the door as if I could stifle the noise of the bell....My bare feet ran across the floor as if it were cracking ice. As I grasped the doorknob, I suddenly glimpsed myself in the mirror of the hall closet: a fat man, panting, in a nightshirt too short for him....But it was just the good-natured sergeant from the local precinct who stood before my apartment door, an empty staircase behind him. We were old acquaintances, so to speak, and until yesterday we would have greeted each other when we met in the street. His voice was soft and sympathetic as he said: "I have to arrest you, Mr. Littner!" Then he sized me up with a look that gradually became more severe, as if it annoyed him to see me in a nightshirt, and he snapped harshly: "Get dressed!"

Where Littner was content to state the facts—when and who and what—Koeppen has spun the episode of Littner's first arrest into a drama of its own. From the "old rumor" that superstitiously bodes ill to the ringing bell and bare feet, Koeppen has fleshed out and dramatized the terse original, and in the process he has given it more emotional impact. This is especially evident in the detail of the nightshirt, which allows the embarrassment that the narrator feels at the beginning of the passage to spin into full shame by the end.

Koeppen's changes—not unlike Spielberg's alterations to *Schindler's Ark*—most commonly consist in making events either more ironic or more dramatic than they actually were. Later in the book, Littner receives a heartbreaking series of letters from his son and daughter-in-law in the Warsaw ghetto lamenting their horrible circumstances. In the original manuscript, Littner answers their cries for help with letters and money transfers, but his responses to his daugher-in-law's final letter go unanswered. In Koeppen's version, a decree forbidding Jews to use the postal services is passed the day after Littner received his daughter-in-law's last letter, rendering him unable to respond. (In fact, Littner writes that the prohibition came down a few days later.) At another point, Koeppen and Littner use nearly identical words to describe SS soldiers cutting off the beards of elderly Jews, but Koeppen adds a final twist: "The leader of the synagogue, an elderly, pious Jew, hanged himself on the evening of that same day."

At other points, Koeppen's additions, in the clear light of hindsight, sound like the work of an outsider, a person at a greater remove from the events of the war than a survivor could be. This is evident in the following passage, identical in the two texts, in which Littner cites the letter he received from the *Judenrat* in the town of Borszczów (now Borshchiv) in response to an inquiry about his siblings:

> In response to your communication of December 5 we inform you that Sida Littner, Irma Littner and Victor Blum died on November 11, 1941 in Borszczów and were buried that day in the local Jewish cemetery.
> For the *Judenrat*
> (signature illegible)

Koeppen's text quotes this letter word for word, but he adds at the end: "Who would want to sign his name legibly at the bottom of such a document?" Where Littner reports the illegibility of the signature simply as a matter of fact, Koeppen reads into it a certain confession of shame.

Finally, one of the most striking departures from the original involves Koeppen's treatment of Littner's spiritual life. A dominant theme of the original manuscript is Littner's profound religiosity. "In overcoming seemingly inescapable situations, faith in God must play a crucial role," Littner writes in the typescript. "True faith in God produces an unshakable sense of security and superhuman powers." But Koeppen has Littner start out as an extremely secular Jew—so assimilated, in fact, that he is accustomed to celebrating Christmas with his non-Jewish friends, and laments not being in the mood for it after the events of November 1938. Instead, he goes for a walk on Christmas Eve, and winds up at the burnt-out synagogue, destroyed on *Kristallnacht*. "Should I stand before the wall and say my New Year's prayer here, like my brethren at the Wailing Wall in Jerusalem?" he wonders. Only now does a glimmer of devoutness awaken in him: "I, a quiet businessman in our century of progress, feel a sense of piety, of reverie, a breath of the spirit world." This passage might well have been what inspired Littner's horrified letter to Kluger disavowing the book: any religious Jew, not to mention a religious Jew who had survived the Holocaust, would be appalled at the thought of celebrating Christmas. But again, there is no doubt that the character that emerges as a result is more complex, more human for his imperfections.

In light of the allegations that Zachau, Grübler, and others have made against Koeppen, it should be pointed out that there are certain adjustments to Littner's text of which he is *not* guilty. He did not, as has been frequently and predictably claimed, portray the Germans with greater sympathy than Littner had. As evidence for this Zachau cites Koeppen's addition of "praise" of the first commandant in Zbaracz: "How desirable it would be if all German masters were like this one. We would race through the countryside and give up our last belongings." These lines are extremely misleading out of context. Here is a more complete version of the passage, in my translation:

The local commandant is a man who concerns himself with nothing, for better or for worse. He sits in his slippers in his requisitioned house and eats roasted duck. How we wish that all German masters were like this one! We would rush about all over the countryside, selling and trading our last possessions to provide them with ducks on which to satisfy all their lust for cruelty, their cannibalistic longing for human flesh, as the song goes: "When Jewish blood streams from the knife."

Clearly the reason Koeppen's narrator wishes that "all German masters were like this one" has nothing to do with any positive personal attributes that the commandant possesses, even in Koeppen's version. (The detail of the ducks, incidentally, appears to be Koeppen's invention.) The point is that it is a rare good fortune to have a commandant who is more interested in eating ducks than in killing Jews. Certainly the other details that Koeppen has added—the Germans' "cannibalistic longing for human flesh," the gruesome line of the song that he cites—cannot be perceived as in any way constituting "praise" of the German commandant, as Zachau would have it.

Moreover, the claim that Koeppen "displays a tendency to emphasize the role of 'good Germans'" seems truly bizarre in light of one of the most surprising elements of Littner's text: his close relationship with his business partner Christine (Christa in Koeppen's version), whom he praises, often effusively, at every possible opportunity. Repeatedly Littner calls Christine "this good spirit," "this faithful soul," and "our Munich angel," among other endearments. Just a few sentences after Littner laments the deaths of his son and daughter-in-law, he mentions that Christine has just sent him the news of the death of her mother, and writes, "Her pain was also mine." So close were the two that just a short time after suffering his own tragic loss, Littner was able to sympathize with hers. He also details Christine's efforts to help him: her gifts of money and food, her extremely risky visit to the ghetto, her collaboration on his behalf with a sympathetic local doctor, and her continual bribes to the man in whose cellar he is hiding. The memoir ends with Littner's reunion with Christine after the war: "We had reached our goal: to shake, in eternal grati-tude, the hand of the noble person who had saved our lives. Without Chris-tine we would certainly not be alive today! May God reward Christine for everything, which we certainly cannot do ourselves." Koeppen not only short-ens the character's name to Christa, he also downgrades her role in Littner's survival and omits the closing encomium to her: in his version they do not meet again. The novel ends, rather, with those lines that would so distress the German critics: "Only God can judge that which is entirely lacking in human-ity, and may he judge mercifully, even when human compassion would be too much to ask for."

In fact, the appearance of Littner's original manuscript actually had the effect of exonerating Koeppen of one of the more damning claims that the German press had leveled against him: that the work's conclusion was unbe-lievably and unforgivably exculpatory. In fact, the same sentiment appeared nearly verbatim in a postscript that Littner appended to his testimony. Koep-pen's alterations went far, but not that far.

It is worth remembering that Koeppen never presented his book as anything other than a novel—an imaginative adaptation drawing from real-life events. In contrast, Kurt Grübler goes out of his way to convince the reader of the authenticity of *Journey through the Night,* his translation of Jakob Littner's original manuscript. The book's subtitle is "Jakob Littner's Holocaust Memoir." The jacket copy states that the contents are Littner's "own true story, appear-ing for the first time in any language, with additional family and historical material provided by a younger relative." Zachau's foreword summarizing the book's history is intended to validate Grübler's version. He notes that Grübler added information from his interviews with Littner's stepson and daughter, but emphasizes that Grübler, like any careful scholar, took pains to distinguish this extraneous material by setting it in italics and within brackets. (Remember that Grübler is an amateur historian and not a trained scholar.) Yet when *Journey through the Night* is compared with the original German manuscript (the title of which, of course, is *Mein Weg durch die Nacht*—My journey through the night), a number of discrepancies become apparent.

Grübler substantially shortened Littner's original text, deleting sentences and entire scenes. No ellipses or other markings appear in the English version to indicate that such cuts have been made. Instead, the lines that fall before and after the deletions are simply slapped together, which gives the text a choppy, disconnected feel. (In an interview with the *Frankfurter Allgemeine Zeitung*, Grübler acknowledged that about one-third of the text had been cut at the behest of the publishers, who he claims were more interested in Littner's life story than in his experiences in Zbaracz.) In addition, Grübler often condenses Littner's language, and he cuts significant details that help the reader visualize the scene. Grübler's version of Littner's story, in addition to rendering the text less readable, is at times actually misleading.

Consider, for example, the passage that describes Littner's departure from Munich. Here is Littner:

On March 1, 1939, I finally left Munich with ten marks in my bag (I was not permitted to take any more with me) and a suitcase of clothing and linen.

Farewell to Munich! For me this was farewell not only to the beautiful city, but also to the people whom over the course of some twenty-six years had been important to me. I knew that our separation hurt them no less than it hurt me; I was certain that despite all the acts of discrimination that I had to suffer, they stuck by me and abhorred such acts of violence. But what can that mean in a "totalitarian state"! The fact that I also had to leave behind Christine and her family was particularly painful for me.

Though my papers were entirely in order, I was harassed at the border by an SS inspection. But this last humiliation, too, was quickly endured and I was permitted to cross into a free land. It is impossible even approximately to describe the feeling I had at that moment. What good fortune to be a free person again, with no more torture, never again having to see the symbol of racial hatred. It was as if I could once again breathe easily. What meaning did economic difficulties or other such problems have in view of the fact: I am free!

Having arrived in Prague, at first I stood perplexed in front of the station....

And here is Grübler:

On March 1, 1939, I left Munich, on a train bound for Prague, with ten Reichsmark in my pocket and a piece of hand luggage filled with spare clothes. Several fellow passengers with Polish passports sought to reach the same destination. At the border several SS officers came to inspect passports. They asked routine questions and after stamping the vital documents returned them to their owners. As soon as the train left the station and crossed over into the still free country, I felt greatly relieved. Upon my arrival in Prague, I stood next to the terminal not knowing where to go.

More than a few details have simply disappeared from Grübler's version—and others have been added. What has happened to the two long and quite moving paragraphs in which Littner laments having to leave his city and yet rejoices in his newfound freedom? In sharp contrast with Grübler's clipped summary, his language is specific, even flowery. Gone are Littner's somewhat complicated thoughts about leaving behind his non-Jewish friends in Munich, and the omnipresent encomium to Christine. In their place have been inserted some apparently counterfactual lines about the presence of other passengers with Polish passports (if there were such passengers, Littner does not mention them) and the ease with which Littner crossed the border (in fact, as we learn from the original manuscript, he suffered a "last humiliation" at the hands of the SS). Although Grübler's English is obviously unidiomatic, this constitutes more than just bad translation.

Grübler's text is least faithful to the original when the events taking place involve the Germans, which, needless to say, is fairly often. Ironically, considering the allegations made against Koeppen, Grübler takes it upon himself to sharpen Littner's often completely neutral language regarding his persecutors. In one instance where the original text reads simply *die Deutschen,* "the Germans," Grübler has rendered it in English as "the butchers." Two pages later, where the original manuscript has *die Behörde,* "the authorities," the English reads "the callous despots." And Grübler's embellishments are not limited to Germans: on the next page, *dem Beamten der Ukrainischen Miliz,* "the Ukrainian militia official," is translated as "the Ukrainian puppet." At another point, where there is no reference in the original to the SS at all, Grübler has added a phrase calling them "malevolent demons."

Even when Grübler is neither adding nor leaving out material, his translations are often so poor as to entirely obscure important details of subtext.

In Littner's description of the SS invasion of Zbaracz, for instance, there is a clear biblical reference that Grübler skips over. "Robbery, murder, violence came over us like a destructive hailstorm," Littner writes. "No Jewish home was spared." This should ring in the ears of anyone who has attended a Passover seder as an ironic reference to the sufferings of the Egyptians, who were tormented by a series of plagues, including hail, and finally by the tenth plague, the slaying of the firstborn. Since the Jews had marked their homes with the blood of the lamb, the angel of death passed them over, but no Egyptian house was spared. These lines have dropped out of Grübler; instead, we have: "A reign of terror commenced afterwards. Initially, several Jewish dwellings were ransacked." He misses another reference to the ten plagues a few pages later.

Grübler's translation suffers from a myriad of careless errors, as well as from its author's evidently loose grasp of English idiom, grammar, and even spelling. Sloppy mistakes such as these, together with the more systematic conceptual problems with this translation, confirm that *Journey through the Night* is no more reliable a representation of Jakob Littner's manuscript than Wolfgang Koeppen's novelization of it. If indeed it is a crime to tamper in any way with a Holocaust memoir, then Grübler is as guilty as Koeppen.

Unfortunately, the people who took it upon themselves to certify *Journey through the Night* as the true, authentic Holocaust memoir of Jakob Littner—Grübler's publisher, Zachau, the journalists who made inaccurate or grandiose statements—were either unable or unwilling to perform the due diligence necessary to justify their own claims. As a result, scholars repeat misinformation stemming from Grübler's book and continue to misrepresent Koeppen's role. In an essay about Holocaust memoirs published in the *Sewanee Review* in 2002, Heinz R. Kuehn writes that Littner's original manuscript "was virtually identical to Koeppen's book and proved his 'novel' to be a falsification." It is not identical, and it "proved" no such thing. Rather, it showed his novel to be a *novelization*—and a well-crafted one, at that—which is exactly what Koeppen always said it was. As we know, Littner himself rejected Koeppen's version as bearing no relation to his own life story. This fact alone should demonstrate that Koeppen was no plagiarist. His literary crime, if it can be called that, was a now-familiar one: the crime of fictionalizing the Holocaust.

I ate from American cans and wrote the story of a German Jew's sufferings. And so it became my story. This extraordinary statement got lost in the hubbub over Jakob Littner's original manuscript, but it is perhaps the key to the entire strange affair. How could Koeppen, a German non-Jew whose "sufferings" during the war were obviously on a different scale than those of his protagonist, feel that Littner's story was his own? As Cynthia Ozick would write a few years later in reference to a controversy over the authorship of a Holocaust memoir by the Ecuadorean Jew Salomón Isacovici—a controversy with many surface similarities to the Koeppen/Littner debacle, but which forces a conclusion that is very different—"How may we regard what appears to be an act of usurpation?" When a narrative of survival is declared to be fiction, Ozick continued, "is the Holocaust being denied? Or is it being affirmed in terms of art?"

What makes these questions so difficult is that the answers rest on the ever-elusive matter of authorial intention. As we saw with regard to Rawicz, Kosinski, Kertész, and Keneally, what makes a work about the Holocaust a novel is not the percentage of its material that can be designated "fact" or "fiction"—which can be determined only by reference to the author's biography and other things outside the book itself, things about which our knowledge is imperfect at best. What matters, rather, is the work's own internal dynamic: its creative ambition, its motivations. As Koeppen himself wrote in his introduction to *The Hothouse,* the "scope" of a novel "lies beyond any connections with individuals, organizations, and events of the present time"; it must have "its own poetic truthfulness." Is a book's reason for being to offer the most effective reportage on an actual event, adhering as closely to the facts as possible, as Keneally does in *Schindler's Ark?* Or does it seek—as those other writers do, and as I believe Koeppen does in *Jakob Littners Aufzeichnungen*—to create an artistically coherent text, one that rises above the specific circumstances of its narrator to present a vision of humanity in extremis? If it does, and does so successfully, there is no danger in another person—writer or reader—laying claim to it as his or her own story. Put another way: if Jakob Littner disavowed Koeppen's text as his own memoir, then how could it *not* be Wolfgang Koeppen's story?

But if Littner *had* claimed Koeppen's ghostwritten version as his own memoir, the questions raised would have to be very different. This is precisely what happened in the case of the book to which Ozick was referring, over which a struggle took place nearly simultaneously with the controversy over *Jakob Littners Aufzeichnungen*. In 1990, *A7393: Hombre de Cenizas* was published by Editorial Diana in Mexico. (The title of the English translation, leaving out the concentration camp number, is *Man of Ashes*.) A blurb on the cover identified it as a "cruel and truthful testimony of the Nazi concentration camps." Readers might have thought it strange that equal prominence on the cover was given to the names of two authors, Salomón Isacovici and Juan Manuel Rodríguez—surely two people cannot bear witness with a single testimony! But the book's content is evidently the memoirs of Isacovici: the protagonist bears his name, and the book tells of his childhood in Sighet, now in Romania (also Wiesel's hometown); his experiences at various concentration camps, including Auschwitz and Jaworzno; and his emigration to Quito after the war and subsequent life in Ecuador.

While it is undisputed that Isacovici provided Rodríguez with a rough draft to edit and polish, the other details of the book's genesis remain unclear. Isacovici's son Ricardo has said that Rodríguez—a former priest who was born in Spain in 1945—worked as Isacovici's amanuensis, taking down his thoughts during long hours of conversation. They had a contract in which Rodríguez agreed to be paid a flat sum per finished page, and in which they are treated as coauthors. In a statement Isacovici made shortly before his death in 1998, he said that he "hired Mr. Rodríguez after [the manuscript] was written, in order to help me with the literary and structural parts of the book." But, he stated plainly, "I, Salomón Isacovici, am the legitimate author of [*Man of Ashes*]. After all, it is my autobiography."

After the book was authorized for English translation by the scholar Dick Gerdes, however, Rodríguez apparently had second thoughts. He retracted his authorization, arguing that his name should appear more prominently on the cover than Isacovici's and protesting against an introduction by Gerdes that mentioned him only in passing. As Ricardo Isacovici put it, "He insist[ed] on being the author and my father a mere prop." More than that, he issued the claim that *Man of Ashes* should be considered a novel—his novel. "Salomón is my novel's protagonist, I am *his* author," he told Ilan Stavans, who first brought the controversy to public attention in the *Forward*. He referred to the process by which he had come to possess Isacovici's life as "transubstantiation"—an extraordinary word, especially coming from a former priest:

> [Salomón] simply wanted me to put his experiences in regular Spanish....I refused on the grounds that I am not a *corrector*, that is, a spell- and style-checker....I asked to borrow the first few pages and in a single night I turned them into part of the first chapter, which came out almost without need of revision. When I showed it to him, Salomón realized the material had potential. We started to work. I wrote the entire work, its title included, in six months, grounding myself in his manuscript and in mutual conversations....I would use my memories in the Iberian

countryside as inspiration. When I would show Salomón the result, he would be amazed at how much I knew about his past. To the point that I invented passages and details and afterward he believed he had lived through them. For him the book is an autobiography; for me it is a charming novel.

No one appears to have believed Rodríguez's claims. Not Stavans, who began his article with the bold statement that "A shameless moral theft has taken place: a Holocaust survivor's voice is being silenced by a Jesuit ex-priest." Isacovici's son Ricardo told Stavans that "everything in [the book] is absolutely true. Not a single iota of it is fiction." Rodríguez had a tendency to "overwrite and fantasize," he says, "but Papa would bring him to his senses, eliminating all embellishments." Isacovici's secretary told the Omaha *World-Herald* that the book, which she helped to transcribe, was Isacovici's "testimony, his auto-biography, and not a novel from the imagination of that person." Daniel Ross, then the director of the University of Nebraska Press—which had contracted the English translation by Gerdes and which Rodríguez was threatening to sue if his demands were not met—told the *World-Herald* that he had "no doubt about…Isacovici being the real author of an authentic autobiography." Despite all this, copies of the book, which had been printed but not yet assem-bled, were held in a warehouse for more than a year and a half on the advice of the press's lawyers, who demanded $25,000 in escrow from Isacovici's heirs as protection against Rodríguez. The book was finally released after the lawyers gained confidence in the strength of the press's case in the event of a lawsuit.

Is one man's "shameless moral theft" another man's legitimate creative license? Why should Koeppen's adaptation of Littner's story be legitimate while Rodríguez's assertions of ownership are not? In both cases, other writers (both of whom happened to be non-Jews) performed editorial adaptation on a survivor's original memoir; Koeppen even went as far as Rodríguez in his claim of authority over Littner's story. But the fundamental difference is that while Koeppen's book is demonstrably a novel, *Man of Ashes* is not. There is no original manuscript, no *Urtext* against which the "novel" can assert its auton-omy. No source material can be brandished as evidence of authentic testimony, because *Man of Ashes* is itself Isacovici's testimony.

The Littner and the Koeppen versions of Littner's story can exist simultane-ously, because they are two different texts: one a memoir, the other a novel—albeit a novel based on a true story. But a single book cannot be simultaneously one man's testimony and another man's novel. To believe Isacovici—as it would seem everybody knowledgeable about the situation does—is to disbelieve Rodríguez. And while *Jakob Littners Aufzeichnungen* reads like a novel—its literary, fragmented style; its psychological and its literary-historical depth— *Man of Ashes* does not. It reads, rather, like a fairly typical Holocaust testimony. It reads, in other words, like *Mein Weg durch die Nacht.* The paradox, of course, is that what makes it persuasive as a memoir also makes it unimpressive as a work of fiction. "As a novel," Stavans wrote, "the volume is predictable and unimaginative; as a memoir, instead, it is not only harrowing but essential." Yes, Rodríguez could possibly have contrived this style in an effort to make his book more believable as a testimony. But it is far more plausible simply to conclude that the book is what it appears to be, and that Isacovici is its rightful author.

And yet, no matter how meritless Rodríguez's claims appear, the doubts they raise cannot be completely dispelled. This has less to do with the content of this particular book than with the inherent qualities of memory itself: its malleability, its susceptibility to suggestion, its inevitable failures. Which of us has not at one point confused a story told by a parent with our own childhood memories, or an action that took place in a dream with waking life? It is not hard to imagine that some of what Rodríguez said might be true—that Isacovici truly might have incorporated some of his collaborator's suggestions into his own memories.

I spoke to Dick Gerdes to confirm some details of the Isacovici/Rodríguez controversy and to hear his perspective on it. I was particularly interested in how the holdup over the book's publication was finally resolved, as none of the press reports I had consulted provided any details. Gerdes initially declined to answer, telling me that he didn't remember many of the particulars of the case, which after all took place about a decade ago. I then recounted some of what I had gleaned from the newspaper accounts. Gerdes's tone changed; he sounded immediately more sure. "Now that you mention that," he said, "I do remember it."

9

The Effect of the Real: W. G. Sebald

Over the years I had puzzled out a good deal in my own mind, but in spite of that, far from becoming clearer, things now appeared to me more incomprehensible than ever. The more images I gathered from the past, I said, the more unlikely it seemed to me that the past had actually happened in this or that way, for nothing about it could be called normal: most of it was absurd, and if not absurd, then appalling.

—from *Vertigo*

After the publication, in 2001, of *Austerlitz,* the novel that solidified his international reputation as one of the most important of all contemporary writers, W. G. Sebald turned to what would become his final completed project. Together with the artist Jan Peter Tripp, his close friend since childhood, he created a book called *Unerzählt* (*Unrecounted*), consisting of thirty-three lithographs by Tripp accompanied by the same number of Sebald's "micropoems." Never more than twenty or so words long, these poems, like haiku or the imagism of Ezra Pound, flash with the lightest lyricism. "Seven years / in a foreign place / and the cock has ceased / to crow." "Blue / grass / seen / through a thin / layer / of frozen / water." "Please send me / the brown overcoat / from the Rhine valley / in which at one time / I used to ramble by night." "Like a dog / Cézanne says / that's how a painter / must see, the eye / fixed & almost / averted." (Around the time of his sudden death, in a car accident in December 2001, Sebald was working on the translation of this book.)

This last poem aptly describes Tripp's lithographs, all of which depict pairs of eyes, often viewed from the side, with one eye deeply in shadow. Even when we see the eyes face-on, their gaze rarely focuses directly on the viewer, but rather seems fixed on a point off the page, somewhere just beyond the world contained in the image. Tripp works in the style often called hyperrealism, in which, as Sebald described it in an essay on the artist, "faithfulness to reality is taken to an almost unimaginable extreme." The wrinkles around the eyes are deeply chiseled; you can count the hairs in the eyebrows that frame them; the irises shine with light reflected from some unseen source. "Everyone looking at a picture of Tripp's is immediately struck by the seemingly unfailing accuracy of the representation," Sebald wrote. "Paradoxically, it is just the stupendous skill that prevents us from seeing his true achievement."

Any reader of Sebald's work knows that this description applies equally well to his own incomparable prose, with its distinctive blend of novel, essay, travel journal, encyclopedia, and dream. Marked by an extraordinary profusion of facts—sketches from Stendhal's diary, notes on the mating practices of herrings, a comprehensive list of the trees to be found in an English garden—the books, nonetheless, are in an essential way fiction, with untruths lurking amid all the dazzling particulars. The black-and-white photographs that Sebald strews throughout all his prose works seem particularly to attest to the "seemingly unfailing accuracy" of his representations, as do the reproductions of train tickets and restaurant receipts that appear to document the narrator's journeys. But starting with *Vertigo,* which combines fictionalized sketches of Kafka and Stendhal with a record (also presumably fictionalized) of the writer's own travels in Italy and Germany, and ending with *Austerlitz,* the story of a Czech boy sent to England via *Kindertransport* in 1939 and brought up under a false identity, all of Sebald's works balance uneasily on the tightrope separating fiction and reality, occasionally shifting to one side or the other, but always finally remaining upright.

Despite the high level of detail in his stories, which helps to convince the reader of their "faithfulness to reality," Sebald was fond of describing his working method as indirect—"the eye / fixed & almost / averted"—and similar to the way in which "a dog runs through a field." As he once said in an interview, "If you look at a dog following the advice of his nose, he traverses a patch of land in a completely unplottable manner. And he invariably finds what he is looking for." Weaving apparently at random from topic to topic, pursuing links that at first seem tenuous but grow to feel inevitable, Sebald himself invariably circles back to the subject that underlies all his works: "the marks of pain," as he wrote in *Austerlitz,* "that trace countless fine lines through history." His characters are all destroyed souls, fractured under the burden of their anguish. There is the tortured Kafka in *Vertigo,* sick and disoriented as he travels through Austria and Italy, tormented by dreams "in which everything was forever splitting and multiplying, over and again, in the most terrifying manner." There is the painter Max Ferber in *The Emigrants,* a Jew sent to England as a child during the war, whose parents were killed by the Nazis: "That tragedy in my youth struck such deep roots within me that it later shot up again, put forth evil flowers, and spread the poisonous canopy over me which has kept me so much in the shade and dark in recent years." There is the Ashbury family in *The Rings of Saturn,* embroidering cloth all day and undoing their work each night, who feel that they "never got used to being on this earth and life is just one great, ongoing incomprehensible blunder." And there is Jacques Austerlitz, whose life journey is driven by a blind and insatiable longing to recapture the childhood memories he has entirely, yet unwillingly, suppressed.

Though coincidence is one of the emblems of Sebald's work, one of its other most conspicuous characteristics cannot be accidental: the fact that so many of his characters are Jewish. Born in the penultimate year of the war in a remote German village, Sebald was shielded from the destruction by virtue of his youth; but even as a child, he says, he "grew up with the feeling that something had been withheld from me—at home, in school, and also by the German writers whose books I read in the hope of being able to find out more about the enormity in the background of my own life." Nearly all his books feature characters whose lives were altered, directly or indirectly, by the war against the Jews—especially the enigmatic narrator of these works, who shares certain characteristics in common with Sebald but is by no means identical to him. Time after time his meandering path leads him back to the Holocaust, though his approach to it is always indirect, as if to suggest, like Appelfeld, that the catastrophe can be glimpsed only in peripheral vision. "I don't think you can focus on the horror of the Holocaust," Sebald said in an interview with the *Guardian.* "It's like the head of the Medusa: you carry it with you in a sack, but if you looked at it you'd be petrified."

In the same interview, Sebald condemned the "obscenity" of literal attempts to re-create events of the Holocaust, as in *Schindler's List,* "where you know the extras who get mown down will be drinking Coca-Cola after the filming." Though one of the central motifs of his work is the permeability of borders—between memory and forgetting, between art and reality, between the living and the dead—there is one border that he will not cross: like Claude

Lanzmann, whose work he admired, he refuses to travel imaginatively into the sites of the persecution, choosing instead to depict places such as the concentration camp Terezín only through textual and visual quotations from other sources. Richard Eder has written that "Sebald stands with Primo Levi as the prime speaker of the Holocaust," but the description misses a crucial distinction. Sebald's concern is not the actual events so much as their aftereffects, which cascade down out of history into the lives of anyone touched even obliquely by the war.

It would be more accurate to think of Sebald as a "post-Holocaust writer," as the scholar Bryan Cheyette has termed him, except that such a phrase implies that there is such a thing as the "post-Holocaust," which Sebald, like Imre Kertész, would likely have adamantly denied. Human existence, as he depicts it, is characterized by the endless repetition of patterns, so that nothing ever truly ends. Even the dead are "ever returning to us," as in the first story from *The Emigrants,* in which Dr. Henry Selwyn, the subject of its portrait, confesses to the narrator his enduring love for the mountain guide Johannes Naegeli, whom he had known as a youth before Naegeli's sudden disappearance in the Alps. Years later, the narrator reads in a newspaper report that Naegeli's body, frozen beneath the surface of the glacier for seventy-two years, has suddenly been "released." "Certain things, as I am increasingly becoming aware, have a way of returning unexpectedly, often after a lengthy absence," he dryly remarks.

The Holocaust is unimaginable, we have frequently been told by writers and critics: Elie Wiesel, George Steiner, Terrence Des Pres. Sebald, too, often suggests that the Holocaust, together with other catastrophes of enormous magnitude, exists in a realm inaccessible to imagination alone, referring to it often as "unspeakable" or beyond human comprehension. Yet for him this is never a cliché, as it has often become in the hands of other writers. As he depicts people who are uncomprehending of their own traumas—"What was it that so darkened our world?" laments one character in *Austerlitz*—the narrator's own struggle is palpable and painful. A. S. Byatt has remarked that Sebald "connects with immense pain, only to say you can't connect; he tries to make you imagine things that he then delicately says are unimaginable." And yet all the while he continues on, representing the moments of suffering as if somehow occluded, reflected in the imperfect vision of those who endured them, and who continue to endure them.

How much of it is true? This question has always dogged writers who make use of their own lives in their fiction, from Jerzy Kosinski to Philip Roth;

but for Sebald it has a special piquancy. His work has often been described as "documentary fiction," in that it springs from the roots of actual documents—postcards, letters, diaries—but blossoms into its own creation, in which the original source might recognize itself, as Sebald once put it, as if "through a dark mirror." Many critics have argued that it makes no difference whether Sebald's stories are mostly factual, mostly fictional, or anywhere in between: the books present themselves as deliberately ambiguous facsimiles of reality, and they should be understood as such. To parse the differences is "tiresome," as Sebald himself remarked of critics' emphasis on the realism in Tripp's work, the focus on which (in his view) obscures the painter's true accomplishment. "It's almost impossible to tell how much of *The Emigrants* is real," Bill Vourvoulias wrote in a review of that book in the *Village Voice*. "At various points the narrative suggests that the percentage could be awfully low, indeed.... It doesn't really matter whether or not these characters and stories are true, for Sebald has done a miraculous job of making their lives ring true."

But I have always had the opposite suspicion: that the percentage of authentic material in these texts could actually be quite high. And this impression is confirmed by various hints that Sebald let drop, particularly his own persistent reluctance to refer to his work as fiction. Speaking to Carole Angier shortly after *The Emigrants* appeared in English (it was published in Germany in 1992, and in England in 1996), he said that the four portrait subjects were "essentially" real: the germ of the book, he said, was a phone call from his mother telling him that a childhood schoolteacher (who appears as the character Paul Bereyter) had committed suicide. He said also that Max Ferber, the painter in the final episode, was based on two people: his landlord in Manchester and a "well-known artist." (That would be Frank Auerbach, who apparently has enough in common with the character modeled upon him that he objected to the painter's original surname, Aurach, as too similar to his own. For the English edition, Sebald changed the character's name to Ferber.) A few years ago, Sebald's widow took me to see the house where they had lived early in their marriage, the setting of the first story of *The Emigrants,* and when I asked her how much of the story had really happened she said, simply, "Everything."

This isn't literally true, of course. Sebald changed both the town's name and the name of his wife, and he told Angier that while Selwyn had described his friendship with a certain Swiss mountain guide, he couldn't recall "the name he'd mentioned, or if he'd mentioned any name at all.... But I did find that article on a train, just when I was starting to write the story. A mountain guide, in the same year, in the same place... It just needed a tiny little rapprochement to make it fit." As the interview with Angier continues, he admits to more and more such "falsifications" (his word), including—to her great surprise—the page supposedly reproduced from his great-uncle Ambrose's diary. "I wrote it," Sebald tells Angier. But he continues: "What matters is all true. The big events—the schoolteacher putting his head on the railway line, for instance— you might think those were made up for dramatic effect. But on the contrary, they are all real. The invention comes in at the level of minor detail most of the time, to provide *l'effet du réel*."

Exactly the same phrase appears in Sebald's essay about Tripp, which he opens with a discussion of trompe l'œil painting, "a manner capable of conjuring forth out of virtually nothing...what is called the '*effet du réel*.'" He continues: "The suspicion of a confidence trick, and a meaningless one, attached to an artistic practice whose effects are randomly applicable—the more so since the rise of photography and the beginnings of modernism connected with that—later extended to the entirety of representational painting." And also to representational literature, he might have added. The rise of modernism and then postmodernism shook the concept of literary realism, and with it the nineteenth-century trope of the omniscient narrator, down to its foundations. Sebald often expressed his dissatisfaction with traditional fiction forms. "W. G. Sebald once said to me, 'I think that fiction writing which does not acknowledge the uncertainty of the narrator himself is a form of imposture which I find very, very difficult to take,'" James Wood writes in *How Fiction Works*. "'If you refer to Jane Austen, you refer to a world where there were set standards of propriety which were accepted by everyone....But I think these certainties have been taken from us by the course of history, and that we do have to acknowledge our own sense of ignorance and insufficiency in these matters and therefore to try and write accordingly.'"

So Sebald's inherently destabilizing writing, like Tripp's paintings, can also be seen as a form of hyperrealism, in which the documentary evidence presented by his texts—particularly the often-ambiguous photographs—simultaneously supports and undermines the works' authority. Sebald's narrator is always excruciatingly aware of the limitations of his knowledge: he sees the events of his books, which consist in large part of the life stories of other people, only in his peripheral vision, with averted gaze. And yet, as with Tripp, it is his skill in representing these characters with "seemingly unfailing accuracy" that often fools his readers into thinking that the illusion is real, as Angier believed of the diary entry. Richard Eder commented that "Sebald invariably uses a narrator whose voice we want to think of as his," that he "flirts with us" by presenting, for example, on the cover of *Austerlitz,* a photograph of a child whom Eder suspects is Sebald himself. (It's not.) Reviewing *Vertigo,* W. S. Di Piero spoke confidently of the book as "a log of Sebald's inner life," yet stumbled over basic facts of its author's biography.

The constant discrepancies between fact and fiction, art and life, induce in the reader his or her own sense of vertigo—the state in which Sebald's narrator, too, continually finds himself as he gazes down at the past from his eyrie in the present. And as Sebald pointed out to Maya Jaggi in the *Guardian,* the German word for vertigo, *Schwindel,* can also mean "swindle." If the illusion of reality in art is a kind of confidence trick, then the act of producing it becomes tantamount to a crime. "What right do you have to write about any of these things?" Sebald asks rhetorically. "Have you been there, and felt these things for yourself?" To focus exclusively on the documentary—to write only of facts—would imply a statement of narrative authority that he finds untenable. But to assert through fiction the complete and perfect knowledge of a character is similarly impossible. And so the only option that remains is for him to enact the uneasy balance between fact and fiction that constitutes his unique way of getting around these problems—"the arrival at the truth on a crooked route," as he put it.

At the beginning of the second story in *The Emigrants,* which tells the life story of the schoolteacher Paul Bereyter, the narrator pulls back to describe his emotions upon learning of the man's suicide. He wanted to write something about Bereyter's life, he said, but any attempts he made to imagine it felt like a kind of "wrongful trespass." Speculation failed to bring him any closer to his subject, "except at best for brief emotional moments of the kind that seemed presumptuous to me." For Sebald, the only way to resolve the moral problem, to create literature that is neither "wrongful" nor "presumptuous," is to ground it in fact: in interviews with people who were close to his subjects, or in the documents they left behind. So the question of the line between fact and fiction in Sebald's work is finally not simply a biographical one. It is also a moral question.

The "Max Ferber" story from *The Emigrants* offers perhaps the best laboratory of Sebald's methods, because it is the only story, so far, for which Sebald's sources have been comprehensively traced. The story begins in 1966 with the narrator's own emigration to England. Shortly after his arrival in Manchester, he meets the painter Max Ferber, a Jew of German origins who becomes his close friend. More than twenty years later, the narrator comes across a newspaper profile of the artist, from which he learns that Ferber's parents were deported from Munich to Riga in 1941 and murdered there. He thinks back on their acquaintance with a sense of shame—"It seemed unforgivable that I should have omitted, or failed, in those Manchester times, to ask Ferber the questions he must surely have expected of me"—and returns at once to Manchester to visit Ferber. The two men talk for days about Ferber's experiences growing up in Germany and as a child refugee, and at the end of it Ferber gives the narrator a package containing photographs and "almost a hundred pages of handwritten memoirs penned by his mother…between 1939 and 1941," which mention nothing about current events but are, rather, a rhapsodic description of her childhood in the rural village of Steinach and, later, in Bad Kissingen. "The memoirs," Sebald writes, "which at points were truly wonderful, had seemed to him like one of those evil German fairy tales in which, once you are under the spell, you have to carry on to the finish, till your heart breaks, with whatever work you have begun—in this case, the remembering, writing and reading. That is why I would rather you took this package, Ferber said."

The next twenty-five pages of the story present what seems to be a reconstruction of these memoirs. Sebald attributes them to Ferber's mother, to whom he has given the name "Luisa Lanzberg," but he retells them in his own words and with his characteristic slippage of narrator, in which third person almost invisibly becomes first person. A passage from the beginning gives a good idea of both the style and this process:

From Bad Kissingen the road to Steinach goes by way of Grossenbrach, Kleinbrach, and Aschach with its castle and Graf Luxburg's brewery. From there it climbs the steep Aschacher Leite, where Lazarus (Luisa writes) always got down from his *calèche* so that the horses would not have so hard a job of it. From the top, the road runs down, along the edge of the wood, to Höhn, where the fields open out and the hills of the Rhön can be seen in the distance. The Saale meadows spread before you, the Windheim woods nestle in a gentle curve, and there are the tip of the church tower and the old castle—Steinach! Now the road crosses the stream and enters the village, up to the square by the inn, then down to the right to the lower part of the village, which Luisa calls her real home. That is where the Lions live, she writes, where we get oil for the lamps.… By way of Federgasse, which (Luisa writes) was always full of geese and which she was afraid to walk down as a child, past Simon Feldhahn's haberdashery and Fröhlich the plumber's house with its green tin shingle cladding, you come to a square shaded by a gigantic chestnut tree. In the house on the other side—before which the square divides into two roads like waves at the bow of a ship, and behind which the Windheim woods rise—I was born and grew up (so the memoir in front of me reads), and there I lived until my sixteenth year, when, in January 1905, we moved to Kissingen.

Now I am standing in the living room once again, writes Luisa. I have walked through the gloomy, stone-flagged hall, have placed my hand cautiously on the handle, as I do almost every morning at that time, I have pushed it down and opened the door, and inside, standing barefoot on the white scrubbed floorboards, I look around in amazement.

Notice how in the first paragraph the narrator is still careful to remind the reader of his source, with notes such as "Luisa writes," "so the memoir in front of me reads," and so forth. But by the second paragraph these attributions disappear; the one in the first sentence will be the last. From here the narrator continues the story in Luisa's voice: "I have walked," "I look around." The lack of quotation marks to denote dialogue or excerpts from other texts has often been remarked upon as a vertigo-inducing feature of Sebald's books, as the reader must occasionally look back to figure out exactly who is speaking. It is also, of course, one of his deceptive verisimilitudes, a verbal trompe l'œil in which the actual speaker is concealed behind a screen of words.

In his interview with Angier, Sebald said he had used a manuscript given to him by the aunt of "Max Ferber" as a model for the Luisa Lanzberg memoir. Through a virtually Sebaldian chain of coincidences, abetted by thorough detective work, the German critic Klaus Gasseleder came upon the memoirs of Julius Frank, a Jew from Steinach who later emigrated to New York, and realized that he must have been the model for Leo Lanzberg, Luisa's twin brother: his birth year, his twin sister Paula, and some other biographical details about his early childhood all coincide. (There were also three other siblings—Thea, Nathan, and Irma—whom Sebald omits from his narrative.) Researching the family's history in Bad Kissingen, Gasseleder discovered documents pertaining to the sale of the "Lanzberg Villa" (actually the Frank villa) that match the way Sebald described it, as well as the record of a cattle- and horse-trader named Lazarus Frank, the children's father, who appears in the text as Lazarus Lanzberg. Then he followed the "idiosyncratic directions" from Sebald's story to the Jewish cemetery ("proceed southwards in a straight line from the town hall for a thousand paces") and discovered there the Frank family grave: Lazarus's place of death is given as Theresienstadt (Terezín), 1942, while Paula and her husband Fritz (presumably for reasons of discretion, Gasseleder gives their true last name only as "J.") "were deported in November 1941 and perished," just as Sebald writes. From there he was able to track down Peter J., an "octogenarian from Manchester" who must have been Sebald's landlord. Finally Thea's daughter—the niece of Paula and Julius—showed Gasseleder a copy of memoirs written by her mother, which prove to be obviously Sebald's source.

As Gasseleder shows, certain passages from the Luisa memoir, particularly those describing life in the village, are taken nearly verbatim from the original. He jokes that nothing reveals a plagiarist better than his mistakes, and this proves true also of Sebald, who, following Thea, listed the villages between Bad Kissingen and Steinach in the wrong order; later, he repeats Thea's report of a total eclipse of the sun, which astronomical records show (Gasseleder writes) to have been actually an annular eclipse. But hardly a sentence goes by in which Sebald does not make an alteration, large or small—from changing a letter in the name of a town to making Leo/Julius a scholar of modern, rather than ancient, languages. He removed family jokes and other elements that give the text a cheerful air, emphasizing the melancholy aura of an unrecoverable idyll. Often he elaborates where the original is reticent: Thea describes a neighbor simply as "industrious," while in Sebald she becomes "terribly busy...always hard at work, even on Sundays....We even saw [her] up on the roof once, fixing the weather vane, and we watched with bated breath, expecting her to fall off at any moment and land on the balcony with every bone in her body broken." And as the text progresses and Luisa gets older, the story diverges more and more from the memoir, which ends in 1916. Thus it contains nothing of the most distinctive part of Sebald's story: Luisa's two lovers, the blind war veteran Friedrich and her eventual husband, Fritz J. (Of Luisa's passionate engagement to a French-horn player there is also no trace in the original text, though Thea does report that Paula had many admirers and struck up a particular "friendship" with a violist.)

But the most significant change has to do with the story's authorship. The actual memoir was written by Thea—Paula and Julius's sister—who survived the war; the older twins, Paula (Luisa) and Julius (Leo), the ones who were deported and killed, appear in it only sporadically. And Thea wrote the memoir years later—not "between 1939 and 1941," as a last offering before deportation. But in Sebald's story, Thea does not exist; it is Luisa (Paula) who writes the memoir about herself and her brother. Gasseleder, noting that "Sebald named the *usurpation of another person's life*—a problem for almost every narrative with a biographical background—as the basis for his oft-mentioned scruples in his writing," asks whether it matters that "Sebald's model is not the report of a murdered Jew, as it is claimed to be in *The Emigrants,* but rather the report of one who survived," but declines to answer the question. No matter how scrupulous Sebald is about his dates and place names, the key switch from Thea to Paula inescapably has the effect of wiping out one of them. Is it the survivor who is erased, because her memoir is attributed to the victim? Or is it the victim, since the text conflates her autobiography with that of the survivor? A living Jew takes the place of a dead Jew; or a dead Jew takes the place of the living. The boundary between the two, as always, is porous.

"Seen from the outside, some stories have more truth than others, but the truth value of the story does not depend on its actual truth content," Sebald told one of his interviewers. "The truth value depends on how it is framed and phrased. If a story is aesthetically right, then it is probably also morally right. You cannot really translate one to one from reality. If you try to do that, in order to get at a truth value through writing, you have to falsify and lie. And that is one of the moral quandaries of the whole business."

"*À quoi bon la littérature?*"—What good is literature?—Sebald asked in one of the last public speeches he was to give, delivered on the occasion of the opening of a new Literaturhaus in Stuttgart. He offered an idiosyncratic answer: "There are many forms of writing; only in literature, however, can there be an attempt at restitution over and above the mere recital of facts, and over and above scholarship." By preserving the "memory of those to whom the greatest injustice was done," he said, the writer can restore to them something of what was stolen.

It may not matter which of the ticket stubs and visiting cards Sebald reproduces are actual souvenirs or artificial constructions, which anecdotes are drawn directly from the memoir of Thea Frank and which are invented. But it *is* important to know, as he told Carole Angier, that "what matters is all true." Sebald's fictional project cannot be properly understood without the knowledge that the characters at the center of these stories actually existed—at least in some form. Because for Sebald, the purpose of literature is the excavation of a secret history, of stories covered up by myths or taboos but trackable in documents, buildings, people. The storyteller becomes a kind of detective, who must return to the scene of the crime to discover the traces of personal history in the landscape or in a random photograph, and then retell them in his own words. As Andreas Huyssen has written, Sebald's aim was "to compensate for an undeniable German deficit of memory and experience by practicing a kind of narrative mimesis of the victims of Nazism."

It seems significant that Sebald used in both the body and the title of his speech the word *Restitution*—the text appears in his book *Campo Santo* as "Ein Versuch zur Restitution," An attempt at restitution. The German word, like its English cognate, encompasses multiple meanings, including the restoration of art (which often involves cleaning off the layers of dust left by the passage of time) and the return of anything to its rightful owner. But it also has a specific legal meaning: the restoration of not only property but also of a person's legal status, taken away in violation of international law. In the context of the Nazi era, *Restitution* generally refers to the return of cultural goods that were taken from the Jews as part of their persecution. (At the end of the war, five million cultural artifacts were discovered in German territory. That number does not include the many famous paintings and other works of art that simply "disappeared" and have still not been located.)

What does literary restitution involve? If fiction inescapably takes something away, then what does it return—"over and above the mere recital of facts, over and above scholarship"—to the Jews and other victims of history who appear in Sebald's work? This question, which goes far beyond the word-for-word parsing of one text against another, speaks to the heart of Sebald's project. And the answer, I think, lies in the power of the "narrative mimesis" that Huyssen locates in Sebald's writing. In short, the writer restores them to life— although in somewhat different form.

The experiences that serve best to characterize Luisa Lanzberg, which are all deviations from the life of either Thea or Paula, are her three successive tragedies in love. It is these tragedies—not her eventual deportation and murder, about which, for obvious reasons, the text is necessarily silent—that link her to the rest of Sebald's secret sufferers and offer her admission into their melancholic community. The first is Luisa's engagement to Fritz Waldhof, the French-horn player, whom she meets on a beautiful summer day after a zeppelin ominously passes above, casting a huge shadow. We know this story is fictional not only because Thea identifies Paula's admirer as a violist, but also from the evidence to be found in the text: it is here that Nabokov, who flits through the stories of *The Emigrants* like a guardian angel of fiction, appears to Luisa. Walking together outside town, she and Fritz encounter "two very refined Russian gentlemen" and "a boy of about ten who had been chasing butterflies." (Angier asked Sebald, somewhat ridiculously, if he had found this in his source. He explained that he had taken an episode from *Speak, Memory* that had reminded him of an excursion to the country in the memoir: "What you need is just a tiny little shift to make it match up. I think that's allowed.") When Fritz asks her to marry him several years later, Nabokov's image appears to Luisa again: "I did not know what to reply, but I nodded, and, though everything else around me blurred, I saw that long-forgotten Russian boy as clearly as anything, leaping about the meadows with his butterfly net; I saw him as a messenger of joy." Alas, World War I begins soon afterwards, and Fritz, called up to serve with the Austrian Musicians' Corps, dies of a freak stroke while playing his horn. "I really cannot say how I went on living," Luisa writes, "or how I got over the terrible pain of parting that tormented me day and night after Fritz's death, or indeed whether I have ever got over it."

Whether I have ever got over it: here is the private suffering that connects Luisa to her fictional nephew Max Ferber ("that tragedy in my youth…which has kept me so much in the shade and dark in recent years"), to Henry Selwyn forever mourning the loss of Naegeli, to Austerlitz with his indefinable melancholy for a childhood erased by World War II—the tragic turn that forever alters the course of a person's life. Luisa goes to work as a nurse, but with each new arrival that reminds her of Fritz, she is "overwhelmed afresh by my tragedy." She imagines that by taking care of these men, she might somehow restore him to life, and she becomes especially close to a blind lieutenant, Friedrich Frohmann, whose eyes remind her of her lover's. The two of them play chess together, Friedrich entirely from memory; "and if his memory did fail him, he resorted to his sense of touch.…His fingers moved across the pieces…with a delicate care that I found devastating." In this beautifully poignant image, memory and touch work perfectly in tandem, with touch sufficing to restore memory—an analogue to the subtle and yet direct way the characters in *The Emigrants* are all "touched" by the image of Nabokov, or indeed the way all of Sebald's stories "touch" each other, temporally or thematically. It recurs again in the final image of Luisa's memoir, which ends with her ice skating on the Theresienwiese in Bad Kissingenwith Fritz Ferber, who will become her husband. "When I think back to those days," she writes, "I see shades of blue everywhere—a single empty space, stretching out in the twilight of late afternoon, crisscrossed by the tracks of ice-skaters long vanished." Here is another metaphor for Sebald's endeavor, the somber cartography in which he maps out in his own works of art the crossing paths, real or imagined, of Stendhal, Kafka, Luisa, and the countless others whose suffering is stenciled there.

In his long poem *After Nature,* Sebald wrote of the painter Matthias Grünewald, whose face "emerges again and again / in his work," displaying "always the same / gentleness, the same burden of grief, / the same irregularity of the eyes, veiled / and sliding sideways down into loneliness." Holbein the Younger, too, depicts him in a painting of a female saint:

These were strangely disguised
instances of resemblance, wrote Fraenger
whose books were burned by the fascists.
Indeed it seemed as though in such works of art
men had revered each other like brothers, and
often made monuments in each other's
image where their paths had crossed.

If there is something discomfiting about the way in which Sebald remakes all these figures into secular saints, venerated for their suffering, there is also something deeply consoling about his vision of art as capable of offering some sort of recompense. Like Holbein disguising Grünewald as a woman and a saint, Sebald's portrayal of Paula/Thea Frank is far from representational, but still it offers a kind of monument in the place where these paths cross.

A monument, of course, is erected as an act of remembrance. Sebald, in his Stuttgart speech, spoke of his desire to preserve "the memory of those to whom the greatest injustice was done." But narrative mimesis is not quite the same thing as remembrance. How, exactly, does it preserve the memory of those who came before to recreate them in fictional form, as someone other than who they were? Sebald spoke, however, of "literature," not of fiction—in that speech and always. He refused to identify even *Austerlitz,* his most novelistic work, as a novel, preferring to call it "a prose text of indefinite form."[1] Huyssen's description of Sebald's work might be the most accurate: he calls it "a unique style of memory narrative, located at the breaking point between documentary and fiction." Huyssen continues: "As a German of the postwar generation, he accepts his responsibility to remember while fully acknowledging the difficulty of such remembering across an abyss of violence and pain."

---

1. To the best of my knowledge, he is on record referring to himself as a novelist only once, in Maya Jaggi's profile in *The Guardian.*

Remembering is more than difficult; it might well be impossible. This might sound like an odd thing to say about a writer whose preoccupation with memory is the deepest of his obsessions, who spoke of "appointments to keep in the past," who has been compared to a Proust with a poisoned madeleine. But in fact Sebald is equally (if not more) interested in the *absence* of memory: the inevitable holes that dot even our most straightforward recollections. In *Vertigo* there is an episode in which the narrator, riding on a bus in Italy, encounters two boys who look exactly like the young Kafka, but his interest in them disturbs their parents, who take him for a pedophile. It is one of the more surreal moments in the book, but "that particular episode actually happened, as it is described," he said in an interview with Joe Cuomo. Even so, he continues, "sometimes one asks oneself later on whether one's made it up or not. And it's not always clear."

The biggest gap in Sebald's memory, of course, concerns the event that took place largely before he was born, which he saw only with his face averted, as it were. "At the end of the war I was just one year old, so I can hardly have any impressions of that period of destruction based on personal experience," he writes in *On the Natural History of Destruction,* his book about the effects of the Allied air war on the German cities. "Yet to this day, when I see photographs or documentary films dating from the war, I feel as if I were its child, so to speak, as if those horrors I did not experience cast a shadow over me, and one from which I shall never entirely emerge." It is the drive to fill in this gap that animates all of Sebald's creative works, starting with his first, the poetry cycle *After Nature.* Here he settles on the day before his father left to serve in Dresden, "of whose beauty his memory, as he / remarks when I question him, / retains no trace." The next night Nuremberg was attacked, and his mother, on her way back to the Allgäu, discovered that she was pregnant. The narrator's life, then, is indelibly intertwined with the last days of the war. But he can retain no memory of it; he was too young.

And yet art alone is no substitute for memory. Elsewhere in *Vertigo,* Sebald traces the adventures of the young Stendhal (then known as Marie Henri Beyle) in Napoleon's army, and comments on the novelist's own difficulty in recollecting them: "At times his view of the past consists of nothing but grey patches, then at others images appear of such extraordinary clarity he feels he can scarce credit them." He finds also that "even when the images supplied by memory are true to life, one can place little confidence in them"—years later Beyle will discover that he had replaced his own mental image of the Italian town Ivrea with that of an engraving. "This being so," Sebald concludes,

"Beyle's advice is not to purchase engravings of fine views and prospects seen on one's travels, since before very long they will displace our memories completely, indeed one might say they destroy them." Art, in other words, is every bit as uncertain as memory, and can even act as its destroyer.

There is one exception, and Sebald describes it in his essay on Jan Peter Tripp, which includes his meticulous observations on a few of Tripp's paintings. In one, the painter has depicted a still life that includes the corner of a painting of a boat, that painting's frame, a miniature portrait of an unidentifiable person, a dried flower, and a page torn out of a diary showing the date May 15 (Tripp's birthday). Sebald interprets this painting as a kind of monument. "Time lost, the pain of remembering and the figure of death have there been assembled in a memorial shrine as quotations from the painter's own life," he writes. And he continues: "Remembrance, after all, in essence is nothing other than a quotation. And the quotation incorporated in a text (or painting) by montage compels us—so Eco writes—to probe our knowledge of other texts and pictures and our knowledge of the world. This, in turn, takes time. By spending it, we enter into time recounted and into the time of culture."

Sebald is discussing a painting; but notice that when he speaks of "the quotation incorporated in a text (or painting)," the painting is an afterthought. What he is truly describing is his own working method: to create a "montage" of unidentified pictures and allusions that will compel the reader to probe—perhaps to exhaust—his or her own knowledge of the world. Through this process, we "enter into time recounted...the time of culture," just as Sebald seeks to situate the characters in his works in the context of literary and cultural history. But like fact and fiction, art and reality, memory and forgetting, the recounted must always exist side by side with the unrecounted—and the unrecountable. As the book's final micropoem tells us: *Unerzählt / bleibt die Geschichte / der abgewandten / Gesichter.* "Unrecounted / remains the story / of the averted / faces."

10

Willing Executioners: Bernhard Schlink

State Attorney Kügler: "Did you investigate who was responsible for the killings?"

Former SS Judge Wiebeck: "Back then that did not interest us. Those were supreme acts beyond justice (*justizfreie Hoheitsakte*)."

—Hermann Langbein, *Der Auschwitz-Prozess,* quoted by Rebecca Wittmann

Near the end of 1995, the year of the fiftieth anniversary of the liberation of the concentration camps and the end of World War II, the *New York Times Magazine* published a long article by Peter Schneider, the German playwright and novelist, titled "The Sins of the Grandfathers." During that year of memorial services and symbolic commemorations, Schneider interviewed roughly three hundred Germans between the ages of fifteen and twenty-two, asking them what they knew about the Holocaust and what that chapter of their country's history meant to them. He found them to be open to his questions and well informed about the events of the war, thanks to a comprehensive school curriculum that often introduces the Holocaust by the fifth or sixth grade. But when it came to the moral implications, they ranged from tone-deaf to entirely oblivious.

One boy, speaking of the memorial site at Ravensbrück, near his home-town, told Schneider, "You know, that oven, where they used to burn 'em—it's cool, it's kind of funny." Another teenager who lived near Sachsenhausen complained that her class had to visit the camp every year: "All this obligatory you-have-to-see-this and you-ought-to-feel-that. I can't deal with it anymore." And a twelfth-grader, when asked what he would think of someone who had participated in a massacre that took place in his hometown just a few days before the war's end, during which concentration-camp prisoners escaping from a bombed train were beaten and shot by residents, replied, "You don't have a right to judge if you're not in the situation yourself. I, today, would say, 'Don't shoot!' But I would not judge someone who acted differently."

Is this what decades of reckoning with the past (the Germans, needless to say, have a word for it, *Vergangenheitsbewältigung*) has produced: a generation that finds itself incapable of differentiating right from wrong, so paralyzed by its perceived obligation to historical context—"You don't have a right to judge if you're not in the situation yourself"—that it cannot condemn even an act of unspeakable brutality that would be wrong in any context? The problem is not unique to Germany: witness the defensiveness and denial that greeted the publication of both *Neighbors: The Destruction of the Jewish Community in Jedwabne, Poland* and *Fear: Anti-Semitism in Poland After Auschwitz*—Jan T. Gross's sobering studies of massacres committed by so-called ordinary Poles during the war and after. But in Germany, of course, the judgment of the perpetrators takes on a more complicated emotional dimension. Schneider, who was born in April 1940, reports that he was "lucky" that his father, a composer and opera conductor who was able to continue practicing his profession during the war years, was "no resistance fighter but a genuine pacifist." (Less lucky was Rolf Mengele, who was just a few years younger than Schneider and attended high school in a town not far from where Schneider grew up.) Schneider recalls that he first became aware of the "crimes against humanity" during the mid-1960s, presumably around the time of the Auschwitz Trial, and that he and his siblings joined the wave of student activism in 1968. "But even then we rebels tried to protect our families," he admits. "We never asked my father the one obvious question: What did you do when, one by one, all those Jewish musicians were taken away forever?"

Bernhard Schlink has made this moral confusion his fictional territory. A professor of constitutional law with a sideline writing mystery novels, he burst onto the global publishing scene in 1995 with *Der Vorleser* (*The Reader*), a surprise best-seller in England and America as well as in Germany.[1] The

1. The German title has a somewhat different connotation that cannot be conveyed in translation: a *Vorleser* is specifically a person who reads aloud.

book ranks among the best-selling German paperbacks of all time, and more than two million copies have sold in the United States alone, fueled by Oprah Winfrey's endorsement and the movie adaptation starring Kate Winslet. *Der Spiegel* counted Schlink's novel as "one of the greatest triumphs of German literature since… *The Tin Drum*."

If Günter Grass's epic was the quintessential novel of the wartime generation, *The Reader* was aimed squarely at the generation Brecht named, in one of his poems, *die Nachgeborenen*—those born after. Written in a style of icy clarity that simultaneously reveals and conceals, the novel tells the story of a German teenager in the decade after the war who falls into an erotic affair with Hanna, a woman twenty years older than he. Years later, as a law student, he meets her again: she is on trial for war crimes committed while she was a guard at a women's concentration camp. It is hard to think of a more perfect dramatization of Germany's conflicted relationship with its past: at once lover and mother, seductive and nurturing and brutal.

Yet the novel's investigation of Nazi guilt is problematic. For Hanna turns out to have been an accidental Nazi, stumbling into the SS as a way of covering up her secret shame, which is that she is illiterate. Although she is guilty of a terrible crime—allowing a group of prisoners to burn to death inside a church—the novel treats her as primarily a victim of circumstance. Does it matter that Hanna merely followed orders rather than instigated the crime? Even if we accept her illiteracy as a metaphor (as we must, since Germany had the highest literacy rate in Europe), is it fair to assert that her sin is primarily ignorance? In the midst of the ceremonies and the public apologies and the discussions of reparations that took place with the post-unification resurgence of the *Vergangenheitsbewältigung* movement, when the Holocaust was once again at the forefront of the German psyche, *The Reader* hinted at very serious ethical questions but did not make an effort to provoke any kind of rigorous thought. Instead, it offered an alternative: a way to feel as though one were therapeutically "working through" the problems of the past while in fact remaining comfortably aloof. Perhaps it is unfair to expect a novel to answer unanswerable questions. But it does have an obligation to attend to the skeletons it removes from the closet rather than stuffing them under the rug.

From the start, *The Reader* presents itself as a parable. The setting is sometime during the 1950s. Michael, the narrator, is ill with hepatitis: *Gelbsucht*, literally "yellow mania," a word as reminiscent of the yellow star of the doomed Jews as of the jaundice associated with the disease. The town where he lives could be anywhere in West Germany, with street names that are the run-of-the-mill equivalents of Main Street or Elm Street. His illness begins in the fall and ends with the coming of spring: "The colder and darker the old year turned, the weaker I became. Not until the new year did things start looking up." He meets Hanna when she discovers him vomiting in the courtyard of her apartment building; she makes him help her clean up the mess and then leads him home. The implications are clear: postwar Germany is sick, and it can begin to heal only through its encounter with the Nazi past.

Michael's relationship with Hanna is steeped in moral quandary from the start. After his recovery, he takes her a bouquet of flowers to thank her, but flees her apartment after she catches him watching her change clothes. Afterward he berates himself for being unable to stop fantasizing about her, while simultaneously devising excuses to see her again. "Did my moral upbringing somehow turn against itself?" he wonders. "If looking at someone with desire was as bad as satisfying the desire…then why not the satisfaction and the act itself?…That is how I rationalized it back then, making my desire an entry in a strange moral accounting, and silencing my bad conscience." Considering Hanna's past—not yet revealed, but heavily implied—these justifications for action against one's better judgment have an ominous tone. And so does Michael's explanation for finally going to see her again: "I don't mean to say that thinking and reaching decisions have no influence on behavior. But behavior does not merely enact whatever has already been thought through and decided. It has its own sources."

Does intending to commit a crime make a person as guilty as actually committing it? Of course, this is a moral and theological problem that has persisted for centuries. Most of us would say no: we no longer believe—as, for example, Augustine, following the Gospels, once did—that the fantasy of a sin such as adultery is equivalent to the act. But conversely, does committing a crime without personally desiring to do so—the "just following orders" explanation—mitigate a person's guilt? On this question, one of the most crucial in assessing how we distribute the responsibility for the crimes of the Holocaust, The Reader is disturbingly hazy.

Much has been made of the erotic nature of Michael and Hanna's relationship—particularly by the Oprah audience, which found the prospect of sex between a fifteen-year-old boy and a thirty-six-year-old woman "unhealthy." (Schlink has mocked this American preoccupation, commenting that "I have never experienced a discussion like this with readers in Germany or France.") But Schlink, layering on the symbolism, repeatedly associates Hanna with the maternal. Before Michael and Hanna have sex for the first time, she greets him from the bath—an accident in the coal cellar left him covered in black dust, and she sent him to the tub—with an outstretched towel and dries him. Throughout the narrative Michael makes reference to the twenty-one-year gap between their ages, noting again and again that "she could be my mother." References to milk and to milkiness also are scattered throughout the novel. And then there is the central motif of reading aloud, typically an activity in which parents engage with their children, though *The Reader* reverses the roles (Hanna asks Michael to read novels aloud to her as a precursor to sex). Germans will easily make the connection with *Germany, Pale Mother,* a critically acclaimed film made in 1980 that dealt graphically and hauntingly with the aftermath of the war, taking its title from a famous poem by Brecht. The "mother," of course, is the Nazi past, of which Michael, like all Germans of his generation, is a child.

The questions of inheritance and filial obligation become even more explicit in the second part of the novel, in which Michael, now a law student, recognizes Hanna among the concentration camp guards in a trial that his seminar is observing. By now it is the 1960s, and the second wave of inquiries into the Nazi past is just getting under way. "We students in the seminar considered ourselves radical explorers," Michael says. "We all condemned our parents to shame, even if the only charge we could bring was that after 1945 they had tolerated the perpetrators in their midst." That is the classic dilemma of the second generation in Germany, which Peter Schneider and many others have explored: that the "perpetrators" were in many cases one's own parents. (Schneider's novella *Vati* [Papa] imagines an encounter between the adult Rolf Mengele and his father.) Even if, as in Michael's case, one's parents were technically guilty of no crime—Michael's father was fired from his job as a philosophy professor for teaching Spinoza, and spent the war years editing hiking maps—they still fell under the umbrella of collective guilt.

But Hanna, it turns out, is guilty of a heinous crime. With a few other guards, she led a group of several hundred women prisoners on a death march, and on the way the prisoners were permitted to take shelter in a church for the night. The church caught fire in a bombing raid, and the guards, who had remained outside, allowed the prisoners to burn to death rather than unlock the doors and risk their escape. Hanna conducts herself oddly in the courtroom, appearing to have no knowledge of normal procedure and speaking more candidly than she should, and the lawyers for the other defendants take advantage of her weakness to portray her as the ringleader. Finally the judge demands that Hanna give a handwriting sample so that the court can determine whether it was she who wrote a report about the incident. Rather than do so, she confesses to writing the report and receives a life sentence.

Suddenly Michael realizes that Hanna is covering up the fact that she can neither read nor write—and more: that her need to conceal her illiteracy has guided her steps throughout her life. For she joined the SS only after being offered a promotion from her factory job to a position in which she would be unable to hide her illiteracy. The SS had been recruiting at her factory at the time, and so she signed up. The same situation repeated itself during her affair with Michael: the streetcar company offered her a promotion, and to avoid being found out, she abruptly left town without saying goodbye, wounding him forever.

"Why," Michael wonders, would Hanna "opt for the horrible exposure as a criminal over the harmless exposure as an illiterate?" With its attempts to answer this question, which constitutes the moral center of *The Reader,* the novel falters in such a way that it cannot recover. The problem is not only that it is quite implausible that anyone would prefer to be exposed as a Nazi rather than as an illiterate. It is also that Michael views Hanna's unusual career trajectory—the fact that, owing to her illiteracy, she made truly terrible life decisions—as exonerating. "No, Hanna had not decided in favor of crime. She had decided against a promotion at Siemens, and fell into a job as a guard." But this is a ludicrous distinction. Michael has already acknowledged the truism that to decide against something is, practically speaking, as good as deciding for its alternative. And what about the people of his parents' generation whom he has already criticized for "tolerating the perpetrators in their midst"? One could easily argue that they simply happened to live next door to Nazi Party members—that they just "fell into" their circumstances as well.

If we accept Michael's assessment of Hanna's accidental Nazism, we have to choose between two explanations. Either she is the tender exception to the usual brutishness—the book seems to support this interpretation, since the other defendants are represented as crude and harsh—and so she is not really a Nazi, and so Michael's love for her does not really present that much of a problem. Or perhaps others—many others—were, like her, victims of circumstance; and they, too, were motivated by convenience and the need for employment, not by ideology. Is it fair, then, or is it even possible, to punish those who regarded the SS as simply a line of work?

Schlink offers no guidance out of this morass, and perhaps there is none. "The pain I went through because of my love for Hanna was, in a way, the fate of my generation, a German fate.... I was guilty of having loved a criminal," Michael continues, thus implicating the entire second generation in Germany—for who among them is not "guilty" of having loved a parent or friend or relative or lover who was either a Nazi or a Nazi sympathizer? But this, too, is wrong. One can love a criminal without also taking on the responsibility for his or her crime. Is the mother of a convicted murderer who pleads for mercy for her son then guilty? One assumes a measure of guilt only by abetting a crime, or by supporting the criminal in its conception or its execution. The second generation certainly has a responsibility to try to understand the crimes of its parents, but it is not guilty of them. These are distinctions, however, that Schlink will not make.

What may be the most disturbing thing about *The Reader* is that Michael seems to believe that by learning to read, as she does in prison, Hanna takes an important step toward repentance for her crimes. Michael himself plays a major role in this development: he records books on tape and sends them to her, and by following along she teaches herself to read. Michael selects the books carefully—during their affair, he had enjoyed reading her Russian literature, but now he puts Hanna on a strict diet of German classics, starting with Goethe, Fontane, and Heine and progressing up to the mid-twentieth century. He notes the title of each one:

> Taken together, the titles in the notebook testify to a great and fundamental confidence in bourgeois culture. I do not ever remember asking myself whether I should go beyond Kafka, Frisch, Johnson, Bachmann, and Lenz, and read experimental literature, literature in which I did not recognize the story or like any of the characters. To me it was obvious that experimental literature was experimenting with the reader, and Hanna didn't need that and neither did I.

(It's possible that Schlink may not have intended this comment on "experimenting" as an allusion to the Nazi doctors, but the comparison is tasteless nonetheless.)

Yet the evidence of history demonstrates that Michael's "confidence in bourgeois culture" is misplaced. It is well known that Hitler enjoyed Wagner and that Goebbels was a fan of Shakespeare; the "ordinary Germans," as well, had the highest rate of literacy in Europe. In the face of this evidence, only a naïf could have such faith in literacy's inherent goodness, in literature's humanizing power. Cynthia Ozick has concluded for this reason that Schlink's characterization of Hanna is calculated, suspecting that she is "the product, conscious or not, of a desire to divert from the culpability of a normally educated population in a nation famed for *Kultur*." Once Hanna is able to read, she turns systematically to books about the Holocaust, of which she manages to amass a small library—Primo Levi, Elie Wiesel, *Eichmann in Jerusalem,* "books on women in the camps, both prisoners and guards." Michael interprets this as a sign that Hanna has "dealt with it [her past] intensively." And this, again, poses a contradiction. For Michael himself has acknowledged that books can have the effect of distancing us from history:

> Today there are so many books and films that the world of the camps is part of our collective imagination and completes our ordinary everyday one. Our imagination knows its way around in it, and since the television series *Holocaust* and movies like *Sophie's Choice* and especially *Schindler's List,* actually moves in it, not just registering, but supplementing and embellishing it. Back then, the imagination was almost static: the shattering fact of the world of the camps seemed properly beyond its operations. The few images derived from Allied photographs and the testimony of survivors flashed on the mind again and again, until they froze into clichés.

The references to *Sophie's Choice* and *Schindler's List* suggest that Schlink is aware of the thematic thread that connects his novel to those particular precedents. As an illiterate, Hanna is a case even more unusual than those two characters in Holocaust literature most often criticized as "unrepresentative": Schindler (a rare righteous gentile) and Sophie (a Polish Catholic at Auschwitz). Faced with the knowledge of how unlikely a case Hanna's would have been in wartime Germany, we may conclude that her illiteracy, then, is meant to be a symbolic representation of the blindness of the German people to what was happening in their midst. But the metaphor fails. All the evidence shows that in fact the Germans were not blind or ignorant. They were perpetrators, they were bystanders, they were resistance fighters, they were victims of the terrible Allied bombing campaign; but whatever they were, they were not unknowing.

In Germany in the 1950s and 1960s, the question of intent was not an academic one—it played a crucial role in the Nazi trials. Starting in 1963, as the statute of limitations for murder was starting to run out, twenty of the "order followers" from Auschwitz—including administrators, dentists, barracks commanders, medical orderlies, a doctor, a pharmacist, and a "disinfector"—were tried in

Frankfurt. The West German attorney general Fritz Bauer, a Jew who had taken refuge from the Nazis in Scandinavia and then returned to his homeland to seek justice for war crimes, intended to put the entire "Auschwitz complex" on trial. But West Germany prohibited retroactive legislation, which meant that the defendants could not be charged with crimes against humanity, like the Nazis at Nuremberg or Eichmann in Jerusalem. Eichmann had been tried and convicted under the Israeli "Nazi and Nazi Collaborators (Punishment) Law," established in 1950, which was designed to apply retroactively to crimes committed "in an enemy country" during the period of the Nazi regime, specifically including "crimes against the Jewish people," crimes against humanity, and war crimes. There was never any question that Eichmann, as the chief administrator of the Final Solution—the ultimate *Schreibtischtäter,* or "desk murderer"— was guilty of these crimes; Eichmann himself did not dispute the prosecution's account. But he notoriously insisted that he was nonetheless not truly responsible, since he undertook these acts not of his own initiative but at the direction of his superiors—the same defense invoked at the Nuremberg Trials.

The prosecutors in the Frankfurt Auschwitz Trial, by contrast, were stuck with a definition of murder dating from 1871, which required that they prove the individual motivation and initiative of each perpetrator in order to convict him. This definition, as Rebecca Wittmann explains in her excellent book *Beyond Justice: The Auschwitz Trial,* had the unfortunate effect of hindering the prosecution of precisely the "order followers" whom Bauer had targeted. If the perpetrator of murder was the person who willed or intended the crime rather than the person who pulled the trigger or turned on the gas, then the murder of millions in gas chambers had to call for a lighter sentence than the murder of a single person performed under one's own initiative. In a supreme irony, the prosecutors thus implicitly legitimated the Nazi bureaucratization of evil, with the witnesses sometimes forced to validate the "innocence" of "those who did not act brutally or on personal initiative, describing those who murdered reluctantly as, relatively speaking, 'decent men'...and inadvertently diminishing the criminal nature of the camp system itself," Wittmann writes. The shift in attention away from the systematization of Nazi brutality to individual acts of cruelty "consequently implied—again paradoxically—that Nazi orders were 'acceptable' and 'legal.'" One of the defendants, for instance, was accused of carrying out an execution "without a valid death sentence"—as if such an execution in accordance with a death sentence would have been justified. "As a result," Wittmann concludes, "only the most grotesque and shocking of crimes were severely punished, while mass murder conducted through the machinery of genocide, the gas chambers and the crematoriums, receded into the background."

Though her crime was obviously of a different category, Hanna is depicted, in certain peculiar ways, as a kind of Eichmann figure. Eichmann, too, joined the SS not of his own initiative, but at the encouragement of a friend (Ernst Kaltenbrunner, who would later become chief of the *Reichssicherheitshauptamt*, the Chief Office of Reich Security). He claimed that a "misunderstanding" had led him to enter the SD, or Security Service: "I had mistaken the Security Service of the Reichsführer SS for the Reich Security Service...and no one set me right and no one told me anything," Hannah Arendt quotes him as saying. During his trial, Arendt reports, he appeared embarrassed by his lack of skills and education, and tried to conceal these deficiencies. Despite the fact that it hurt his defense, Eichmann (again like Hanna) even claimed to have been responsible for atrocities that he did not commit—perhaps preferring, Arendt suggested, to be executed as a war criminal rather than to live as a nonentity.

Most importantly, as Arendt famously reported, the psychologists who examined Eichmann found him to be "normal," with a "psychological outlook" and attitude toward his family that was "not only normal but most desirable." It was this aspect of his personality that led her to her famous statement about the "banality of evil"; throughout her report, she remains incredulous that this quotidian man—who finally appeared to her more of a clown than a monster—could have been responsible for such extraordinary crimes. And ordinariness, too, is an important element of Schlink's characterization of Hanna, who is, more than anything else, commonplace: she works at an unexceptional job, lives in a typical apartment building, and engages in everyday activities such as cooking and bicycling. The only abnormal thing about her is her inability to read.

But Hanna, we know, is not an Eichmann. The intellectual and moral confusion of *The Reader* comes from the fact that Schlink simultaneously tries to use the defenses from both trials to exonerate a single figure. For if Hanna is an Eichmann, she cannot also be an ordinary order follower. But if we accept the defense that she was an ordinary guard—a "small cog" in the killing machine, in Arendt's words, neither more brutal nor more generous than the majority— then we indirectly validate the entire system. After all, as Arendt wrote, if it "meant no more than giving unquestioning obedience to the Führer's orders, then they had all been small cogs." By this logic, either all the cogs are guilty— which is impossible; or none of them are—which is untenable. If only Hitler himself can bear responsibility for the crimes against the Jews, the machinery of genocide is, in effect, unpunishable: and this is equally impossible.

Over the fifteen-plus years since *The Reader,* Schlink's thinking on these matters has only become more muddled. His most recent book, *Homecoming* (published in the United States in 2008), also probes tantalizingly yet unsatisfyingly into the Nazi past. The novel begins with Peter Debauer's nostalgic reminiscences of the summers he spent as a child at his grandparents' farmhouse in Switzerland. The grandparents are his only connection to his father, who died during the war, and they treat him with an affection that is absent from his rather formal relationship with his mother, welcoming his help with their farm chores and, later, his company in the evenings while they pursue their other line of work: editing a popular-fiction series. The grandparents forbid him to read the books, saying that they have no literary value, but they give him the galleys to use as scrap paper. "Because I was a good boy," Peter says, "I refrained from reading the printed sides of the pages for years." But one day—perhaps feeling rebellious, perhaps just bored—he turns them over and reads the story of a soldier who escapes from a POW camp and returns home to find his wife married to someone else, with a child in her arms and another hiding behind her apron. Because he has already torn out the last pages of the book, he cannot find out how the story ends, and he is inexplicably haunted by it.

Years later, after graduating from law school, Peter moves to a new town to take a job as a legal editor, and discovers while unpacking his boxes that his childhood possessions were wrapped in the galleys of the soldier's story, now out of order and missing even more pages. Piecing them together, he realizes that the story is modeled on *The Odyssey,* that archetypal homecoming narrative. And more: he recognizes the apartment building the soldier comes home to as one by the square in the town where he now lives. After unsuccessfully placing newspaper ads in an attempt to locate the author, he visits the building to interview the current residents. The door is opened by Barbara, an attractive blonde, and they soon become romantically involved. But Barbara is married to a globetrotting journalist, and when he returns home one morning, Peter is summarily dismissed.

Schlink tries his best to paper over the absurdities of the plot. "I later learned," Peter tells us, "to give an ironic account of having tried to reconstruct the end of a story of a man who returns home after a long absence, climbs the stairs, and sees his wife in the doorway standing next to another man and of my having stood next to a woman as her husband climbs the stairs, returning home after a long absence." But this is insufficient rationalization for the long series of coincidences on which this novel awkwardly rests. Are we really meant to believe that, of all the cities in Germany, Peter just happened to move to the one where the story of his childhood obsession takes place, where he finds the pages of that story again among his belongings? Or that he is able to recognize the (fairly nondescript) apartment house from the book, its details faithfully recorded by the author and preserved unchanged over all the years? Just as no reader of *The Reader* could have gotten very far without guessing Hanna's secret, no reader of *Homecoming* will fail to realize by this point that the author of the mysterious novel must be Peter's father, not dead in the war after all but vanished into a life of which his son knows nothing. It is hard to fathom why Schlink, who is said to be a skilled writer of mysteries, crafts his plot so clumsily.

But fine: let us accept that the central secret does not really need to be a secret, and that pleasure can still be taken in the journey even if one already knows its destination. *The Odyssey* is indeed an evocative model for a story about the aftermath of World War II, if not a new one: Primo Levi used it effectively in *The Reawakening,* his memoir about his adventure-laden journey back to Turin from Auschwitz. (In his *New York Times Magazine* article, Peter Schneider, reflecting on his own childhood, remembers that "we talked more about the Trojan War of Homer, which we were studying in the original Greek, than about the war that had just ended.") Peter's journey—too convoluted to describe here, and again pinned to crucial and highly implausible coincidences—eventually leads him to John de Baur (as his father now calls himself), a law professor at Columbia who has written a book called *The Odyssey of Law.* De Baur has founded the school of deconstructionist legal theory (*bauen* is German for "build," so his name itself carries deconstructionist connotations), which takes the notorious relativism of literary deconstruction and applies it to the law: "its goals, its upswings and downswings, what it saw as good and evil, as rational and irrational, as truth or falsehood. All that remained of the odyssey of law were the abstract quantities of justice and injustice and the fact that decisions were constantly to be made." Peter, who argued in his doctoral dissertation for *fiat iustitia, pereat mundus*—"justice be done though the world perish"—recognizes in de Baur's philosophy the ring of the Nazi propaganda that de Baur wrote under a pseudonym during the war. But he is drawn to it anyway. (A possible model for de Baur is the deconstructionist literary critic Paul de Man, who was revealed after his death to have written anti-Semitic articles for a Belgian collaborationist newspaper during the war.)

As in *The Reader,* the ideas driving *Homecoming* are thought provoking, if at times a little wooly. But the novel fails to dramatize them in a believable way: it is all scaffolding, with no structure at its core. There is no shortage of scenarios in which the justice of acts committed during the war could be called into question: the most debated in recent years is the Allied carpet bombing of German cities, which resulted in the deaths of hundreds of thousands of civilians with debatable value to the war effort. But justice in this novel remains largely an abstraction. The book's ideas finally take on some life in the strange final section, in which the moral relativism of the postwar generation ("I would not judge someone who acted differently") is cruelly put to the test. But this episode is a disturbing summation of the problems presented both here and in *The Reader.*

De Baur holds an exclusive retreat for favored students at the end of each term, and Peter is invited. The driver designated to bring the group to a remote hotel in upstate New York gets lost; it begins to snow hard; and when they finally arrive, in the middle of the night, the hotel is deserted and de Baur is nowhere to be found. Unable to turn on the heat, they make do as best they can, but by the next day they begin to grow nervous. Suddenly four men show up and effectively take the group hostage: they use abusive language, order the students to prepare food for them, and threaten them physically. At first the group bands together, but after a few days of this they grow suspicious, paranoid, and desperate. Finally Peter, noticing the video cameras set up in each room, realizes that the men are actors in a game designed by de Baur, who is monitoring the action from a distance. He confronts de Baur by speaking into a hidden camera in his room, asks to be excused, and is released.

This episode is clearly modeled after the notorious Stanford Prison Experiment conducted by psychologist Philip Zimbardo in 1971. Building on the well-known experiments of Stanley Milgram in the 1960s, in which ordinary people obeyed orders to administer what they believed were severe electric shocks to another person sitting nearby, Zimbardo selected a group of normal college students and assigned them randomly to act as either prisoners or guards in a mock prison. After only a few days, the "guards" turned cruel and sadistic, and the "prisoners" began to break down mentally under the stress. Zimbardo terminated what he had intended to be a two-week experiment after six days.

Milgram had begun his own experiments in 1961, soon after the start of the Eichmann trial, intending to investigate people's compulsion to "just follow orders." He had predicted, he wrote in an article in *Harper's* magazine describing his findings, that most subjects would not continue beyond the recipient's first request to be freed, and that "only a pathological fringe of about one in a thousand would administer the highest shock." Instead, as is now well known, he discovered that no matter where the experiments were conducted, regardless of the subjects' education level or social class, at least 60 percent were willing to carry the experiment to its conclusion. (A scientist in Munich, Milgram reports chillingly, found that 85 percent of his subjects complied.) If the choice was left to the subjects, they preferred to deliver what they believed to be were very low or even painless shocks; but if they were ordered to give the highest shocks, the majority of them obeyed. In his *Harper's* article, Milgram drew an explicit connection between his experiment and Arendt's conclusion in *Eichmann in Jerusalem*. "After witnessing hundreds of ordinary persons submit to the authority in our own experiments, I must conclude that Arendt's conception of the banality of evil comes closer to the truth than one might dare imagine," he wrote. A social worker who participated in the experiment was even more direct, reporting that his wife told him afterward, "You can call yourself Eichmann." Asked whether something like the Holocaust could occur here, Milgram answered that "if a system of death camps were set up in the United States of the sort we had seen in Nazi Germany, one would be able to find sufficient personnel for those camps in any medium-sized American town."

Milgram's conclusion is stark: when given orders by an authority figure whom they believe to be legitimate, people will do basically anything. This was duplicated by Zimbardo, who found that his guards, given the vague instruction to control prisoners who resisted their commands, resorted immediately to aggressive and humiliating tactics: they forced the prisoners to strip naked, deprived them of basic comforts such as food and bedding, and put them in solitary confinement. Some of the prisoners began to exhibit "acute stress reactions"; others turned subdued and "zombie-like." Meanwhile, the guards' tactics became ever more sadistic, including hooding the prisoners, forcing them to clean toilet bowls with their bare hands, and humiliating them sexually. When Zimbardo's girlfriend, then a graduate student (she is now a professor of psychology at Berkeley), came to observe the experiment, she was sickened to see "the line of hooded, shuffling, chained prisoners, with guards shouting orders at them." Zimbardo insisted to her that this was "amazing stuff," but she eventually convinced him to end it.

Zimbardo calls himself a "situationist," arguing that good and evil are largely a function of context and societal roles, and that the line between them, "once thought to be impermeable, proved instead to be quite permeable." In a recent book called *The Lucifer Effect: Understanding How Good People Turn Evil*, he revisits the experiment in great detail and extrapolates its conclusions to the crimes at Abu Ghraib, which he believes resulted not from the sadism of a few rogue guards but because the situation in which they found themselves made it nearly inevitable. And Schlink seems to subscribe to this conclusion as well. Hanna, if not exactly innocent, is not exactly guilty, either: the circumstances in which she found herself dictated her actions more than any personal compulsion to do evil. In *Homecoming*, it takes only hours for the group from de Baur's seminar to degenerate into a *Lord of the Flies*–like dystopia. As Milgram concluded, "Even when the destructive effects of their work become patently clear, and they are asked to carry out actions incompatible with fundamental standards of morality, relatively few people have the resources needed to resist authority."

Still, there are those "relatively few." And they might not be as few as they appear. As Cass Sunstein points out in a review of Zimbardo's book in the *New Republic*, there were also some "good guards" in the experiment, who performed their tasks without cruelty and even did favors for the prisoners. Zimbardo recognizes this, differentiating between the "perpetrators of evil" and "passive contributors." But the framework of his experiment cannot account for the presence of goodness; and the difference between the perpetrators and the bystanders seems to be more significant than he—or Schlink—acknowledges. "Different people," Sunstein points out, "have radically different 'thresholds' that must be met before they will be willing to harm others." (This was also evident in Milgram's experiments.) Some people have a dispositional tendency to sadism; others have a dispositional tendency to heroism. But "there is a continuum of thresholds from the sadists to the heroes, or from the devils to the saints." Arendt agreed: "Under conditions of terror most people will comply but some people will not," she wrote, "just as the lesson of the countries to which the Final Solution was proposed is that 'it could happen' in most places but *it did not happen everywhere*." Thus, she concludes, such an argument cannot be used to exonerate Eichmann—nor does it work, as Schlink seems to want it to, for Hanna or de Baur.

At the same time, one has to wonder where all those high-threshold guards were in Nazi Germany. The recent book *Tapping Hitler's Generals* presents transcripts of conversations among captured high-ranking German officers between 1942 and 1945, secretly recorded by British intelligence. These conversations are a surreal mix of defensiveness, rationalization, and true horror at the things that were done. One general, upon hearing that another destroyed the town of Brest completely, cried out, "But that's a war crime!" "Of course!" replies the other. "But I was only following the example of the English, when Nelson burned down the whole of Toulon." Others, however, seem to have known that a line had to be drawn somewhere. In another passage, a son asks his father whether Himmler "hasn't achieved a hell of a lot" in addition to the harm he did. "No, no—one must have a certain amount of humanity and decency, otherwise the pendulum of history swings against you," the father replies. It is a bit dispiriting, however, to discover the limit of his threshold. "One can even go so far as to say that the killing of those million Jews, or however many it was, was necessary in the interests of our people," the father continues. "But to kill the women and children wasn't necessary. That is going too far."

11

Identity Theft: The Second Generation

It was as though Duncan and his kind had all somehow been resettled on Earth from Planet Auschwitz, a universe unknown to astronomers and beyond the sight of telescopes or NASA's curiosity. Often these children of survivors looked and acted very much like everyone else. But in their most private and desperate moments, their eyes would become vacant, their heads shaven, their skin reduced to mere bone wrappings, their cavities suddenly unfilled and goldless. They breathed in the rarefied, choking vapors of an atmosphere known only to their parents. What had killed the survivors had somehow become oxygen for their children.
—Thane Rosenbaum, *Second Hand Smoke*

More than ten years ago, a man calling himself Binjamin Wilkomirski published a book titled *Fragments,* a memoir of his experiences in Majdanek and Auschwitz written as an impressionistic collage of scenes from childhood. The book was initially well received, both in Germany and in the United States, and Wilkomirski became something of a celebrity on the Holocaust circuit. He would appear on stage for readings wearing a tallis-like shawl and perform an adaptation of Max Bruch's "Kol Nidre" on the clarinet. At a meeting in Los Angeles for an organization of child Holocaust survivors, he publicly embraced a woman who, he tearfully claimed, had been a childhood friend of his in the camps.

We now know that Wilkomirski was a fraud. He turned out to be Bruno Grosjean, the Protestant son of a Swiss factory worker, who had been obsessed with the Holocaust for much of his life. In 1972, he saw a poster for a concert by the Polish violinist Wanda Wiłkomirska, and a friend remarked that he could pass for her brother. The idea apparently lodged in Grosjean's mind, and he concocted the story that appeared in *Fragments* "after two decades of psychological labor on the materials of this invented self," in the words of critic Robert Alter.

Wilkomirski was not the first Holocaust fraud, but his name has since become synonymous with the phenomenon. As long as there has been survivor literature, there have been survivor impostors. The most famous (if significantly more ambiguous) case is probably that of Jerzy Kosinski, author of *The Painted Bird,* another supposedly autobiographical book about a child survivor that has long since been revealed to be fictional, and from which Wilkomirski apparently borrowed. As the years have gone by, the frauds have become more outlandish. The past few years saw the discrediting of *Misha: A Memoire [sic] of the Holocaust Years,* in which the author claimed she had walked from Belgium to Ukraine and spent time living with packs of wolves; and *Angel at the Fence,* whose author said he had been saved in Buchenwald by a girl who threw apples to him over the barbed-wire fence, whom he then met years later in New York on a blind date and married. (Both books were recommended by Oprah Winfrey.) But what makes Wilkomirski's story particularly interesting, from a psychological perspective, is that fact and fiction may actually have fused in his mind: he seems to have truly believed that he was a victim of the camps.

Not surprisingly, Holocaust survivors and their families have been among the angriest debunkers of these frauds. In the introduction to *Nothing Makes You Free: Writings by Descendants of Jewish Holocaust Survivors,* Melvin Jules Bukiet, a child of survivors himself, named Wilkomirski as an example of "survivor-wannabeness at its grossest." Writing in the *Jewish Week,* novelist Thane Rosenbaum complained that "Holocaust envy" has become so pervasive that non-Jews fabricate their memoirs and Jews who "fled long before the camps were even built" pass themselves off as "tattooed victims."

Ironically, though, Bukiet and Rosenbaum have been at the forefront of what is surely one of the most disturbing trends in contemporary Jewish literature. Call it Wilkomirski-ism: driven by ambition, guilt, envy, or sheer narcissism, a number of the children of survivors—commonly referred to as "the second generation"—have constructed elaborate literary fictions in which they identify so strongly with the sufferings of their parents as to assert themselves as witnesses to the Holocaust. They do not actually believe that they suffered in the camps, obviously. They are not quite as deluded as Wilkomirski, though some deck themselves out in trappings of pseudo authenticity not unlike Wilkomirski's yarmulke and shawl. But they have convinced themselves, often by means of complicated maneuverings in postmodernism and trauma theory, that they are in some essential way primary in this dark story—that the second generation's "memories" of the Holocaust are as valid as those of the survivors. Bukiet is perhaps the most outrageous case: he writes with deranged pride that he uses the number of his father's concentration camp tattoo as his ATM passcode; when he presented former German chancellor Helmut Kohl with a copy of one of his novels, he signed the number instead of his name. He would gladly use it as his phone number, he says, if the phone company would cooperate. In a story by Lily Brett, one of the writers in Bukiet's anthology, one character says about another: "She said that she sometimes had not been sure that she too hadn't been in Auschwitz. It sounds crazy but I knew what she meant."

It does sound crazy. But in many ways this grotesque solipsism is an inevitable consequence of a movement that seems to have sprung from the psychotherapy craze of the 1970s, which convinced Americans that validation is more important than analysis, sympathy more constructive than critique. There is no denying, of course, that survivors emerged from the war with terrible scars, both physical and psychological. The first organized psychiatric evaluations of survivors were undertaken during the late 1950s, as part of the requirements for the *Wiedergutmachung* (reparation) payments offered by the German government. The journalist Helen Epstein, who began interviewing the children of survivors for an article in the *New York Times Magazine* in 1977 that she eventually expanded into her book *Children of the Holocaust: Conversations with Sons and Daughters of Survivors,* writes that "so many survivors had to be examined...that some individual practitioners had soon compiled more than one thousand case histories. At a time when the Holocaust survivors had dropped out of public sight, this psychiatric material provided the only comprehensive account of survivors as a group." It's hard to remember this now, but during the first decades after the war the survivors had an extremely low public profile. Especially in Israel, there was even a fair amount of hostility towards them: survivors were considered to be not quite right in the head or, worse, even criminal. No doubt they also presented an awkward reminder of a pre-Zionist ethos. Now we tend to emphasize the heroic stories of survival, but then some people—along the lines of Primo Levi's theory that "Only the worst survived"—thought that it was possible to survive the camps only through corruption.

Epstein points out that while we talk about them as a collectivity—"the survivors"—they were a heterogeneous group. They ranged from *shtetl* Jews who had never lived among gentiles to assimilated big-city professionals; they came from every class and level of education; and they had had entirely different experiences during the war. German and Polish Jews might have lived in ghettos or camps for as many as seven years; Hungarian Jews, for less than one. And of course some survivors didn't experience the camps at all, but spent the war in hiding or living under false identities. These widely differing experiences make generalizing about survivors very difficult. As Epstein writes, "Psychiatrists found a bewildering variety of people and problems, scattered throughout the world." Some had been hospitalized for psychiatric treatment; others had milder forms of depression or posttraumatic stress disorder (PTSD); others seemed to have adapted well to normal life but manifested symptoms of suppressed trauma years later. Others showed no ill effects: the psychiatrist in New York who examined Epstein's mother wrote in 1961 that Holocaust survivors as a group had a lower rate of mental illness than New Yorkers. One of his colleagues scoffed that he seemed to be arguing that persecution was good for people's mental health. But what it could mean instead is that those whose mental constitutions were already strong were more likely to survive in the first place. It is the cases of survivor suicide that attract the most attention, as proof that the Holocaust drove survivors insane; but certainly a person with preexisting mental illness stood little chance in the camps.

Despite the diversity of symptoms, in the early 1960s psychiatrist William Niederland established the criteria for what he called "Survivor Syndrome," describing it as characterized by "insomnia, nightmares, personality changes, chronic depressive states, disturbances of memory, anxiety, and psychosomatic ailments." At a conference on "massive psychic trauma" at Wayne State University in 1968, Epstein reports, specialists "reiterated that they were describing a 'clinical' picture of Holocaust survivors, but [their] conclusions came to be ascribed to the whole group." These psychiatrists did not distinguish between survivors of the Holocaust and survivors of other historical traumas: the survivors of Hiroshima and Nagasaki; prisoners of war who came home after being interned in Korea and Vietnam; or the Roma, Armenians, Africans, and others who had escaped slaughter but had been forced to emigrate and start new lives elsewhere. "All these people," Epstein points out, "had developed extraordinary survival skills as well as suffering trauma," which the concept of "Survivor Syndrome," focusing as it did on pathology, did not recognize. Rather, it suggested that the survivors were defective. And this portrait was reinforced in the media and in popular culture, which portrayed survivors "either as saints and martyrs, people who had survived the worst and could do no wrong; or, alternatively, as little more than shells of their former selves, near-criminals who had stooped to inhuman measures in order to prolong their lives." Elie Wiesel wrote in his 1962 novel *The Accident* that "anyone who has seen what they have seen cannot be like the others, cannot laugh, love, pray, bargain, suffer, have fun, or forget.... They aren't normal human beings. A spring snapped inside them from the shock."

Is a child of a manic-depressive more likely to develop manic depression? Yes, because the disease has a genetic component. Is the child of an alcoholic or a drug addict more likely to become addicted? Again yes, for the same reason. But what about the child of someone who suffers from a nonorganic psychiatric disorder such as PTSD? Is it possible to inherit trauma, or somehow to absorb it from the atmosphere? As early as the late 1960s, some psychiatrists were arguing that, with regard to the children of Holocaust survivors, it was. "We now see increasing numbers of children of survivors suffering from problems of depression and inhibition of their own function," psychiatrist Henry Krystal wrote in a book called *Massive Psychic Trauma*. "This is a clear example of social pathology being transmitted to the next generation." Another researcher went even further, writing that "it would almost be easier to believe that [the children], rather than their parents, had suffered the corrupted, searing hell." Epstein echoed this conclusion in the first paragraph of her *Times* magazine article, in which she quotes the director of a psychiatric hospital in Tel Aviv: "The trauma of the Nazi concentration camp is re-experienced in the lives of the children and even the grandchildren of camp survivors. The effects of systematic dehumanization are being transmitted from one generation to the next through severe disturbances in the parent-child relationship."

What kinds of disturbances? An article about the psychiatric consequences to children of survivors published in the *Times* in 1979—by now the term "second generation" had come into use, though some abbreviate it flippantly to "2G"—reported that survivor parents tended alternately to overprotect and overcriticize their children. Some called their offspring "little Hitlers." Epstein's father explodes at his children when they don't finish their dinner: "Do you know what we would have given for a meal like this? Seven hundred calories a day we were given! And we didn't spend the day in school!" A friend who is the child of survivors tells me that when the kitchen was dirty, his father would compare it to the conditions in a concentration camp. One of Epstein's interviewees says that when his mother was angry at him, she would throw up her hands and say: "Did I leave Auschwitz for *you?*" But rather than signs of abuse, these sound more like variations—albeit extreme ones—on the manipulations of which all parents are at times guilty.

The difference is in how such rebukes are perceived by the children—whether they shrug them off or take them as a route to existential conundrums. The latter seems to be more common. Whether they see it as a blessing or a curse, the members of the second generation lay claim to an intimate relationship with the Holocaust, an understanding of it that outsiders cannot achieve. "I feel the Holocaust in a different way from someone who watches a documentary about it or studies it from books," says one of Epstein's interviewees. Bukiet puts it more crassly: "To be shabbily proprietary, we own it. Our parents owned it, and they gave it to us." (Thane Rosenbaum, to his credit, has distanced himself from this position: "The Holocaust is nothing but a black hole to me," he has said.) But while they feel an almost organic connection to the Holocaust, obviously they have no personal recollections of it, and they tend to be hazy on the particulars. Many of Epstein's interviewees confess that they have trouble remembering the details of their parents' stories. "I could never follow [them] all the way through," one says. And in contrast to Bukiet's obsession with his father's tattoo, Epstein writes rather surprisingly that of the hundreds of children of survivors she interviewed, none could remember the numbers in a parent's tattoo or even which arm it was on.

Another paradox comes up frequently among Epstein's subjects. On the one hand, their parents tell them that their presence on earth is nearly miraculous, that it has an almost cosmic significance. "My life was not just another life, I thought often when I was a child, it was an assignation," one child of survivors tells her. " 'Every one of you is a miracle,' my mother would say about children of the people she had known in [the] camp." At the same time, they cannot shake the conviction that the vicissitudes of their own lives are insignificant compared to what their parents went through. Epstein writes that "every story they told was a matter of life and death, of loyalty or betrayal. Nothing that upset me—the fact that my boyfriend had asked another girl to a dance...or that I could not fathom some homework assignment—was important compared to the upsets my parents had known. 'Worse things have happened, you know,' they said, and I saw the war rise like a great tidal wave in the air, dwarfing my trouble, making it trivial." In *After Such Knowledge: Memory, History, and the Legacy of the Holocaust,* her book about the second generation, Eva Hoffman writes of having internalized this attitude. " 'It's not the Holocaust,' I would think in my adolescence as I met with some small but hurtful problem—an awkward social encounter, a summer job interview, a friend's rejection, a rebuke from a teacher." Indeed, such problems are "not the Holocaust," but that does not make them undeserving of sympathy, and one can imagine the sadness of a child who grows up with parents who are unable to empathize with her travails, however minor. Even so, is such behavior actually traumatizing?

"I'm of no comparable stature. I didn't suffer," says one of Epstein's subjects. This feeling of lack can go so far as to impinge on the children's very sense of existence. Another man she interviews reports that he was thrilled when a psychologist he consulted gave him a sheet of typed notes on his personal attributes: his abilities, his ideal profession, and so forth. He stored the piece of paper in a safe deposit box, so crucial to him was this visual, verbal proof of his own identity. Hoffman more trenchantly diagnoses the second generation with what she calls "significance envy." "Envy has been one of the taboos, or at least untouched areas of second-generation experience, perhaps because it is so hard to fit into any credible scheme of human perception," she writes. "For how can you envy someone for having gone through hell? But this, too, has to be acknowledged: that aside from its enormity, the Holocaust had enormousness, and that the enormousness was awe inspiring as well as awful. The sojourn in hell and the drama of survival conferred on these parents a kind of existential grandeur that no ordinary experience could match."

When Epstein first started interviewing children of survivors, many were speaking about their feelings regarding the Holocaust and their parents for the first time. Her stark transcriptions of these conversations reveal the rawness of voices that had not yet assimilated their experiences into smoothly coherent accounts. But the very premise of her investigation—the definition of the children of survivors as "children of the Holocaust"—set the preconditions for the most pernicious aspect of the second-generation phenomenon: the virtual displacement of the survivors by their own descendants through the appropriation of Holocaust narratives.

In the thirty years since Epstein's book was published, the "2Gs" have coalesced into an organized movement, whose members gather at conferences and on Internet forums, and are quoted by reporters seeking appropriately somber comments at Holocaust remembrance ceremonies. Their rise has coincided, not entirely coincidentally, with the saturation of American culture and society with all things Holocaust. The American public's "Holocaust consciousness," as Gary Weissman calls it in *Fantasies of Witnessing*, is usually dated to 1978, when the miniseries *Holocaust* was broadcast on network television. Two years later, Elie Wiesel was already wondering in the *New York Times* "whether a saturation point has been reached" at which "mention of the Holocaust produces only apathy." Anxiety about "Holocaust fatigue" increasingly became a theme in the media during the 1980s and 1990s, even as the public's appetite for the Holocaust raged undiminished: Art Spiegelman's graphic novel *Maus* became a best seller; the United States Holocaust Memorial Museum in Washington, D.C., opened to great acclaim; *Schindler's List* won seven Oscars, including Best Picture. If there were actually such a thing as "Holocaust fatigue," it would have long ago rendered us all comatose.

Amid this profusion of creative work in all genres, Adorno's famous remark that "to write a poem after Auschwitz is barbaric" has become the straw man of Holocaust studies, invoked only to be knocked down; Adorno himself modified his position in the 1960s. Now, more than sixty years after the liberation of the camps, it is rarely suggested that the Holocaust might not always be an appropriate subject for artistic expression. Only the most outrageous instances provoke any sort of outcry, as in the controversy that arose several years ago over an exhibition mounted by the Jewish Museum in New York, in which one artist juxtaposed a swastika with the Prada logo and another digitally inserted an image of himself holding a can of Diet Coke into a photograph of inmates at Buchenwald. By and large, it is a given that the Holocaust is a valid, even important topic for art, even if most would hesitate to call it "the greatest opportunity of our era," as Bukiet does.

But as we know, the voracious cultural hunger for novels, films, plays, and other art about the Holocaust has provoked a backlash from some critics, who worry that any attempt to represent the Holocaust necessarily trivializes it. The antirationalism of this belief is particularly disturbing, since in addition to discouraging art, it essentially prohibits scholarship. More than that, it puts not only the members of the second generation, but anyone who feels it is important to study the Holocaust, in a terrible bind. We who came after—*die Nachgeborenen,* to use Brecht's evocative term—by definition did not experience the Holocaust. Yet we are told by no less a figure than Elie Wiesel that only those who "lived it in their flesh and in their minds" are entitled even to think about it. And so it is no wonder that a common feature among second-generation and other recent texts about the Holocaust is a desire, either repressed or explicit, to somehow witness the Holocaust as if one had been there. This phenomenon is not limited to the children of survivors, but can also be found among people like the critic Gary Weissman, who uses the term "nonwitnesses" to categorize those members of the postwar generation whose familial connection with the Holocaust is faint or nonexistent, but who are nonetheless "deeply interested in studying, remembering, and memorializing it."

In the desire to gain imaginative access to the Holocaust, the zeal of identification can turn to overidentification. Some do this through elaborate, almost legalistic reasoning: "The desire to feel more connected to the Holocaust leads some Jewish Americans to regard *themselves* as Holocaust survivors, their rationale being that 'Hitler meant to kill all Jews,'" Weissman writes. Carolyn J. Dean has written about the way "Jewish memory exemplifies a pathological cultural attachment to having been or being a victim." As a result of the rise of identity politics, she argues, "victimization now confers social recognition." In rare cases, the unconscious need of children of survivors to justify their own sufferings in terms of the Holocaust has manifested itself physically. In her memoir *The War After: Living with the Holocaust,* the British journalist Anne Karpf writes about the disabling eczema that struck her after she became romantically involved with a non-Jew, to which her mother responded that she was "doing what Hitler hadn't managed." She was unable to control her scratching, and her skin became so inflamed that she had to go out entirely covered up. Nevertheless, her parents refused to comment on her condition, which "only served to inflame my rage, because by now I desperately wanted them to acknowledge my distress." Finally a friend pointed out to her that she tended to injure her forearm in the same place as her mother's tattoo. This is Holocaust obsession literally enacted by the body.

Epstein wrote that the children of survivors are "possessed by a history they never lived." As Weissman points out, her language is dated. No one speaks of "history" in this way anymore. Today's buzzword is "memory," in all its forms. While one might have expected the second generation, of all groups, to be painfully aware of the difference between the two, they have led the charge in blurring the line. Hoffman has stated plainly that "It is important to be precise: we who came after do not have memories of the Holocaust." But this distinction has generally been lost. In her influential book *Family Frames,* which was published in 1997 and quickly became a staple of the Holocaust studies curriculum, Marianne Hirsch, also a child of survivors, coined the term "postmemory" to describe her response to her parents' accounts of the war. Though her "experience" of the Holocaust came only via secondary sources such as stories and photographs, she argues that it was for her "no less present, no less vivid, and perhaps because of the constructed and deeply invested nature of memory itself, no less accurate" than her parents.' Hirsch's students have carried her idea much further, creating a "Sorcerer's Apprentice"–style nightmare of multiplying memory typologies, each less coherent and more diluted than the last: "prosthetic memory," "vicarious memory," "memory of the witness's memory," "hypermediated experiences of memory" (this last one being the result of such indirect experiences as viewing photographs or film footage of the Holocaust).

The multiplications of memory are largely dependent upon trauma theory, which began to develop in the 1990s and is still a dominant force in Holocaust studies. This school of psychoanalytic literary criticism, championed by the literary scholars Cathy Caruth, Shoshana Felman, and Elaine Scarry, finds its basis in Freud, who theorized that a traumatic event cannot be assimilated by the psyche when it is first experienced; it must be repeated and reexperienced, insistently and against the victim's will, often in dreams or flashbacks in which the original event returns in its literal form. One can often see this in survivor memoirs or literature, in which the narrative tense can shift suddenly to the present when a moment of extreme trauma is being described, almost as if the writer were reliving it.

The trouble arises when it comes to the audience for such stories. For testimony requires a listener; the person who bears witness speaks, in the words of the poet Paul Celan, in search of "an addressable you." But if the trauma is repeated and reexperienced each time, does the listener experience it as well? This is the argument of psychologist Dori Laub, another leading figure in trauma theory:

> The listener to the narrative of extreme human pain faces a unique situation. While historical evidence to the event which constitutes the trauma may be abundant and documents in vast supply, the trauma—as a known event and not simply as an overwhelming shock—has not been truly witnessed yet, not been taken cognizance of. The emergence of the narrative which is being listened to—and heard—is, therefore, the process and the place wherein the cognizance, the "knowing," of the event is given birth to. The listener, therefore, is a party to the creation of knowledge *de novo*. The testimony to the trauma thus includes its hearer, who is, so to speak, the blank screen on which the event comes to be inscribed for the first time. By extension, the listener to trauma comes to be a participant and a co-owner of the traumatic event: through his very listening, he comes to partially experience trauma in himself. The relation of the victim to the event of the trauma, therefore, impacts on the relation of the listener to

it, and the latter comes to feel the bewilderment, injury, confusion, dread and conflicts that the trauma victim feels.... The listener, therefore, by definition partakes of the struggle of the victim with the memories and residues of his or her traumatic past.

In a therapeutic context, this is basically a definition of the phenomenon of countertransference, in which the therapist's appropriate empathy with his or her patient inappropriately shades into overidentification. Jung described extreme cases in which the therapist literally takes on the suffering of the patient, even his or her psychosis. Obviously a therapist who responds in this way—who also becomes a victim—is unable to meet the patient's needs. In the same way, a listener who assumes the trauma of the witness is unable to meet the witness's needs, because he or she is too preoccupied with his or her own. Bukiet has compared the effect of the Holocaust on Europe to a rock dropped into the center of a pond. This metaphor is unintentionally powerful, since each of these writers, gazing in, sees only his or her own reflection.

In an effort to stake out their place on this rough terrain, some writers of the second generation have appropriated the rhetoric of the survivors—particularly the assertion that the Holocaust is a sacrosanct topic, taboo to anyone but the initiated. The difference is that in their efforts to establish themselves among the initiated, they construct their identity—at least their literary identity—in a way that displaces the actual survivors. "I kept thinking it was time for Elie Wiesel to move over. That there was another generation coming up behind him," says an anonymous child of survivors quoted in Helen Epstein's book. Bukiet goes so far as to question the authority of anyone outside the second generation to write about the Holocaust—even the survivors themselves:

> In the midst of this festive free-for-all, the 2G's occupy a special place. Whatever wisdom others bring to it comes from the heart and head, but for us it's genetic. To be shabbily proprietary, we own it. Our parents owned it, and they gave it to us. Just as John Quincy Adams and Ken Griffey Jr. followed in their parents' footsteps, we go into Shoah business. I'd like to tell everyone from the Bellows and the Ozicks to the Styrons and the Wilkomirskis, "Bug off. Find your own bad news," but no one can legislate artistic imperative, and perhaps no one should.... We have been given an obscene gift, a subject of predetermined value that no one can deny.

It's difficult to say what is most offensive about this passage: that a writer like Bukiet is asserting moral authority over Saul Bellow; that the survivors somehow bequeath their stake in the Holocaust to their descendants; that anybody "owns" anything about the Holocaust. But to be precise, the writers of the second generation do not normally write "about" the Holocaust at all. Their subject, and their inspiration, is their family life. Bukiet is unsure whether members of the second generation were "born writers" or "compelled to write by our proximity to extremity." He gives an example from his family, a story about the liquidation of the Kraków Ghetto that his uncle would tell at the dinner table. Separated into a group of men destined to be shot, his uncle sneaked back into a group of workers. He caught the eye of Amon Goeth, who asked suspiciously where he worked and warned that if he turned out to be lying, he would be hanged. "I'd rather be hung tomorrow than shot today," the uncle decides.

It is a good story. But that's all it is, a story. Or at least that's all the use Bukiet tries to make of it: "Rendering life with people who are capable of saying, 'I'd rather be hung tomorrow than shot today. Pass the salt,' becomes one's most enduring subject." Eva Hoffman wisely cautions against using such material as a crutch. "Writers of the second generation cannot count on the primary power or persuasiveness of their material, on which survivors' memoirs often rely," she remarks, adding that such writers "may end up not so much illuminating the past as turning the searchlight on [their] own narcissism."

Perhaps Hoffman was thinking of some of the writers in *Nothing Makes You Free,* which, on the whole, is as tendentious as its title. (If the appropriation of Auschwitz were not already awful enough, the book's jacket depicts the camp's infamous gate, with the words of the title in place of *Arbeit macht frei.* Could the analogy between the survivors and the second generation be more blatantly asserted?) With their didactic language, clunky dialogue, and transparent metaphors, some of Bukiet's selections sound like rough drafts from an undergraduate fiction-writing workshop. One wonders whether Adorno was right after all: a certain kind of writing about the Holocaust may indeed be barbaric. In one story, the daughter-in-law of a survivor reacts with fury when the elderly woman, left to babysit, shaves her infant granddaughter's head. "Those stories are prehistory by now," she fumes at her husband. "You must realize that your mother is crazy. I told you a long time ago. She lost some screws in her head in the Holocaust." In J. J. Steinfeld's "Dancing at the Club Holocaust," the weirdest story in this extremely weird collection, a man named Reuben has hallucinations—and very stilted conversations with his therapist—about going to a club where neo-Nazis watch German propaganda films and Jewish boys perform sex acts on men dressed up as SS officers. In the end he sets fire to the club, sending it all up in smoke and creating another Holocaust of his own. (Fire, not surprisingly, is a frequent motif in this fiction.)

The kitsch of these stories reveals itself in their usage of details that the writers believe to be authentic but which in fact reveal their ignorance. Yiddish, Polish, or German words intended to give the flavor of the old country are misspelled. Reuben in one deranged moment imagines his mother's tattoo appearing on his own hand—but his mother would have been tattooed on her arm, not her hand. (Perhaps he got somebody's phone number at the Club Holocaust?) In another story, a family invited to a Passover seder enjoys a supposedly "traditional" dinner that includes challah and kreplach—two foods that contain leavening and are thus forbidden on Passover.

No reader can overlook how frequently and stridently these stories assert one overriding theme: that the Holocaust was not simply an event that happened to the previous generation, but something, as one second-generation character puts it, "that *we* went through." To be sure, there is precedent for this in Jewish tradition: when the story of the Jews' liberation from Egypt is told during Passover, listeners are urged to feel that they too were slaves in Egypt who are now free. The Haggadah, the prayer book used at the seder, instructs that "in every generation one must look upon himself as if he personally had come out from Egypt, as the Bible says: 'And thou shalt tell thy son on that day, saying, it is because of that which God did for me when I went forth from Egypt.'" But there is a somewhat complicated theological basis for this that cannot simply be transposed onto the Holocaust. In a literary context, it is simply bad taste.

Thane Rosenbaum's story "Cattle Car Complex," the most blatant example of persecution fantasy in Bukiet's volume, goes the furthest to assert the identity of the second generation's experiences with those of the first. This story is the starting point for Rosenbaum's first book, a collection of linked stories called *Elijah Visible*. Adam Posner, a lawyer working late in his glitzy Manhattan office, has a panic attack when he gets stuck in the elevator—an understandable reaction. But he quickly spirals out of control. "Adam himself knew a little something about tight, confining spaces," Rosenbaum writes ominously. "The legacy that flowed through his veins." When the security guard asks him over the intercom if he is all right, he shouts back: "This is not life—being trapped in a box made for animals!...Why should we be forced to resettle? This is our home." When the repairmen arrive, the irritated guard tells them,

"De guy in de elevator thinks he's in some fuckin' World War Two movie." But when the door opens, Adam emerges literally transformed into a Holocaust victim:

> Light filtered into the car. The stench of amassed filth was evident. It had been a long journey. An unfathomable end.
>
> Adam was sitting on the floor, dressed in soiled rags. Silvery flecks of stubble dappled his bearded face.... As he lifted himself to his feet, he reached for a suitcase stuffed with a life's worth of possessions, held together by leather straps fastened like rope. Grabbing his hat and pressing it on his head, Adam emerged, each step the punctuation of an uncertain sentence. His eyes were wide open as he awaited the pronouncement: right or left, in which line was he required to stand?

Critics more sympathetic than I have viewed this as an attempt at magic realism or a metaphor for "how present the Holocaust is in the lives of the survivors' children"—which, to be sure, it certainly is. But I read it primarily as exactly the sort of second-generation wish-fulfillment drama that Weissman describes—the desire "to witness the Holocaust as if one were there." Rosenbaum has said that "the transformation that is alluded to throughout the story, with [Adam's] cries for help, his warped time frame, his complete incomprehension of reality, finally takes on a physical, material, literal dimension as the elevator door opens." The suggestion of literal transformation is precisely the problem. If Adam's appropriation of the survivor's identity were allowed to remain metaphorical, the story would simply be ponderously unironic. The fact that Rosenbaum intends the transformation to be literal—which he indicates through the shift in perspective, at the end, to the men who witness the opening of the elevator doors—pushes it across the line from homage to appropriation.

Rosenbaum has said that as a matter of principle he does not write about the actual events of the Holocaust—his creative passion is for the aftermath: "I have no claims to the Holocaust as an event, only its generational consequences. Nor do I welcome any suggestion that I am a witness to anything other than my own experience as a child of survivors." But his follow-up to *Elijah Visible,* tastelessly titled *Second Hand Smoke,* determinedly asserts the opposite. Here the protagonist is Duncan, which you don't need to be a Shakespearean to connect to the name Thane. His parents, resettled in America, are a caricature of survivors, pathologically secretive and at once overbearing and belittling of their son. (In a typical comment, his mother refuses to put wine on the baby's tongue to anesthetize him for his circumcision, saying she wants him "to feel it.") Duncan cannot break away from the Holocaust either: it continues to obsess him as an adult, and he works for the Department of Justice tracking down fugitive ex-Nazis.

The novel's prologue has the tone of a manifesto:

He was a child of trauma....He certainly wasn't pleased by the hand dealt to him, the straw that he nervously drew from the lot of random legacies....This wasn't a badge of honor, not the sort of thing that registered—even in his own morbid vision of the world—as a source of personal pride....Without the workings of a will or a bequest, he had received an inheritance that he would have rather done without, the kind of legacy he'd just as soon give back. But it doesn't work that way. What his parents gave him, he couldn't pass off on someone else. He couldn't even explain or understand what it was that he had. Splintered, disembodied memories that once belonged to them were now his alone, as though their two lives couldn't exhaust the outrage. The pain lived on as a family heirloom of unknown origins. What he saw he couldn't exactly identify; what he remembered was not something he actually ever knew. It was all interior—like a prison, like a cage.

Duncan had not been a witness to the Holocaust, only to its aftermath. His testimony was merely secondhand. Yet the staggering reality of the cattle cars, the gas chambers, and the crematoria did not feel remote to him, either....

What to expect from such pedigrees, such misbreeds? Children of smoke and skeletons.

The Holocaust shaped those who were survivors of survivors. Inexorably, cruelly, and unfairly so. The choices and compromises made, the relationships cultivated and broken, the psychic demons and grotesque muses that mockingly interfered with everyday life.

It's conceivable that this novel might be less offensive if it weren't so ridiculously overwritten. In the world of Rosenbaum's fiction, a man can't just wave a fork: he "spear[s] the air, making his point, beating back any rebuttal." Duncan's eyes are "a bloodshot blue, like a wounded sunset." The Jewish Nostra "combined the unusual smell of cigarettes and chicken-fat vapors scaling the walls in search of a diet." This kind of sloppiness and imprecision is one thing when the subject is chicken fat, but it leads Rosenbaum into deeper mistakes. Musing on his mother's illness, Duncan thinks: "Imprisoned and dehumanized in the camps, she was now incontinent and equally disgraced at Mt. Sinai Hospital." Equally disgraced? In the ironic voice of a writer like Philip Roth or even Gary Shteyngart, a line like this might work, but Rosenbaum cannot marshal their wicked humor.

Another, more significant slip is Rosenbaum's reference to the "staggering reality" of the gas chambers and the crematoria, neither of which is something his parents could possibly have remembered themselves, much less passed the memory on to him. A similar substitution of imagination for memory appears in Epstein's interviews, in which some children of survivors confess that images of fake showers figure prominently in their fantasies, despite the fact that—by definition—the memory of the gas chamber could *not* have been passed on to them by their parents. These are tropes, familiar images from the countless ways in which the Holocaust has been represented in books and movies for the past six-ty-plus years. They belong no more to Rosenbaum than they do to anyone else.

To be clear, I do not take issue with the idea that the children of survivors are affected by the experiences of their parents. Obviously they are. My prob-lem is with the literalization of the metaphor: the idea that this is somehow an organic experience, that it comes out of their blood and inevitably shapes everything they do for the rest of their lives. Perhaps in extreme cases this may be true, as with Anne Karpf, the woman with eczema. But if not all survivors suffer from "Survivor Syndrome," then their children can't either. The homo-geneous vision of survivors presented in the works of their children is precisely what Epstein warned about thirty years ago.

Bukiet, a professor of creative writing at Sarah Lawrence College who has served as literary editor of *Tikkun* and on the board of Yad Vashem, is the author of many novels and short stories, most related in some way to the Holocaust. His story "The Library of Moloch," which he selected for his own anthology, describes Dr. Ricardo, the director of a collection of videotaped survivors' testimony (obvi-ously a stand-in for Yale's Fortunoff Video Archive) who treats the tapes as if they were butterflies, obsessed with obtaining "each and every one of the particular species he collects." His interest is pathological, obsessive: his wife wants babies, but "he would not breed. The tapes were his children." As for the survivors them-selves, "the individuals whose lives and memories were condensed onto half-inch tape, wound onto spools, stacked on shelves—the hell with them."

One day Dr. Ricardo is confronted by a survivor who is apparently the first ever to challenge him or make him question his assumptions. "Why do you wish to know?" she asks in response to his request that she tell him about herself. Surprised, he falls back on a platitude: "To prevent such a thing from ever happening again.... Don't you think it is important to remember? Never to forget?" "Did you ever think we might prefer to forget?" she retorts. "We are not survivors, but merely remainders, or the remains. And you are jackals, feasting on the last tasty flesh that sticks to our bones." Dr. Ricardo is unswayed, still convinced that "his register of martyrs hallowed them, and that his recordings of their lives saved them." When the woman warns him that "there is only one sentence for those who tamper with forbidden mysteries," he grows defensive. "Like it or not," he tells his recalcitrant subject, "we are in the archival era. This library does not exist in order to examine experience. Here experience exists in order to be examined." Inevitably, he is punished for his arrogance: after he falls asleep with a cigarette in his hand, it ignites the arm of his chair, which an agitated survivor, unobserved by him, had scratched all the way through to the stuffing. The tapes, and he, are consumed in the flames.

Moloch was the name of a Semitic god who was believed to demand sacrifices by fire, especially of children. Obviously Bukiet means to ask some provocative and disturbing questions about the intensity of our culture's interest in survivor testimony and the uses to which we put it; and in this he succeeds. Can we really demand that they offer "a moral explication of the universe," which the library's goal is said to be? But his tone, which wavers somewhere between satirizing and hectoring, is so off-putting as to alienate the reader. Does Bukiet truly believe that this unsubtle farce should serve as the last word on the Holocaust—that it should draw a line across which Saul Bellow and Cynthia Ozick, much less anybody else, dare not cross?

To be fair, there are some talented and vital writers of the second generation. In his graphic novel *Maus,* Art Spiegelman not only retold his father's wartime story, but also unsparingly examined his own experiences as the child of survivors and the moral implications of using his father's testimony as the subject of his art. (One panel depicts the artist sitting at his drawing table, which is perched atop a pile of corpses; flies buzz around his head.) The novel *Nightfather,* by Carl Friedman—a Dutch woman writer who is largely unknown in America—is a collection of vignettes that shows what it really is like to grow up in a household where the Holocaust is discussed at the dinner table. The narrator is a little girl who badly wants to understand what plagues her father, what causes his depression and fits of temper, but all she knows is that he "has camp," as her mother calls it. At school, the girl's teacher praises her drawing of "a man flying through the air." "He isn't flying, he's hanging," the girl corrects

her. "See, he's dead, his tongue is blue. And these prisoners have to look at him
as punishment. My father is there, too. Here, he's the one with the big ears."

It is hard to convey the peculiar dark humor that sometimes accompanies
the juxtaposition of the Holocaust with the tropes of daily life. (Spiegelman
also has done it well.) Friedman's writing is often simply funny—not melodra-
matic, not self-aggrandizing, not explicitly analytical. In one of the vignettes,
the children clamor for their father to tell them a story, to which he responds
with the familiar tale of how he once stole dog food to eat.

> "That isn't a story," Simon [the girl's brother] grumbles with disappoint-
> ment. "That really happened."
> "Do you want a story then? Okay, have it your way!" says my father.
> "Little Red Riding Hood is walking with her basket through the woods.
> Suddenly a vicious dog jumps out of the *Hundezwinger*. "Hello, Little Red
> Riding Hood, where are you going?" "I'm going to see my grandmother,"
> says Little Red Riding Hood. "She's in the hospital block with typhus."
> "No," says Simon. "That's not how it goes."

So I was astounded to learn that Carl Friedman—who after the success of
Nightfather had gone on to publish several other works of fiction on themes
related to the Holocaust, as well as to become a respected newspaper columnist—was recently unmasked as a fraud. Her real name turned out to be Caro-
lina Klop; she was a non-Jew whose father had served as a political prisoner in
Sachsenhausen. To be sure, she never actually claimed to be Jewish. But critics who read *Nightfather* assumed she was Jewish—perhaps because the father
in the novel has a recognizably Jewish name. Not only did she never correct
them, she played into their hands by often speaking of Jewish subjects in her
interviews and her newspaper columns.

Now, in my opinion this does not discredit *Nightfather*.[1] Rather, it
goes to prove that the second-generation experience is not explicitly Jewish.
While political prisoners often had it easier in the camps, Sachsenhausen was

---

1. It does, however, present a problem for Bukiet, who excerpted the novel in his anthology. He
wrote in the introduction to his book (which, we recall, was subtitled "Writings by Descendants of
Jewish Holocaust Survivors") that while he had not investigated the backgrounds of his contributors, if a "second generation Wilkomirski" was discovered among them, he would delete that section
from future editions and leave blank pages in its place. Through his agent, he declined to respond to
my request for clarification on the case of Carl Friedman.

Sachsenhausen. Helen Epstein realized this in her book, noting that studies of victims of trauma did not differentiate between Holocaust survivors and those who had come through other atrocities. But what is interesting is that Klop herself appears to have found her experience somehow inadequate by virtue of not being Jewish; and so she felt the need to embellish her personal story. (I conjecture; she has given no interviews since the scandal broke.) Her "memory envy" led her to appropriate not the identity of a survivor, but the identity of the Jewish descendants. She appears to be the first second-generation fraud. Paradoxically, her writing feels more direct, more honest, than that of "legitimate" Holocaust descendants such as Bukiet and Rosenbaum.

Hoffman concludes that "the best that we can ask for, as we contemplate the Shoah from our lengthening distance, is that we distinguish authentic from inauthentic response, genuine perception from varieties of bad faith." But how exactly do we distinguish between the authentic and the inauthentic—or, more broadly speaking, ethical appropriation from unethical appropriation? Is it all just a matter of taste? Would the self-portrait with Diet Coke at Buchenwald be more acceptable if it were a more brilliant work of art? And does it matter that, as one rabbi who denounced the exhibition said, "there wasn't any Diet Coke at Buchenwald"? (Is there really any danger, sixty years later, that someone would look at that photograph and come to such a conclusion?) Critics of Holocaust literature have often worried that the fictional representation of the camps can give fodder to Holocaust deniers. While art cannot take on the responsibilities of history, it does have responsibilities of its own.

What is our obligation, as members of the next generations, to the responsible representation of the Holocaust? Or, as Hoffman puts it, "What, then, from our vantage point and moment in time, shall we do about the Holocaust?" Well, there is nothing we can "do" about the Holocaust. But "we"—and by that I mean not only the children and grandchildren of survivors, but also nonwitnesses, post-witnesses, pseudo witnesses, and anyone else who did not experience the greatest catastrophe of the twentieth century—do have an obligation: not only to remember the Holocaust, but also by now, at our vantage point and moment in time, to situate it properly in historical perspective.

If there can be said to be a defining characteristic of the second-generation writers, it is that the Holocaust lies at the very foundation of their consciousness. Their locutions are strikingly similar. "My parents' generation grew up in a world without a Holocaust, but for us there could be no such world," says the Israeli psychoanalyst Dan Bar-On. Or, as Rosenbaum more crudely puts it,

"The world had been reborn with Auschwitz. The Big Bang that doubled as a Second Coming....God spoke; the ovens of Auschwitz swallowed." Hoffman recalls an epiphany she had during a visit to the Holocaust Memorial Museum in Washington. "As I walked through this most daunting of museum exhibitions, and as I entered into its hellish world as into a familiar element, I suddenly thought: but there must also be something outside of this," she writes. "There must be a reality that is not horror, but that is equally foundational. The Holocaust cannot be the norm that defines the world."

The idea that the Holocaust might actually be the "norm that defines the world" is a common, and disturbing, theme in survivor memoirs, where it bespeaks a terrible and perfectly plausible fatalism. Primo Levi offers one of the starkest images of it in *The Reawakening,* in his description of "a dream full of horror" that continues to visit him long after the war's end, in which "everything collapses and disintegrates around me, the scenery, the walls, the people....I am alone in the center of a gray and turbid nothing....I am in the Lager once more, and nothing is true outside the Lager." In survivors, this degree of possession by the Holocaust is tragic—but in their descendants it is shockingly defeatist. The slogan "Arbeit macht frei" was a cruel joke, but the idea that "nothing makes you free" is in its way just as sickening. Like Melvin Jules Bukiet's appropriation of his father's concentration-camp number, or the facsimiles of Auschwitz tattoos that some younger Jews have reportedly had inscribed on their arms, it is worse than fraudulent—it is cheaply perverse.

In her conclusion, Hoffman mentions the Jewish rituals surrounding death, noting that after the dead have been grieved for "fully and deeply," mourning must come to an end. This, as she rightly understands, is a blessing of having been born after the Holocaust: that we are able to see the world both before and beyond it; to understand it as a terrible catastrophe, but not one that marks our daily lives. "How we turn away from the Holocaust matters," she argues, but it matters equally that we do at last turn away. Otherwise, as she discovered, we make of the world our own personal Holocaust museum, a dreadful cabinet of horrors in which the worst evils of the twentieth century are allowed to wreak their private havoc.

Conclusion: The Third Generation

"Touch, taste, sight, smell, hearing…memory. While Gentiles experience and process the world through the traditional senses, and use memory only as a second-order means of interpreting events, for Jews memory is no less primary than the prick of a pin, or its silver glimmer, or the taste of the blood it pulls from the finger. The Jew is pricked by a pin and remembers other pins. It is only by tracing the pinprick back to other pinpricks—when his mother tried to fix his sleeve while his arm was still in it, when his grandfather's fingers fell asleep from stroking his great-grandfather's damp forehead, when Abraham tested the knife point to be sure Isaac would feel no pain—that the Jew is able to know why it hurts.

When a Jew encounters a pin, he asks: *What does it remember like?*"
—Jonathan Safran Foer, *Everything Is Illuminated*

"You want your characters to breathe," the cheerful workshop leader urges, leading a group of twenty or so survivors through a writing exercise designed to help them get started on their memoirs. Begin with specific details, the instructor encourages the would-be autobiographers, and don't worry about getting down all the facts of what happened. But her students are confused by this advice. What could be more important than what happened? One woman tries to read aloud her account of hiding out in the woods with a dog, but she soon puts her paper aside and tells the tale from memory. A man breaks into tears while reading his story of liberation by a Russian soldier: "I threw my arms around him and said, 'Thank you, you saved my life, I am Jewish.' He pushed me away and said, 'Of all the people in the world, I had to save a Jew.'"

This workshop took place at the United States Holocaust Memorial Museum in November 2003, as part of a weekend celebration to mark the museum's tenth anniversary. Around two thousand survivors, accompanied by nearly five thousand friends and family members, came to Washington to join in the museum's Tribute to Holocaust Survivors, billed as a "reunion of a special family." I joined them, as a journalist but also as a not-entirely-impartial observer: I count myself a member of this family. My grandparents, originally from Poland, are survivors, and my mother was born in a displaced-persons camp in Germany shortly after the war. Like all families, this "special family" has its customs and secrets, its taboos and private jokes. The moderator of one panel I attended, apologizing for running out of time for questions, invited anyone with a "burning issue" to approach him afterward. Then he grimaced in embarrassment: "Did I really say that?" The laughter was forgiving.

Most of the events that weekend were carefully designed to keep the survivors in the foreground. A banquet tent behind the museum was transformed into a "Survivor Village," with people gathering for lunch in clusters around tables marked "Kindertransports," "Bessarabia," "Ravensbrück." A bulletin board quickly became a collage of notes handwritten in black marker on index cards, many with the idiosyncratic punctuation and spelling of immigrants still uncomfortable in English: "Does anyone know what happened to a 16 year old boy Moshe Fogel from Munkcs Ghetto and Btyu, Btngy, arrived to Auschwitz May 1944." But palpable, if largely undiscussed, was the fact that this was almost certainly the last such gathering. As the generation of survivors disappears, the question of what role their descendants must play in the years to come takes on a new urgency.

At the tribute weekend, I felt this in an extremely personal way: I was nine months pregnant with my first child. Still struggling to define my own relationship to my grandparents' legacy, a relationship that I hoped might go beyond the usual platitudes ("She will keep the memory of the Holocaust alive," friends of the family would comment upon reading my articles), I also wondered how I would teach my children about the Holocaust. Would they—ought they to—feel a special connection to it, or would it be for them another historical event: geographically remote, barbaric, but with somewhat less personal tragic force than, say, September 11? Would they, like me, someday turn to books to explain it, and, if so, which books would they choose?

You want your characters to breathe. Could there be a more absurd juxtaposition of the demands of literature with the historical exigencies of the Holocaust? The average survivor is no more capable of making his or her characters breathe than of stepping back through time and turning off the gas. And yet this is precisely what a literature about the Holocaust requires, if it is to have any kind of endurance, any hope of creating images and words with lasting power. But to get there we have to overcome our fear that "the telling of beautiful untrue things"—Wilde's classic definition of fiction—is the same as desecration, trespass, lying: a means, even, of Holocaust denial.

It seems somehow perverse to go back to Wilde on this subject, to champion a pure art-for-art's-sake perspective in the one domain where it would seem impossible simply to make art. But the situation Wilde satirized in *The Decay of Lying* is strikingly similar to the recent tendencies in Holocaust literary criticism. Throughout literary history, Wilde argues, even in works that are supposedly biographical or historical, facts have been "either kept in their proper subordinate position, or else entirely excluded on the general ground of dullness." But now, he continues, "everything is changed. Facts are not merely finding a footing-place in history, but they are usurping the domain of Fancy, and have invaded the kingdom of Romance. Their chilling touch is over everything. They are vulgarizing mankind." Wilde overstates, of course, but it is undeniable that in the insistence on adherence to fact in recent memoir—in contrast to the more freewheeling attitudes of earlier autobiographers such as Benvenuto Cellini or Casanova, two of Wilde's models—something important, something literary, has disappeared from view.

Most critics of Holocaust literature have argued that we can't accept, in relation to this subject, a definition of art as complete as Wilde's: "Art takes life as part of her rough material, recreates it, and refashions it in fresh forms, is absolutely indifferent to facts, invents, imagines, dreams, and keeps between herself and reality the impenetrable barrier of beautiful style." Life as the rough material—okay. But indifference to facts? Beautiful style? These are the signal traits that readers of literature about the Holocaust will not abide, the two barriers this literature is never supposed to breach.

And yet this is precisely what the newest generation of writers has been trying to do, to return art to the realm of aesthetics. (I hesitate to call them "Holocaust writers," because although their works do touch on the subject, tangentially or more directly, it is never their main focus. Indeed, this is part of their literary liberation.) The generation to which my contemporaries and I belong is the last generation privileged to learn about the Holocaust from survivors—either from our own family members or from the strangers who were once fixtures at school assemblies or synagogue functions. But we also learned about it from books. As the writers of this generation begin to tell these stories from their own vantage, they have turned Jewish literary tradition inside out. And in doing so, they demonstrate that the stories of the Holocaust remain tellable.

If any work of Holocaust literature could fit Wilde's definition of art, it would be Nathan Englander's short story "The Tumblers," which is to my mind the most brilliant treatment of the Holocaust in contemporary American fiction. (Strangely, this story has been largely overlooked by critics, perhaps because it goes against the main thrust of *For the Relief of Unbearable Urges,* the impressive debut collection in which it appeared, which is mainly concerned with satirizing the mores among the Orthodox Jews of today.) "The Tumblers" riffs on the traditional "Wise Men of Chelm" stories of Jewish folklore, in which Chelm is a town populated by fools known for ridiculous and absurd solutions to problems: for instance, a man avoids disturbing the snow with his footprints by requiring four other men to carry him around on a table. What happens, Englander asks, when the Holocaust comes to Chelm—which was, after all, a real village in eastern Poland? When the world itself is turned upside down, the ridiculousness and absurdity of Chelm transmutes into literary irony.

Forced through the sieve of this dramatically altered perspective, the familiar elements of the Holocaust story—a ghetto established and then liquidated, its residents loaded into trains—have a newly concentrated power. In Englander's version of the Chelm ghetto, the villagers rename the things they have for the things that they lack: potatoes are called "gold," darkness is "freedom," filth is "hope." ("It was only death they could not rename, for they had nothing to put in its place.") By chance or by miracle, some of the villagers are able to sneak away and wind up on a different train, one filled with circus performers. Here they learn about the "feats of magic" currently taking place in Eastern Europe. The trains "go away full—packed so tightly that babies are stuffed in over the heads of the passengers when there's no room for another full grown—and come back empty, as if never before used," a musician tells them. "What trick is performed with the Jews?" one of the men from Chelm asks. "Sleight of hand...a classic illusion," comes the response. "First they are here, and then they are gone." And so the Jews of Chelm decide that they too must become magicians of a sort. "If the good people of Chelm could believe that water was sour cream, if the peasant who woke up that first morning in Mendel's bed and put on Mendel's slippers and padded over to the window could believe, upon throwing back the shutters, that the view he saw had always been his own, then why not pass as acrobats and tumble across the earth until they found a place where they were welcome?"

Jonathan Safran Foer is another contemporary writer who has turned to fantasy to filter the remote, seemingly unprocessable events of family history. In *Everything Is Illuminated,* his sensational debut novel of 2002, a character bearing the novelist's name and demeanor travels to Ukraine in search of a woman named Augustine, who is said to have saved his grandfather's life during the war. What could have easily become a sentimental tale is dramatically altered by Foer's decision about how to tell it: the Ukraine portions of the story are narrated by Alex, a Ukrainian teenager who serves nominally as Foer's translator and gives his account of their trip in a demented, ludicrously thesaurus-inflected English. These chapters alternate with Foer's own magic-realist history of the shtetl Trachimbrod, his grandfather's former home.

The two teenagers (they are accompanied by Alex's grandfather, a taciturn man who turns out, in the story's most sentimental turn, to have his own connection to Jonathan's history) do eventually encounter a woman whom they initially believe to be Augustine. She is a kind of guardian saint of Trachimbrod, the preserver of all the town's memories in a two-room house crammed with clothes, shoes, and boxes bearing odd labels: "Weddings and other celebrations," "Privates: Journals/Diaries/Sketchbooks/Underwear," "Hygiene/Spools/Candles," "Darkness," "Death of the firstborn," "Dust." She tells them the story of Trachimbrod's liquidation, another familiar account of rounding up, torture, desecration, which becomes unfamiliar, remarkably, through the strangeness of its telling, filtered through Alex's alien consciousness. Dropping his bizarre invented dialect, he repeats her words in a process not unlike Lanzmann's in *Shoah:* through repetition, the story regains its force. " 'They made us into lines,' she said. 'They had lists. They were logical.' I translated for the hero as Augustine spoke. 'They burned the synagogue.' 'They burned the synagogue.' 'That was the first thing they did.' 'That was first.' 'Then they made all of the men in lines.' You cannot know how it felt to have to hear these things and then repeat them, because when I repeated them, I felt like I was making them new again."

Critics have expounded on this; there are complicated theories about what Alex feels here, ideas involving trauma theory, and the degree to which the person who listens to a testimony becomes himself a kind of witness, and so on. Foer's novel doesn't take a stand on this, and it doesn't have to. But clearly Alex does express some of his creator's anxiety about how to make such a story new, how to justify its telling again and again and again, at such a late date and by a person whose authority on it is tangential at best. This becomes even clearer later on in the novel, when Alex criticizes Jonathan for asking him to remove certain things from the story. "We are being very nomadic with the truth, yes? The both of us?" he writes in a letter. "Do you think that this is acceptable when we are writing about things that occurred? If your answer is no, then why do you write about Trachimbrod and your grandfather in the manner that you do, and why do you command me to be untruthful? If your answer is yes, then this creates another question, which is if we are to be such nomads with the truth, why do we not make the story more premium than life?...We could even find Augustine, Jonathan, and you could thank her, and Grandfather and I could embrace, and it could be perfect and beautiful, and funny, and usefully sad, as you say." The story, as Foer writes it, is neither perfect nor beautiful, and the bawdy, absurdist style in which he told his fantastic version of the ghetto's history got him in trouble with at least one literal-minded survivor, the writer Henryk Grynberg, who publicly took him to task for writing things that could not possibly have happened. But by now, certainly, a novel about the Holocaust must also be equally about its own telling—something that eschews the demands of a strict adherence to realism.

Michael Chabon, too, has chosen to approach the subject of the Holocaust through a filter of fantasy. In *The Amazing Adventures of Kavalier and Clay,* Joseph Kavalier is a young Czech Jew who takes refuge in New York during the war years and channels his fear for relatives left behind into a cartoon character he calls "the Escapist," a superhero who battles against a Hitler knock-off with greater success than the doomed Czechs. Chabon's novella *The Final Solution* told the story of another boy refugee, this time in the guise of a Sherlock Holmes tale. And in *The Yiddish Policemen's Union,* Chabon went a step further by creating an imagined historical scenario in which the Holocaust never happened. According to this alternate history, the Federal District of Sitka was established on the Alaskan peninsula as a temporary refuge for the Jews of Europe, which turned permanent after the newly created state of Israel was destroyed in 1948. In Chabon's counterfactual telling, two million Jews were still killed by Hitler, but the rest made it to Sitka, "Tel Aviv on the Tundra," where, by the start of Chabon's novel around fifty years later, they are speaking a crazy argot of American-inflected Yiddish, feuding with the Tlingits over land, and eating at cafeterias with names like the Polar-Shtern.

The Holocaust is at once in the background of these novels and central to them: they could not exist without it, but they also feel free to make their own use of it. Chabon has done so in his presumably nonfictional work as well; in a lecture that he used to give titled "Golems I Have Known," he talked about his childhood relationship with Holocaust survivor Joseph Adler, the writer of numerous believe-it-or-not-type books as well as a memoir about the camps. A minor kerfuffle ensued when the writer Paul Maliszewski revealed that Joseph Adler was fictional: Chabon had invented both the books and their author. In Chabon's defense, a spokesperson for Nextbook, which had sponsored Chabon's lecture series, argued that the lecture contained obvious fictional elements, including golems, and that Chabon had repeatedly signaled his turn to fiction with statements such as "I'm still telling lies." I agree with Maliszewski that Chabon went too far: the average listener had no reason to suspect that the Joseph Adler aspect of the lecture—as opposed to the stories about golems—was fictional. But the fact that Chabon felt compelled to insert a fictional Holocaust survivor as a defining figure in his own personal literary history underscores the continued centrality of the Holocaust to his writing.

But will it always be so central? If the legacy of the survivors is to continue in their absence, it must grow larger to fill that void. This has been an issue of constant debate, but never more so than during the creation of the Holocaust Museum in Washington, when there was some discussion of whether it should focus exclusively on the Holocaust or include other instances of genocide, perhaps in a separate wing. Though this idea was quickly rejected, comparisons were unavoidable. The war in the Balkans served as a macabre backdrop to the museum's inauguration, at which Elie Wiesel rebuked President Clinton for his lack of intervention: "We cannot tolerate the excruciating sights of this old new war." For every mention of the Holocaust as a unique event, it seemed, there had to be another reinforcing its relevance to contemporary society. The museum "teaches what needs to be taught," the *New York Times* editorialized at the time. "How can anyone doubt the need for such instruction in a world that produced 'ethnic cleansing'?"

The issue remains divisive. Speaking at the Tribute to Holocaust Survivors, Benjamin Meed, president of a survivors' organization, said that if museums and other institutions dedicated to the Holocaust "are to represent us, they must respect our experience, respect both its Jewishness and its universality." Moments later, he referred to the museum as a "permanent memorial to the Jewish uniqueness of the Holocaust." Inside, an exhibit titled "Decade of Genocide" displayed photographs of atrocities that had taken place since the museum's founding: a pair of eyes staring from a hospital bed in Sarajevo; corpses piled in a mass grave in Rwanda; a little boy, naked from the waist down, crying and clinging to the legless body of a man. Underneath was a quote from Wiesel: "A memorial unresponsive to the future would violate the memory of the past."

It is no accident that those who oppose the idea of literary representation of the Holocaust tend also to be those who argue most forcefully for the Holocaust's uniqueness. For literature, whatever its specific details, ultimately makes a case for universality. Art makes comparisons; it encourages empathy; it awakens the imagination. In short, it emphasizes the fundamental sameness of the human condition. "There is something truly universal about a corpse," Leon Wieseltier wrote upon the museum's opening. "Anybody who looks at these images of corpses and sees only images of Jews has a grave moral problem." It does not detract from the memory of those who died, or from the pain of the survivors, to allow their experiences to remind us of others' suffering. There is enough mourning to go around.

When my son was born, a few weeks after that tribute weekend, friends sent a copy of the children's book *Brundibar,* a retelling of a Czech opera for children originally performed at Terezín. Written by Tony Kushner and illustrated by Maurice Sendak, the story tells of two children who go off in search of milk to feed their dying mother. They sing on the town square in the hopes of making money, but are chased away by the evil organ grinder Brundibar, who accuses them of horning in on his turf. Aided by a friendly group of talking animals, they gather together a band of children and storm back, singing a song of triumph and filling their pail with gold coins. Brundibar slinks off, but we haven't seen the last of him. The book's last page, designed to appear as if it were drawn on the back of an invitation to the original performance of the opera (we can just make out the date and address), is a scrawled note that reads:

> They believe they've won the fight,
> They believe I'm gone—not quite!
> Nothing ever works out neatly—
> bullies don't give up completely.
> One departs, the next appears,
> and we shall meet again, my dears!
> Though I go, I won't go far…
> I'll be back. Love, Brundibar.

To an adult—particularly an adult sensitive to Holocaust allusions—this book is nothing short of terrifying. The Holocaust is never explicitly mentioned, but the Jews in the town wear yellow stars, and the villainous Brundibar is drawn with a Hitler mustache. Towards the end, it becomes clear that the town where this all takes place is Terezín: a sign in one image indicates the entrance to the "Terezínského Ghetta," near another sign reading "Arbeit Macht Frei." I read through the book once and put it away on a high shelf, hoping that my son wouldn't find it. But eventually he did, and he was drawn to it instantly. The book became a regular in his bedtime rotation, even if my hands sometimes shook while turning the pages.

Nothing ever works out neatly—bullies don't give up completely. One departs, the next appears, and we shall meet again, my dears! A difficult lesson for a three-year-old. But this, in the end, is the lesson of all Holocaust literature. In this way, perhaps Wiesel was right to say that "A novel about Auschwitz is not a novel, or else it is not about Auschwitz." For a novel about Auschwitz can never *only* be a novel about Auschwitz: it is a novel also about Armenia, about Siberia, about Cambodia, about Bosnia, about Darfur. *Though I go, I won't go far... I'll be back. Love, Brundibar.*

Index